ANTHRAX WAR

ANTHRAX WAR

DEAD SILENCE . . .

FEAR AND TERROR ON THE ANTHRAX TRAIL

Bob Coen and Eric Nadler

COUNTERPOINT
BERKELEY

Library of Congress Cataloging-in-Publication Data is available.

ISBN: 978-1-58243-509-1

Front cover design by Nadia Coen
Interior design by David Bullen

Printed in the United States of America

Counterpoint
2560 Ninth Street, Suite 318
Berkeley, CA 94710
www.counterpointpress.com

Contents

Preface

When the 2001 anthrax attacks hit the US in the days following 9/11, it was like a one-two punch against the Republic. Workers in New York's media center who had seen the planes swoop too low over their heads en route to the Twin Towers were now terrified of their mail. In Washington, DC, Capitol Hill was evacuated and White House staffers were chewing Cipro tablets.

It was our scariest collective nightmare come to life—the attack of deadly invisible bugs. It seemed like a self-fulfilling prophecy, the preceding years filled as they were with scores of films, best-selling books, TV shows, and articles on the coming of "bioterror." Indeed, for the first time in history, national leaders and the military actually acted out high-tech "germ attack" war games, one of which had a scenario shockingly close to the actual events.

So when the government pledged the most thorough investigation it could muster, we hoped the Feds would get to the bottom of it all. Thus, we were saddened but not really surprised when the attacks disappeared from public discourse—unmentioned, for example, by any major candidate during the 2008 election contest. And when the FBI announced suddenly last summer that the cold case was red-hot, identifying a lone culprit—US Army Scientist Bruce Ivins, just slain by his own hand, and quickly closed its seven-year investigation, it felt to us, and to most polled citizens, that something was not quite right.

In the thirty years we've covered international politics for newspapers, magazines and television networks, rarely, if ever, had we seen such a big story buried so deep. Relying on our network of government, journalistic and intelligence contacts, it soon became clear that the powers that be were for a variety of reasons loathe to open wide the Pandora's box where the real anthrax answers could probably be found. We made a nonfiction film ignited by the germ attacks of 2001. And we wrote this book with Elizabeth Kiem to fill out a story that our 90-minute documentary could only outline. We hope that the open minds that elected the new president are just as open to what we've learned.

Bob Coen and Eric Nadler
Brooklyn, New York
March 2009

ANTHRAX WAR

CHAPTER ONE

The Ghost of Bruce Ivins

A PERFECT FALL GUY

Bruce Ivins wanted no grave and perhaps not even the notoriety that his death generated. In his will he asked simply for his ashes to be scattered. And so, for weeks after he died in the summer of 2008, with his body cremated but not immediately disposed of, Bruce Ivins was in limbo. Reduced to ash, his body languished in a Maryland funeral parlor for more than a month as his wife, a devout Catholic, came to terms with his final request. His will stated that only with "documented proof" that his wishes had been granted would his wife receive her dead spouse's modest bequeathment. It was strangely, morbidly appropriate that Ivins, an anthrax expert, had been reduced to powder.

Dr. Bruce Ivins was a civilian researcher at the US Army Medical Research Institute of Infectious Diseases (USAMRIID) in Fort Detrick—the government's leading biological defense lab. He was a church-going, piano-playing husband and father, a sixty-two-year-old microbiologist from Lebanon, Ohio, and an accomplished amateur juggler. He spent most of his adult life in the Fort Detrick facility or in his modest house just outside its gates. The Ivinses raised two children in that house. Once they were grown, Ivins' wife ran a daycare center there; Ivins cultivated an extravagant garden in the backyard.

But Ivins messed with scary stuff: cholera, plague and then, for the last two decades of his thirty-year career, with anthrax. Scarier than the germs he worked with was the state of his mind as he worked on them. "*I'm a little dream-self, short and stout, I'm the other half of Bruce—when he lets me out*," he wrote during breaks between composing scientific papers on peritoneal macrophages and antibiotic post-exposure prophylaxis. There were other "eccentricities." There was a secret personal post office box. There were threats to his therapist. There was an unhealthy fixation on the star of a reality TV show and with the women of Kappa Kappa Gamma sorority, whom Ivins considered "lovely, highly intelligent campus leaders," who had nonetheless issued a "fatwa" on their adoring fan. There were the multiple e-mail identities: *kingbadger*, *goldenphoenix*, *jimmyflathead*, *prunetacos*. And there was that spiteful condition in the will—have me cremated or fifty grand goes to Planned Parenthood, he instructed his wife, a former president of the local Right to Life chapter in Frederick, Maryland. Years before his suicide, Ivins confided to friends that he suffered paranoid delusions and schizophrenic symptoms.

Then on July 27, 2008, Ivins is said to have taken a heavy dose of prescription Tylenol with codeine and collapsed in his house. Transported to the local hospital, he lay unconscious for two days before he died. Eight days after that, the FBI announced that Ivins was the man they had been hunting for seven years—

the fiend who in the weeks after 9/11 put a highly lethal strain of powdered anthrax in sealed envelopes and sent it through the US mail to Capitol Hill, the network news and a supermarket tabloid, killing five random Americans along the way. Television crews flocked to Fort Detrick; daycare in the Ivinses' house was suspended.

It was a major development in a case that, for most of America, had faded from memory. But for the FBI, burned by bungles and false accusations in the hunt for the anthrax killer, Ivins needed to be more than a break—he needed to be a closer.

"We regret that we will not have the opportunity to present evidence to the jury," said US Attorney Jeffrey Taylor at a news conference meant to slam the door shut on an investigation that had cost taxpayers tens of millions of dollars.

But the bombshell failed to level the many doubts raised during seven years of "Amerithrax," the government's name for what it called one of the largest and most complex investigations in the history of US law enforcement. Indeed, the government's insinuation that the dead man's guilt was the cause of his death was met with instant incredulity and demands to see the evidence Taylor had alluded to. Much of the skepticism surrounding the Ivins revelation was the deserved response to an investigation that had spent valuable time and resources on a false lead that earlier forced a $5.8 million payout to a wronged man. There was also a clear lack of confidence from the scientific community, which even after a four-hour briefing by the FBI and consulting scientists on the methods used to trace the murder weapon to Bruce Ivins' lab counter, was divided on the forensics.

Overriding questionable science and general antagonism towards the FBI probe was the sense that this latest suspect was a product of the bureau's growing desperation to close the case; that time had run out; and that in pinning the anthrax attack on Ivins, investigators had themselves adopted the cynical mantra that the outcome was "good enough for government work." Because no matter how obscure the mysterious scientist appeared to be when he dropped into a late summer news cycle, and no matter how often the FBI spokespeople repeated a scenario in which the suspect had killed himself only when the bureau was days away from an indictment, in fact, Bruce Ivins had been near the radar throughout the investigation.

In October 2001, Ivins was among a select group of experts given a viewing of the anthrax powder sent in an anonymous letter to Senator Tom Daschle. He reportedly marveled at its sophisticated properties. He was among the group of ninety Fort Detrick scientists tasked by the FBI in the following months to analyze the thousands of copycat powders running amok in the mail system. A year later, he was among a group of local Red Cross volunteers who assisted divers looking for discarded contaminants and equipment in a lake not far from Fort Detrick; and for the following six years, right up to the point when he became the Feds' primary suspect, Ivins continued to pass on samples, suggestions and suspicions of his own to investigating officials.

Beyond his physical presence in the labyrinthine investigation, Ivins left other red flags for the Amerithrax investigators: manic e-mails evidencing his unstable mental health; a stash of unmailed letters to congressmen and media outlets; reported outbursts and homicidal threats at his AA meetings. Bruce Ivins, on paper and in fact, was a loose cannon and a stranger neither to anthrax nor to the Amerithrax investigation. So why did it take seven years for this noose to close?

The answer, according to the FBI probe, was in the science. The case against Ivins was circumstantial, but it did have going for it the enticement of cutting-edge microbial forensics involving genetic sequencing not even available until 2005. Only after sequencing more than a thousand different strains, carried out by genomic programs across the country, was the murder weapon identified: a four-mutation blend of multiple anthrax samples that apparently had been prepared at the government's testing site at Dugway Proving Ground in Utah before being shipped to Fort Detrick in Maryland a decade earlier. The blend, coded RMR-1029, was said to have a unique genomic "fingerprint" that could be traced to a "sole creator and custodian." Bruce Ivins, concluded the FBI in early 2007, was that unique individual.

But this was no smoking gun. Yes, Ivins had custody of the lethal blend ten years earlier, but since then RMR-1029 had been distributed to at least 100 other scientists in two dozen labs in a handful of countries, according to the Feds' own estimation. Independent experts wanted to see the data that had ruled out other strains and other anthrax handlers. And they wanted to know how the bureau could be sure that the blend Ivins had allegedly concocted had not been replicated elsewhere by another rogue scientist.

Because the FBI's Quantico facilities are not authorized to work with biohazardous material, the forensic investigation had been farmed out to reputable microbiologists at labs throughout the US. The bureau called a press briefing on August 18, 2008, three weeks after Ivins' death, to quell a rising tide of incredulity among the citizenry. Some of the scientists who played lead roles in the sequencing work found themselves hauled before journalists at the FBI's headquarters in the J. Edgar Hoover Building to help put the FBI indictment to rest along with Ivins himself. But even the experts, who had themselves been kept in the semi-dark about the true purpose of their work until the press briefing identifying Ivins as the anthrax murderer, were unable to provide definitive answers, or even complete unanimity, on the scenarios that could have ended with RMR-1029 in five envelopes in a New Jersey mailbox.

That day, with questions swirling about Ivins, additives,

genomics and, particularly, the investigation's methodology, even the FBI's own bioweapon specialist had to acknowledge the obvious—that the case was not airtight. "There will always be a spore on the grassy knoll," concluded Dr. Vahid Majidi of the FBI's Weapons of Mass Destruction Directorate. With that, he rolled out the red carpet for conspiracy and gave the journalists their headline for the day.

Indeed, paranoia had taken on epic proportions among the bioweapon scientific community in the Amerithrax years. Once the FBI seemed determined to prove in late 2001 that the deadly anthrax most probably had its origins in an American lab and not in some jihadi cave in Afghanistan, Fort Detrick ceased to be a relaxed workplace. By then, 30,000 members of the American Society for Microbiology had received a letter from the Feds, alerting them that "it is very likely that one or more of you know" the anthrax killer. As speculation swirled that only a military lab could have produced the apparently "weaponized" anthrax, Fort Detrick became a Janus-faced hub—at once suspect and expert for the FBI probe. As more and more scientists were drawn into the investigation on a highly secretive, need-to-know-basis, the environment became tenser. There was finger pointing, there was terseness, there were relationships terminated on the advice of lawyers.

Ivins himself reportedly offered up names to the bureau—coworkers he posited as potential suspects. When scientists from Fort Detrick were called to testify before a grand jury they could not be sure whether they were witnesses or suspects. It made for an unpleasant working environment, this failure of investigators to clarify the positions of the various researchers involved. By keeping these relationships to the investigation opaque, the FBI hoped to protect the bureau from the fallout of having an adviser turn out to be a perpetrator. In the end, it didn't work.

As it became clear to Ivins in late 2007 that he had become the Feds' primary suspect, he reportedly turned up the crazy. According to the FBI narrative, he was drinking heavily, stalking his therapist, telling his AA group that he had a list of witnesses he planned to kill. He bought weapons and ammo and hid them in his house. He spent a week in a psych ward and when he came home, he killed himself. The FBI spun this tale into closure. They said they were days from an indictment. But that Ivins beat them to it.

Anthrax was in the headlines again for about a week. The media speculated, and the public recalled an anxious time years ago. Then they both turned the dial—there were Olympic gold medals to be won in Beijing and higher-stakes games to be played in the Caucasus, where fighting in a mountainous enclave between Russians and Georgians promised to bring back the Cold War. But in a small studio office with a river's edge view of the post-9/11 New York skyline, two veteran journalists had a moment of deeper ambivalence. Bob Coen and Eric Nadler were four years into their own investigation; they were working on a documentary on the dangers posed by today's biological weapons, the genesis of which was the 2001 anthrax attacks. Since those attacks, they had tracked the deadly bacteria through numerous covert and overt military and civilian programs to determine just how extensively anthrax has infiltrated the global armory. They found traces of it everywhere. Like the bodies of the five unfortunate victims of the October letters, the twenty-first century map was thoroughly contaminated. And the infection was spreading, fueled by fear, cultured with money.

On the anthrax trail, Coen and Nadler had followed many divergent leads, traveling with their cameras, contacts, and growing suspicions to Siberia, South Africa and London, along paths that always seemed to converge just at the point of an apparent dead end. They had learned to recognize these crossroads by a common landmark—the body of a dead scientist. And they had learned to navigate beyond these crossroads with a dead man's ghost for a guide. Because none of the deaths met so far on the anthrax trail had ended in silence. Indeed, Bob Coen and Eric Nadler had grown adept at hearing the dead speak. Bruce Ivins, they agreed, told them more now than he would have ever told in life.

The journalists embraced the dead scientist as the newest character in a profoundly haunted cast: an erratic vaccine maker whose psychological profile seemed well suited for psychotic behavior. A slim, eccentric man of science who was known to dress up as a clown at county fairs and to put unexplained miles on his family van. A man who had written hundreds of unmailed letters and who had ransomed his own dead body. A man who owned a makeup kit . . . and body armor.

They had seen him coming—sort of. A few weeks earlier, a well placed source within the US military had tipped them off to an imminent breakthrough in the anthrax case—a tip that could possibly prove catastrophic for their working thesis—that there was a cover-up at the highest levels and that a systematic and sincere investigation into the source of the deadly anthrax would lift the veil on a world that the government wanted to remain secret at all costs. So when the FBI trotted out a dead suspect and at the same time slammed the door shut on the seven-year case, the journalists could only laugh in relief.

"We couldn't have scripted it better," said Nadler. "Another dead body and dozens more unanswered questions."

Amerithrax would not be put to rest. Dogged by controversy and an incredulous press, the Justice Department hedged, saying that another three to six months would be needed to take care of "loose ends." Critics balked. "If the case is solved, why isn't it solved?" asked Senator Charles Grassley of Iowa, as prelude to a direct accusation of a cover-up. By mid-September 2008, the clamor for answers forced FBI Director Robert Mueller himself to appear before the House and Senate Judiciary Committees to face questions about anthrax. Coen and Nadler drove to Washington to be in the front row.

Mueller, a career litigator, former marine and pretty tough hombré, had been FBI director for almost exactly as long as there had been an Amerithrax investigation. Since his swearing in one week before 9/11, Mueller had weathered political shitstorms over warrantless wiretaps, whistleblowers, and the so-called National Security Letters, which allowed unprecedented data collection on civilians. Mueller was the first FBI director to send agents into combat zones since World War II, and under his tenure more than 500 investigators would ship out to Iraq and Afghanistan. He displayed an independent streak at times and had the gumption to anger the White House in March 2004 when he publicly threatened to resign over what he interpreted to be an attempt by the Bush administration to subvert the authority of the Department of Justice over a controversial surveillance program run by the National Security Agency. As he made his way to Capitol Hill that morning in September of 2008, a long, fawning profile in a Washington magazine proclaiming him "The Ultimate G-Man" was still on the newsstands.

In the press gallery, Nadler could hardly wait for the action to start. It had already been an unsettling few hours in DC. The Capitol was an uneasy place during the final stage of the regime-changing presidential campaign, and an episode the previous evening had raised its own red flags. Nadler had a run-in with an old acquaintance, a guy he had worked with while investigating Saudi Arabia's nuclear weapons connections back in the day.

This source, hard-wired into the Capitol's military and intelligence circles, was now running an Internet investigative journalism consortium and was all over the Ivins affair. He—we'll call him "Teddy B"—agreed to meet Nadler and Coen at the Ritz Carlton in Arlington, Virginia near the Pentagon. Teddy B arrived in a long black limo leading a small C-list conga-line entourage that starred a provocatively dressed dynamite blonde who he introduced as a "fucking Emmy Award-winning producer for the shit we did together in Somalia." Nadler and Coen took part in the requisite "how you been, man?" But they steadfastly refused the repeated slurred suggestions to "get in the limo and party." When it was clear that Nadler and Coen would not be moving outside the Ritz, Teddy B slurped the dregs of his cocktail, pushed himself well into Nadler's personal space and issued an incoherent stream of invective, slander and threats that promised an IRS audit of Nadler's financial records. Then he stormed out with his posse, the blonde apologizing for the sudden turn of events in the twenty-minute encounter.

"They wanted us in that limo, man," Coen sighed. "They were up to no good." Nadler shrugged. "He was always a party kind of guy, but I'm not real sure which parties Teddy's working for these days," he said. "Maybe it was nothing."

"Or maybe it was something," replied Coen. "This town gives me the creeps," he concluded before heading for his hotel room.

Later that night, Nadler spent some time going over the holes in the Amerithrax science with his brother, a congressman who would be sitting on the House committee questioning Mueller the next day. Despite the promises from the *Washington Post* that the congressional hearing would feature a dramatic anthrax showdown, Representative Jerrold Nadler, as it turned out, was the only member to address the anthrax issue over the course of the hearing. On his kid brother's suggestion, Nadler, a liberal Democrat from New York City, asked Mueller to provide the relative weight of the additive silica reported to have been found in the attack powder. This arcane forensic detail, Coen and Nadler had learned, could help to determine if the anthrax had been manipulated in a highly sophisticated, multi-disciplinary operation, thereby cutting the heart out of the FBI's lone gunman case. But FBI Chief Mueller deferred. He'd have to "get back" to him on that, he said. Representative Nadler pressed on, noting that "only a handful of laboratories" could achieve a silica content over 1 percent. Had the FBI investigated all of those labs? And how had it ruled them out as potential sources of the deadly anthrax?

"You can assume we looked at every lab in the US and several overseas that had people and facilities capable of preparing the anthrax powder," Mueller answered. He said he would soon get back with an answer to Rep. Nadler's follow-up about how his bureau cleared individual labs of suspicion.

In lieu of hard data, Mueller promised an independent review of the science with the aid of the National Academy of Sciences (NAS). But at the Senate hearing the next day, he took heavy flak from politicos on both sides of the aisle who didn't trust him or the lame duck Bush administration to be completely forthcoming about Amerithrax. Ranking GOP committee member Senator Arlen Specter, the one-time district attorney of Philadelphia, blamed the FBI director for the air of distrust that had prompted the hearings. "You can't run a government on separation of power without good faith among the branches," he said, "and you can't pursue the matters to the courts to have them adjudicate disputes between the legislative and executive branches, but that's what it's come to." Specter brought up past episodes of "unsatisfactory relations" between Congress and the bureau and then waved his trump card. "We're not interlopers here, this is an oversight matter," he chided.

Mueller sat facing the grim senator, his mouth set in the

unpleasant half-smile of a man tasked with humoring the guy setting his trap. He noted the "extraordinary and justified public interest" in the investigation and announced the intention to set up an independent review of the Amerithrax conclusions by the National Academy of Sciences. Specter jumped, demanding that the Senate oversight committee be allowed to name scientists to the independent investigation. Mueller hedged, leaving it to the NAS to name panelists. Specter countered, "What's there to consider, Director Mueller? I'm talking about the Judiciary Committee of the US Senate which has a constitutional responsibility." Eric Nadler grinned—he liked the heat in the room. Coen remained stone-faced, his eyes narrow behind his stylish green glasses.

Then it was the turn of Senator Patrick Leahy, head of the committee and himself a target of one of the anthrax letters. Leahy spoke with gravitas in a gravelly, languid voice chiding the director for bureaucratic bamboozlement right out of *Catch-22*. Finally he dropped the detachment: "I have been very reluctant to even ask questions about this because my office and myself were put at risk because of a letter that was addressed to me and I realize we did not suffer like the families of those who had people die . . . I do not believe in any way, shape or manner that [Ivins] is the only person involved in this attack on Congress and the American people. I do not believe that at all. I believe there are others involved, either as accessories before or after the fact. I believe there are others who can be charged with murder."

The chairman of the United States Senate Judiciary Committee was charging conspiracy and cover-up at the center of one of the FBI's biggest cases ever—and it was broadcast live on C-SPAN. This was not Internet chatter, but a powerful challenge to powerful interests by an impeccable source. It was a fantastic and important story—but one that for whatever reasons, would be ignored by the media.

"Even cable," noted Nadler.

DEATH IN THE MAIL

Bob Coen arrived in New York just two months after hijacked jets slammed into the Twin Towers and the Pentagon. It was a hell of a welcome back for a man who had fled the violence of Zimbabwe for the sake of his newborn son. Like many New Yorkers, Coen experienced a certain atmospheric anxiety throughout that extraordinary autumn; some moments of mild panic as he tucked his son in at night, making sure his bedroom window was closed against the choking cloud that still hung over lower Manhattan and draped the river between his Brooklyn apartment and the still-burning pit of Ground Zero.

But it was the anthrax in the letters that made Bob Coen stop sleeping at night.

The first batch of anonymous missives was mailed via regular US Mail the week after 9/11, postmarked September 18 in Trenton, New Jersey. One of the envelopes was addressed to Tom Brokaw at NBC News. Inside was a note that read 09-11-01 THIS IS NEXT / TAKE PENACILIN NOW / DEATH TO AMERICA / DEATH TO ISRAEL / ALLAH IS GREAT. Also inside was a powdered substance. Brokaw never opened the letter, but his assistant did and broke out in a nasty rash. The opened letter, turned over to authorities, tested positive for anthrax spores.

Bacillus anthracis is a bacterium that occurs naturally throughout the world. Just not usually in Rockefeller Center or in Boca Raton, Florida, where the first fatal anthrax infection took its victim. Rather, anthrax is generally found in the blood of grazing animals—cows, goats and sheep. When an animal dies and decomposes in the environment, the bacterium is released as spores that can resist almost any force in nature and linger dormant in the soil for years or decades. The majority of anthrax victims (and there are up to 200,000 a year according to the World Health Organization) are therefore generally farmers, veterinarians and meat-workers. They are usually infected through the skin. Cutaneous anthrax causes blisters and ulcers. It is easily treatable and rarely fatal. But the second wave of letters to find a human target, letters that were sent to the offices of Senators Patrick Leahy and Tom Daschle, contained a fine powder, created to cause pulmonary anthrax, in which the pathogen enters the respiratory system, spreads to the lymph nodes, and from there chases through the blood stream releasing the deadly bacteria throughout the body. Pulmonary anthrax causes lesions, hemorrhaging and in ninety-nine cases out of one hundred, death within a week. Until the deaths that came by mail, there had been only eighteen recorded cases of pulmonary anthrax in the United States in the twentieth century. The last one was in 1978, when a knitter became too enamored with the smell of his imported yarn.

Anthrax was a microbiological breakthrough. It was anthrax that demonstrated, in 1876 to a German biologist named Robert Koch, how bacteria cause disease. One hundred years later it was widely considered the ideal biological weapon—cheap to make, convenient to stockpile and easily modified with modern genetic engineering techniques. Most major nations have experimented, tested or stockpiled the stuff for ostensibly defensive purposes in case of a biological war. Some have actually used it, deliberately or unintentionally. In these state-sponsored labs, each country has developed its strand of anthrax, varying in natural regional mutation or genetically engineered makeup, and therefore, in virulence. But even with these national anthrax "trademarks," it is difficult to track the source of any one strain because transfers from lab to lab and even country to country have gone almost entirely undocumented since the international community outlawed weaponized anthrax thirty years ago. FBI agents hunting the source of the anthrax in the October letters would have almost as tough a time as the Hazmat crews rifling through millions of envelopes in post offices up and down the Atlantic seaboard.

Within ten days of the first mailing, many people were infected, but none of them was diagnosed. Only when Robert Stevens, a photo editor at the tabloid *Sun* in Boca Raton, was confirmed to have died on October 5 from inhalation anthrax did the story grow legs. By then, a second batch of anthrax-tainted letters had been mailed—among them were envelopes addressed to Senators Tom Daschle and Patrick Leahy, postmarked October 9. Daschle's letter appeared to be from a precocious youngster with a social studies assignment—the return address said 4th grade, Greendale School, Franklin Park, New Jersey. The town exists. The school does not. Inside this envelope was a note like those sent to newsrooms in September with a few more helpful lines reading: WE HAVE THIS ANTHRAX. / YOU DIE NOW. Once they arrived, the country was well primed for another panic. Congress shut down for the first time in modern history, newsrooms began plying employees with the antibiotic ciprofloxacin (Cipro), and Senator John McCain told David Letterman that the anthrax might have come from Iraq. Within a week, there were two dead postal workers in Washington, DC.

By the end of October, there were twenty-two anthrax victims. Four of them were dead: They were Robert Stevens, Kathy Nguyen, Thomas Morris and Joseph Curseen. Their names, like those of collateral damage throughout history, have since returned to near obscurity, despite the fact that their deaths sparked a national panic, revived a booming biodefense industry and birthed a federal probe that stretched across six continents, interviewing more than 9,000 people and issuing 6,000 subpoenas.

The fatalities ended in an inexplicable coda one month later, when a ninety-four-year-old woman in Connecticut with no link to the media or to politics died of inhalation anthrax. Her name was Ottilie Lundgren and for a time after her death, many in Oxford, Connecticut wore facemasks. The era of death in the mail was over for now, but the hoaxes had only just begun.

In the aftermath of the anthrax mail scare, there were dead people and sick people, but there was also all of Capitol Hill needing Hazmat cleaning, and four post offices closed indefinitely pending decontamination. Other post offices, government offices and schools would close periodically on bio hoaxes. There was also a rumor mill working overtime to establish a connection between the fictional Greendale School, Al Qaeda and the leg lesion that appeared on one of the 9/11 hijackers while he was taking flying lessons in Florida. And by the way, if somehow these attacks could be linked to Saddam Hussein, so much the better.

Meanwhile, on no budget, Bob Coen had started doing his own investigation from his computer in Brooklyn. Coen knew more about anthrax than most laymen, and what he knew made him less worried about innocent Americans being killed by spore-wielding terrorists, and more worried about the number of significant arsenals that included deadly anthrax. It wasn't fear for his safety or the security of his home and his family that kept him awake . . . it was the reemergence of anthrax as a weapon of choice.

Coen's first encounter with anthrax dated back to his childhood. Growing up in what was then called Rhodesia, Coen had heard of the terrible effects of the bacterium when hundreds died and more than ten thousand were sickened by anthrax in the course of that country's independence war. True, the Rhodesian anthrax outbreak in 1978, the largest in recorded history, killed more cattle than humans, but many have long suspected that it was the result of Rhodesian Special Forces applying biological warfare in the last stages of a lost war. In the case of Rhodesia's civil war, anthrax did not prove to be the ultimate weapon—only a nadir in the code of war and a poor legacy for humanity. But it also served as a very real precedent, and for some scruple-less scientists, a working basis. Rhodesia, in Coen's youth, was a pioneering bioweapons locus.

Now, nearly a quarter century later, Coen felt a familiar sense of distrust and disbelief. Once again, he was living in a society under siege by a shadowy enemy. He recalled his younger self—son of the privileged class, served by a black population with whom he had very little interaction. Only when he went off to high school in the requisite wool blazer and straw boater did Coen become aware that his people were at war. At war against the house "boy," the garden "boy," and the friendly men and women who humored his quiet, curious presence outside their shacks, smelling of wood smoke, ganja and bodies.

"Our headmaster gave speeches at assembly about the evil communists conspiring with black terrorists and about how Rhodesia was on the front line of the battle for Western civilization," he recounted to Nadler during one of their many conversations on the creeping ascendancy of the Bush administration's "Us against Them" mentality. "It was funny how overnight, the racist characterization shifted from treating blacks as backward baboons to branding them subversive and dangerous terrorists."

By the time Coen neared his eighteenth birthday, he was convinced that he was living in a "twisted and schizoid country based on lies and fear." Resolved not to serve in its conscripted army against black insurgents in an increasingly brutal bush war, Coen entered university a year early. His peers took up guns, and he took up political consciousness and the music of cynical disenchantment.

In 1978, after a couple of years of college during which he spent less time attending lectures than he did immersing himself in the lexicon of Frank Zappa and the growing student counter-culture that was questioning the status-quo of white power in southern Africa, Coen emigrated with his family to the United States. For someone arriving from the repressed right-wing society that was Rhodesia, New York at the height of the punk era of sex, drugs and rock and roll was like landing on another planet. Abandoning all academic pursuits, he got a job off-loading books from trucks and devoted the next several years to catching up on everything that had been out of bounds—and to attending as many Frank Zappa concerts as he could (even meeting his hero backstage after one show). Zappa's music began responding to the politics of the times—the growing right-wing religious fanaticism of the Reagan administration. Those policies also became the focus of another major musical influence for Coen—The Clash, with their radical songs calling attention to the proxy wars in Central America, Nicaragua, El Salvador and . . . South Africa and Zimbabwe. He began to understand how these conflicts, separated by oceans, were all connected.

After taking a guerrilla video activist course, Coen returned to the independent Zimbabwe in 1985 determined to make a film about a civil war that was raging in neighboring Mozambique. It was baptism by fire—not only did he have no idea how to make a film but nothing could have prepared him for the brutality he would document over the next eighteen months. In a desperate attempt to hold on to power and halt black liberation, the apartheid regime in South Africa had unleashed a campaign of destabilization across the whole of southern Africa, including supporting the insurgency in Mozambique that specialized in terrorizing civilians by cutting off their lips and noses. The film *Mozambique: The Struggle for Survival* was broadcast by PBS exactly at the time right-wing Republicans were pushing for Washington to cut ties with the socialist government and recognize the rebels—but Coen's camera had documented the war, exposed the South African hand and helped to influence policy.

After a film on the civil war in Angola, Coen turned to television news, becoming the roaming Africa reporter for CNN. For the next decade and a half, he honed his war reporting skills covering dozens of conflicts across the continent: from the Rwandan genocide to religious riots in Nigeria, from Islamic terrorism in Algeria to child soldiers in Liberia and Sierra Leone, interviewing "Blood Diamond" merchants, dictators, warlords and mercenaries along the way and also winning the Bayeux Prize for best television war correspondent in 1997. He became hooked on "the jazz" of pushing the limits as far as he could and together with a strange tribe of war junkies, some of whom eventually caught bullets with their names on them, would move from conflict to conflict.

In 2000, after he was nearly killed by angry war veterans in Zimbabwe, Coen's reporter days came to a crashing halt. The years of violence, bloodshed and suffering had taken their toll and it was time to start afresh. In a new relationship and with a baby on the way he said good-bye to Africa and returned to New York, soon after the Twin Towers came down. Frank Zappa's words were always with him.

This was a devotion of Coen's that Nadler, after years of conspiracy chasing together, had become very aware of. More than once, over breakfast or coffee or a midday stroll along the industrial edge of the East River, they would be talking about facets of their investigation—some troubling revelation of the underbelly of science, progress and innovation, whether it be germ proliferation, pharma profits or targeted genetics, when Coen would stop and smile to himself. "You know Zappa had it right," he would say, and Nadler would wait for the proof. "The government is just a cardboard cutout hiding the real workings of the machine." Nadler would nod.

Nadler, like most Americans, spent the months after September 11 eyeing the skies warily and avoiding the dreadful evening news. For New Yorkers it was a particularly strange moment—a time when the sickest of questions popped into the head: Is that a jet overhead or a missile? Is it flying correctly? What are we breathing? Are we all caught in some death match between Jesus, Allah and the god of Abraham? Now in his early fifties, Nadler was not exempt from this acute weirdness that afflicted New Yorkers.

A city kid from a working class family, Nadler graduated from Brooklyn's public schools and the State University of New York at Binghamton and passed straight into the ranks of Gotham reporters. He covered the police blotters, suburban town corruption, arson fires and the "Son of Sam" for the Gannett Newspapers in Westchester and then signed on as a political writer for the *SoHo Weekly News*, a pretty hip weekly in downtown NYC. In the early 1980s, Nadler worked out of a small apartment he shared with his wife and another couple with an infant son—a communal experiment on the Upper West Side. For a decade, Nadler's work on the more awful maneuvers of the Reagan Revolution could also be found in a host of magazines—*The Nation, The New Republic, Harper's, Mother Jones, Rolling Stone*. He was also on staff with Bob Guccione's *Penthouse*, and co-authored "The United States of America vs. Sex," a lively critique of the Meese Commission on Pornography, which Nadler found to be a scandalous political payoff to Jerry Falwell and the Religious Right. He and his co-author Philip Nobile lampooned the Commission as the "F-Troop of the Erogenous Zone."

He went on to earn heftier field stripes when he joined Danny Schechter and Rory O'Connor's award-winning PBS weekly newsmagazine *South Africa Now* as investigative editor. In the 1990s, he produced several *Frontline* investigations for PBS dealing with the political influence of Rev. Sun Myung Moon, the BCCI banking scandal and the "hidden history" of US and Saudi Arabian relations.

In the fall of 2000, Nadler, living in Jackson Heights, Queens with his wife Elisa Rivlin, the general counsel of Simon and Schuster, and their two kids, sold Court TV on his original documentary series *Confessions*, which aired videotaped confessions of murders supplied to Nadler by the Manhattan District Attorney Robert Morgenthau. It was a very controversial effort at the time. For some reason Nadler has never understood, these real life interrogations—introduced as evidence in murder trials—were greeted hysterically by the media. Even before airing, *Confessions* prompted the *New York Times* to urge in an editorial that the network kill the reality show. Despite an avalanche of publicity and a doubling of Court TV's anemic prime time ratings, the program was yanked after just two episodes. So when a museum in Denmark proposed that Nadler and his co-producer Richard Kroehling bring the *Confessions* tapes to a "censored television" festival in Copenhagen, all expenses paid, he readily agreed. He and Richard were booked on the 12:10 AM flight from Newark International Airport to Copenhagen—the first flight out of Newark slated on September 11, 2001—eight hours before United Airlines Flight 93 was hijacked into infamy from that same terminal.

On the television set at the gate, the New York Giants were in the final moments of a 31–20 loss to the Denver Broncos. Nadler cursed, regretting a bet he had made earlier. When boarding began, he presented his ticket to the attendants and ambled into the jetway with a yawn. But halfway to the door of the plane, a uniformed US Customs official and a fellow in plain clothes were stopping passengers asking to see passports. Nadler produced his and the agent stopped at the Pakistan visa—a stamp from a trip to Islamabad he took in 1994 on assignment for *Rolling Stone*.

"Pakistan!" the Customs officer hissed before hurling questions: "Why were you in Pakistan? What is your business? How long were you there? When were you last there? Where are you going now? Is Denmark your final destination? Where are you staying in Copenhagen? Please step to the side, sir."

In the end, Nadler was allowed to board. He thought it all a bit odd, ordered a drink with dinner and slept until Scandinavia. As he settled into his hotel the next morning, his traveling companion screamed from the next room: "Dude, check this out!" Nadler ran in. For the next twenty-four hours, when not phoning home to make sure all loved ones were okay, he watched the TV. From that moment on, you couldn't mention 9/11 to him without his certainty that the true story had yet to be told.

And then came anthrax.

The death-by-mail anthrax episode three weeks later unhitched itself quite quickly from the September 11 consciousness. After the period in which Cipro, the powerful antibiotic used against anthrax, became a household name invoked by Tom Brokaw signing off the nightly news, the whole affair seemed to go into hiding, under the cover of a federal probe. It was the disappearing act that surprised Nadler. He was intrigued by the discrepancies between events that, on the one hand, suggested a bioterror link to the attacks on the World Trade Center and the Pentagon, and on the other hand, directly benefited drug companies like Bayer, which haggled with the Feds over the price of Cipro as its stock price soared immediately after the attacks. He wondered if the apparent discrepancy was no more than a cynical pretext: if someone within the world's burgeoning biodefense establishments that clearly had the means and profit motive to carry out the attacks, had also seized the opportunity. Nadler, after all, had come of age during the revelations of Woodward and Bernstein; he had spent his career working towards an inexorable conclusion that as a journalist, you can't go wrong if you "follow the money." He thought the twenty-first century's mainstream media was ignoring this maxim too readily.

Nadler had been exploring the international networks behind the proliferation of weapons of mass destruction for years. When the anthrax attacks happened, he was spending hours each day in a fifteenth-floor editing suite a mile north of the smoldering pit of Ground Zero, at work on the final edit of a documentary about the black market spread of nuclear weapon components. The ultimate villains in this film, *Stealing the Fire*, were Germans. Germans with roots in the Third Reich. The Degussa Corporation, a multinational company that had once manufactured Zyklon B—the preferred gas of Auschwitz—had made a good profit helping Pakistan and Iraq with their uranium enrichment program in the 1980s and 1990s. Five years of work had granted Nadler unprecedented access to a German engineer, Karl-Heinz Schaab, the first man convicted of atomic espionage since the 1950s, who sold classified centrifuge blueprints to Saddam Hussein. The spy was convicted of treason in a German court, sentenced just to five years probation and fined $32,000. That spelled Western government complicity to Nadler and his partner John S. Friedman. Nadler remained finely tuned to suspect an untold story behind any news of rogue weapons of mass destruction, especially where corporate interests were involved.

It was during a screening of his documentary on the underground trade of nuclear weapon widgets that Nadler ran into Coen, who literally stepped out of the shadows of a Greenwich

Village theater to greet his old colleague. It had been more than a dozen years since they had worked together on *South Africa Now*. The two headed up the investigative unit, and had produced stories about American diamond merchants violating apartheid-era sanctions and American companies dumping their toxic waste in Zulu villages.

Nadler recalled how Coen was arrested outside the gates of the New Jersey corporate headquarters of American Cyanamid, the chemical giant which shipped its mercury waste to South Africa, and how his shots of New Jersey state cops' boots kicking at his camera landed on the front page of the *Village Voice* three days later. Coen, Nadler knew, was the best kind of troublemaker. He was thrilled to hear he was back in town.

The two went for coffee. By morning, they had a new shared beat. Coen wanted to investigate how and why anthrax had been allowed to rear its head so dramatically, only to slink offstage. Nadler wanted to examine the role of public and private biodefense developers to see what they stood to gain from a germ war panic. They knew that the place to start was with the federal response to October 2001, when someone or some group went postal on America. They started with Amerithrax.

AMERITHRAX

The federal investigation into the anthrax attacks began with an implicit promise that the Feds would leave no stone unturned, no mailbox unswabbed in their effort to find a perpetrator. In early November 2001, about a week after Ottilie Lundgren died in Connecticut, the newly appointed Director of Homeland Security, Tom Ridge, held a news conference at which he alluded to an expansive plan to incorporate expertise and tips from all sectors. There was a $250 million bounty on the head of the anthrax killer to encourage just such help.

"You'd be amazed at the number of, they're not solicitations, but inquiries . . . about the potential application of this or that technology," he said. "Clearly, not only will we look to the private sector to help us identify some of the problems, but also to come up with some solutions . . . We want to explore all potential ideas and suggestions, particularly when they seem to be further along in terms of research and development." As if to emphasize the inclusiveness of the effort to safeguard America, Ridge also noted that the Office of Homeland Security had just welcomed a contingent from the National Organization on Disability to a talk about homeland security—the same talk he gave to the good folks at NASCAR.

But later in the briefing, Ridge told reporters that he was unable, as of yet, to project a hypothesis on whether the anthrax letters were the act of an individual or a group, domestic or foreign. What he could tell reporters was that the spores found in the letters had been identified as the "Ames strain" of anthrax—the "gold standard" for weaponized anthrax because of its virulence. The strain, which was originally from a dead Texan cow, had passed through the National Veterinary Services Laboratory in Ames, Iowa where it got its moniker, and then on to the Unites States Army Medical Research Institute of Infectious Diseases (USAMRIID) at Fort Detrick in 1980. But from there, it is anyone's guess where the Ames strain wandered. Fort Detrick specialists had classified it as one of the most toxic anthrax strains they had seen, and had given some of it to germ researchers in at least three other countries including the United Kingdom and France. And who knows where it went from there?

One of the frightening truths that the Amerithrax probe illuminated over the course of its long life was that for years deadly bacteria and toxins have been shared. Biomaterials were passed between labs and researchers with little documentation, less surveillance and no effective regulation whatsoever. This surprising lack of oversight applied to both content and recipient: in the 1980s the US Centers for Disease Control shipped deadly viruses abroad via express mail. The addressees included the country's foremost ideological foes: Iraq, South Africa, Cuba, the Soviet Union and China. A Senate committee chaired by John McCain and the General Accounting Office opened an investigation into the shipments in the early 1990s but failed to establish whether they represented honest scientific collaboration gone awry or something darker. Nonetheless, with its interest, Congress was signaling the scientific community that the all too routine trading of deadly pathogens was something that would not be tolerated in the new era of preoccupation with weapons of mass destruction—an era ushered in by the fall of the Soviet Union and the rising threat of Saddam Hussein. And even then, one could not really be certain what the scientific community was doing with its viruses and plagues in the name of "research."

When Ames, Iowa was mentioned in context of the anthrax attacks, it was a jolt to the city. Concerned that it might have provided a terrorist with deadly material, on October 12, 2001, the Iowa State University's College of Veterinary Science incinerated its collection of anthrax samples under armed guard. Ironically, none of the samples in Ames were, in fact, the Ames strain (which originated in Texas but was identified by the National Veterinary Services Laboratory in Ames, hence the name), but some dated back to 1928 and were rather regretfully destroyed by the dean, who had hoped to hold a centennial experiment to test their longevity. The USDA ran a laboratory not far from the university but had to retrieve its anthrax collection from a storage closet it rented in a local strip mall under less than standard biohazard safety levels. These samples—crucial baseline samples for "Amerithrax" detectives—were also destroyed (with, astonishingly enough, the approval of the FBI), making it impossible for investigators to compare them when it seemed possible later that the anthrax in the letters may indeed have been linked to Ames, Iowa as well as to the Ames strain.

As the congressional showdown in the fall of 2008 eventually evidenced, the precise nature of the Ames strain anthrax found in the attack powder used in the Daschle and Leahy letters—the most sophisticated powders used in the attacks, and perhaps ever seen—would become one of the most complicated pieces of evidence in the investigation. Years after the attacks, Coen and Nadler found that there was still no unanimity on whether the spores that caused the deaths of five people were easily accessible to individuals with connections to ordinary labs, or whether the anthrax mailer would have needed access to more sophisticated equipment. Though pulmonary anthrax may be a perfect killer, it is not necessarily the perfect weapon. So to find the anthrax murderer, you needed to find the weapon as well as the ammunition. And for a while, the FBI seemed bent on convincing the world that both could be found in a basement lab rigged with about $2,500 worth of equipment. That claim lost credence for many once the Army failed to reverse-engineer a replica of the Senate letters' powder, even with the help of the most high-tech facilities in the country.

The complexities of the science were tough on the media. Reporters often confused the issue, interchanging revelations about the anthrax found in the letters to the senators with news on the samples sent to the media outlets, which were powders of the same derivation, but different grades. Then there was the debate over additives: the heart of the matter. Did almost magical ingredients transform the Senate attack-powders into super lethal anthrax?

Newsweek reported early on that sources found in the powder a "compound previously unknown to bioweapons experts." ABC News in a much-hyped "exclusive" reported that the anthrax contained bentonite, which, it further reported, is a "trademark of Iraqi leader Saddam Hussein's biological weapons program." It took six years for ABC to retract the scoop, which had no factual basis but was useful in the drumbeat for the coming war against Iraq.

The question of additives and silica weight created a sharp schism between the Pentagon and the FBI—one unresolved to this day. Initial analysis of the powder as undertaken by the Armed Forces Institute of Pathology in Bethesda, Maryland suggested to Army scientists that this was a very sophisticated anthrax concoction—milled to an almost infinitesimal size with additives designed to make it float right into the deepest part of human lungs and kill the host.

"Fort Detrick sought our assistance to determine the specific components of the anthrax found in the Daschle letter," Dr. Florabel G. Mullick, the principal deputy director of the Armed

Forces Institute of Pathology (AFIP), was quoted as saying in the Institute's October 31, 2002 newsletter. Mullick described a method using an energy dispersive X-ray spectrometer to detect the presence of otherwise-unseen chemicals. The test identified the previously unknown substance as silica. "This was a key component," Mullick said. "Silica prevents the anthrax from aggregating, making it easier to aerosolize." The AFIP finding was considered by some to be consistent with a multidisciplinary state program. And even if Ivins was culpable, said observers who believed the AFIP was an honest broker, he did not—indeed, *could* not have—acted alone.

Not long after Ivins' death, Coen and Nadler went to see Richard Spertzel, a former deputy commander at Fort Detrick's germ warfare research unit, who had written an op-ed piece in the *Wall Street Journal* soon after Ivins' suicide insisting that the spores in the Daschle and Leahy letters could not have been produced at the USAMRIID by Ivins alone.

"The material that was in the Daschle/Leahy letter, according to FBI releases, was 1.5 to 3 microns in particle size," he told the journalists. Then he characterized the refinement as "super sophisticated . . . phenomenal."

"I'm fully convinced—as are other experts, I'm not alone by any chance—that Dr. Ivins could not have done this with the equipment that he had . . . and I contend that that kind of powder could not be made at Fort Detrick, because they don't have the equipment necessary to get down to that particle size with that kind of refinement," continued Spertzel. "It readily floated off the slides when they tried to examine it in the microscope." Spertzel noted reports that said the spores were "individually coated with a substance called polyglass."

Spertzel was one of several experts who initially credited the idea that the powder came from one of Saddam's suspected germ labs. Even at this late date, he was sticking with that theory.

Leaving his comfortable home in suburban Maryland, Coen and Nadler thanked Spertzel for his time and in particular, for his golden quote about Ivins' death: "He's dead and they can close the case and he can't defend himself. Nice and convenient, isn't it?"

Spertzel's words echoed an interview they had had a year earlier with Stuart Jacobsen, who saw many hands behind the manufacture of the powders. "It's a multi-disciplinary effort," he said during filming in his home on the outskirts of a Texas city. "First of all you need some biologists to understand what kind of strain they need to use the bacteria. In this case *Bacillus anthracis* bacteria. Then you need a chemical engineer to get a high yield of these spores. You then need more chemists to be able to separate these spores, process them and concentrate them."

Coen and Nadler took careful notes, underlining what Jacobsen said about the importance of chemical engineers to the effort. Jacobsen, after all, was one himself.

Jacobsen spoke at length to Coen and Nadler about the complexities of *Bacillus anthracis* and about the effect of friction on electrostatic particles. He speculated about the effect of mail-sorting machines on the anthrax spores' charge. The ghoulishness of the brave new world upon which he reflected was heightened by his matter-of-fact tone of voice, his thick Scottish brogue, even his casual khaki trousers. Outside the window, Coen could see that every house in this featureless subdivision was virtually identical to its neighbor. Like liar's dice, he thought. You would never know from the looks of it which one is empty and which housed folks—like this guy—who claimed important knowledge about the intricacies of mass annihilation.

Jacobsen, an opinionated man waging Internet war battles with critics, explained that the scientific schism could be settled only when the FBI disclosed just how much silica was present in the powder. Some of the researchers who had actually examined the stuff claimed that the silica was naturally occurring. But if there was more than 1 percent, Jacobsen insisted, there could be no doubt that the killer powder had been processed to make it as lethal as possible. Jacobsen considered the anthrax in the letters to Daschle and Leahy to be "weapons grade." This was in alignment with sixteen US government employed biodefense experts who wrote in the Journal of the American Medical Association in May 2002 that the attack powders had the classic weapons signature of "high spore concentration, uniform particle size, low electrostatic charge, [and treatment] to reduce clumping."

But the FBI saw it differently, and called in experts to support its assertion that the Senate letter powder could have been made by a single operator. The agency's post-Ivins briefing panel of scientists reported that the anthrax was not coated with silica, and that if there was some silica in the powder, it was naturally occurring. Like FBI Director Robert Mueller a month later, they would shed no light about the percentage weight of silica in the powder.

One aggressive reporter influenced by Jacobsen and other US Army sources he trusted had a go at the FBI panel at its briefing. Gary Matsumoto, employed in 2008 by Bloomberg News, had grabbed the germ war issue by the short hairs while writing his 2004 book, *Vaccine A*, about the controversial vaccine against anthrax used by the military. He was also one of very few non-scientists to have work published in the prestigious *Science* magazine, when his article on the schism between the FBI and the Department of Defense over the anthrax refinement question was published in November 2003. Matsumoto's intelligence and sources interested Coen and Nadler, who courted the reporter as a source for years after the article appeared. There were phone conversations and coffee meetings and one lunch date for which the journalists were kept waiting for two hours.

During all of these meetings, Matsumoto dropped hints about depths of collusion, secrecy and ultimate significance of his findings. He chided Coen and Nadler for being naïve, for being in over their heads, but he kept returning their phone calls and fishing for their findings.

Matsumoto said his agent was pushing him to write a book on germ warfare and that he had key military co-authors in place. "A Russian general and a US general, you see the level I'm getting at?"

One day in the fall of 2007, Matsumoto announced that he was coming to see them "right now." He arrived bearing a box of chocolates. "I don't know if it's appropriate to bring gifts on the High Holy Days," he said guessing, correctly, his hosts' religious heritage.

Matsumoto was momentarily silenced by the walls of the office, covered as they were with the ephemera of the anthrax trail. Coen and Nadler watched fascinated as the former ROTC cadet, now in his forties, walked over to the whiteboard where they had mocked up the web of players and sources they were cultivating, and began to talk. He recognized key names and spoke for an hour about how the anthrax affair was "very bad business" that he personally wanted out of. "Why are you guys doing this?" he asked almost plaintively. Nadler picked up the box of chocolates and told Matsumoto, "Gary, it's holy work. We're doing it for our kids—all the kids." Matsumoto shook his head and told Nadler and Coen that they were at the tip of an iceberg, that his own book's revelations would "blow them away." Still, he said, they were foolish for thinking their work might make a difference.

"I really don't know why you guys are doing this," he said again, turning to the journalists, who were already regretting at that moment that they didn't have a camera trained on Matsumoto to catch this performance. Matsumoto said he was probably done with anthrax. He spent much of his free time these days dreaming of designing a video game. After an hour or so, he wished his fellow investigative journalists the best of luck and left.

But by the time Bruce Ivins died, it became clear that Matsumoto, despite not having written about anthrax in some time, had not retired from the germ war game. At the 2008 FBI briefing, he went at the experts with detailed questions far beyond the ken of fellow journalists in the room. There were thrusts and parries about the reliability of "silica signal detection capabilities of EDX machines," "dry weight percentages," and the "discrepancy between your findings and those of two US Army laboratories." Under the stern gaze of a government official who conducted the meeting but refused to give his name or position, Matsumoto finally got one FBI consulting scientist to admit that the silica weight percentage was "high"—a victory in the eyes of the *cognoscenti* only.

The debate over additives and silica endures. The more Coen and Nadler listened to the range of expert opinions, the more they became convinced that the anthrax found in the letters to the senators required a skill set and equipment not found even in Ivins' high security lab within Fort Detrick. They tended to believe Jacobsen and his ilk. But they listed to others as well.

In the fall of 2007, they had gone up to Harvard to interview Matthew Meselson, a professor who had advised the CIA and the FBI for decades on germ warfare and who had supported the FBI assertion that the anthrax in question appeared to be free of special weaponized coatings. Meselson had examined micrographic photos of the Senate attack powder and saw no additive. "The spores looked very pure," he said. The journalists pressed him on the findings of the AFIP that *did* find silica in the samples. Meselson said he couldn't really comment because "they haven't released their data for independent verification." The release, he noted, was prevented by the ongoing Amerithrax probe. Nadler then brought up the letter of a UN representative named Kay Mereish that was published in the August 2007 issue of *Applied and Environmental Microbiology*. Mereish's letter noted a recent speech in Paris by an unnamed US scientist who had examined the attack powder and concluded it contained an additive that made it a more effective weapon. At that Meselson rose and extracted a document from a folder nearby. "I can show you this," he said, "but you can't make a copy." Nadler read what he took to be an internal FBI memo, which suggested that the forensic expert who had given that speech may have violated security statutes and could face investigation.

"These are very sensitive areas," said Meselson. "One should be very careful here."

They had been warned. Just as Dallas had its second gunman, Amerithrax had its silica—a forensic detail that implied conspiracy.

Nonetheless, the FBI publicly would contemplate only the theory of a lone mailman. And even before Bruce Ivins, they had one. His name was Steven Hatfill, and by March 2002, they put him on the hot seat.

A PERSON OF INTEREST

Steven Hatfill is broad-shouldered in the way that makes his suit coat sit funny unless his arms are crossed in front of him like a bouncer. He walks with a slight limp that he sometimes attributes to a combat wound. He has a deep cowlick and a grim set to his mouth. He looks like a mashup of a Soviet apparatchik and used car salesman, but he's also gifted with natural charm. Not to mention expertise on scuba and submarine medicine. He could save you if you got the bends. Or got sucked out of a depressurized plane. He can do a skin graft or a C-section and he's worked with monkeys infected with the Ebola and Marburg viruses. When the FBI named Hatfill a "person of interest," a bioweapons specialist who trained CIA agents and commandos in counter-terrorism and germ-warfare preparedness, he fought back.

In October 2001, Steven Hatfill was developing a mobile germ unit similar in schemata to the units the Bush administration would shortly be accusing Iraq of building. The unit would be used for training, it was posited, since it would be "real in all its non-functioning parts," including a mill that would grind anthrax into inhalable powder. The project, contracted out to Hatfill's then-employer Science Applications International Corporation (SAIC), was considered "highly classified," perhaps because it skirted the 1972 ban on biological weapons. Whatever its covert nature, the secret Pentagon project was nothing but suspicious to FBI agents on the hunt for an anthrax assassin. Investigators were also struck by an earlier Hatfill endeavor—a paper outlining bioterrorism scenarios, and detailing, in particular, the most effective method of staging an anthrax attack, using fine powder, delivered in the mail. Hatfill did not author the paper; he only commissioned it from an anthrax specialist who held multiple patents for the weaponization of the bacteria. But soon after its publication someone appeared to follow its blueprint, which, along with the mobile germ unit, had Hatfill's name on it, and so Hatfill became, in August 2002, a target in the Amerithrax investigation. This formal interest-taking by the government happened in a press conference, not in a court of law. Hatfill was never charged with a crime, but he was dogged by the Feds 24/7 for the next five years.

Hatfill made good TV, so camera crews would frequently tag after the agents in their slow-moving pursuit. There were the raids on his apartment and a search of his rented storage facility in Florida, carried out by bloodhounds and men in Hazmat suits. There was heavy machinery for dredging of the pond in the hills of the nature reserves overlooking Fort Detrick with implications that Hatfill himself had dumped his toys in the isolated spot—federal agents helpfully provided a helicopter to the media to film the $250,000 operation from on high. There was the near comic confrontation between Hatfill and his handlers on a Georgetown street, ending in the FBI car running over the suspect's foot and a policeman handing the offended party a ticket for "walking to create a hazard." Everything this guy did, it seemed, was malice aforethought.

Hatfill's resume was curious to be sure. And it was not without its incriminating moments. For starters, much of it was made up. Hatfill's lawyer Tom Connolly admitted as much on the television newsmagazine *60 Minutes* when he said in reference to his client's "forged" PhD diploma: "Listen, if puffing on your resume made you the anthrax killer, then half this town should be suspect."

But Hatfill was bolder. He huffed and he puffed and lambasted the FBI with two back-to-back press conferences in which he accused the bureau of launching a smear campaign. "A person of interest," he told journalists sarcastically, "is someone who comes into being when the government is under intense political pressure to solve a crime but can't do so, either because the crime is too difficult to solve or because the authorities are proceeding in what can mildly be called a wrongheaded manner." He spoke for twenty minutes and declined to take questions. Some reporters said he was close to tears. Other observers saw a man capable of extreme measures of self-defense. Don't mess with Hatfill. He might give you a case of the bends. Or Marburg.

What he did do was sue.

It wasn't Hatfill's germ unit or his ties to "spooky contractors" like SAIC, a well-connected Beltway outfit with military and intelligence contracts (whose acronym, it was frequently pointed out, should be played backwards like a Beatles record), that made him a person of interest to Coen. It was the fact that long before he had become a "rising star in the world of biological defense," an expert tapped by both the Pentagon and by the UN weapons inspectors program, Hatfill was messing around in Africa.

Doing his own research, Coen traced Hatfill's resume: a biology degree from a Kansas college and a short stint at the Army's Fort Bragg installation, followed by a year in Zaire to work with a Methodist missionary doctor. Coen took note. He found that he could never rid his voice of quotation marks when he spoke of Hatfill's unorthodox medical background, since from his time in Rhodesia he knew that one of the favorite covers for CIA operatives based in Zaire supporting the US-backed faction in the civil war next door in Angola, was, in fact, the guise of missionaries.

Africa apparently appealed to Hatfill, as did the nineteen-year-old daughter of the Methodist doctor. Hatfill and Caroline Eschtruth were married in 1976, but less than a year later, Angolan rebels backed by Cubans seized Hatfill's father-in-law, Glenn Eschtruth, during a cross-border incursion into Zaire. His body was found a few weeks later.

In 1978, Hatfill left his wife and moved on to medical school. This is where Coen's interest really picked up. Because the school Hatfill enrolled in was the Godfrey Huggins School of Medicine in Salisbury, Rhodesia.

"What a curious place for an American to do his residency. Curious time too. At the height of one of Africa's bloodiest race wars," Coen noted to Nadler. "It looks like he had quite a temper. When he failed a course, he got pissed off and smashed an office window. But here's the crucial thing. You know who taught at Godfrey Huggins? Bob Symington, that's who."

Robert Symington was the head of anatomy at Godfrey Huggins School of Medicine and considered the father of Rhodesia's biological and chemical weapons program. According to reports, he recruited like-minded students to work on his secret experiments that included crude weaponization of anthrax, ricin, and thallium. Coen took note that around that same time Hatfill has claimed that he was working with Rhodesia's Special Air Service (SAS), an Army special forces unit some say was involved in the deployment of chemical and biological agents.

Later, at the end of the Rhodesian war, Symington joined tens of thousands of other white Rhodesians fleeing south ahead of the transfer of power to a democratically elected black government. Symington reportedly assisted South Africa, the last bastion of white rule on the continent, with its sinister covert germ warfare programs: the apartheid regime's Project Coast.

Steven Hatfill, after completing his medical degree, also moved to South Africa. He was attached at various hospitals as well as a mission to Antarctica. After his adventures in Africa, Hatfill returned to America—not to the heartland, but to the biological weapons orbit around Washington, DC where he worked at the National Institutes of Health, then at Fort Detrick, and then at SAIC where he worked on the mock-up of a "bioterrorist laboratory" for training exercises. Hatfill was apparently connected with well-wired operators on two continents. "This is a guy who's been around some very interesting places," said Nadler.

"And now someone is making him the fall guy," added Coen.

Neither journalist was surprised when in July 2008, Hatfill was awarded $5.8 million for damages in his case against the US government. "He's a rugged man who fought back hard. They're paying him to just go away. I haven't even heard a hint of a book deal—which is par for the course in DC scandals," Nadler summed up. A month later, the FBI officially exonerated the man they had dogged, saying Hatfill "was not involved in the anthrax mailings." But the admission came only after the Ivins death. The contrast between the swaggering virologist punching his way out of his jam, and the brooding tormented dead man who took his place was stark. The FBI had been burned and learned its lesson: Don't tangle with the tough guy.

But Hatfill didn't go too far away. He continued to pound at other parties he held responsible for his lost reputation and career, suing the *New York Times* and *Vanity Fair* for libel and defamation. And when the bureau that had dogged him for years was put on the hotseat and grilled by Specter and Grassley over the Ivins affair in September 2008, Hatfill was sitting in the gallery. Making an entrance not unlike a tomcat fat with canary, the maligned man turned millionaire basked in the flash of cameras before taking his seat next to a brigade of so-called Pink

Ladies—ubiquitous protesters who feel at home when denouncing authority. Hatfill glanced down at his neighbor's sign: "We Don't Trust the FBI," but made no response.

Only when Senator Leahy rebuked Director Mueller for wasting time and money in the Hatfill affair and asked him, "Isn't he owed an apology?" did Hatfill's tough-guy demeanor crack—and he smiled.

The next day Coen and Nadler drove out of the capital and headed for Frederick, Maryland. They drove past Fort Detrick, where both Hatfill and Ivins had risen to prominence in the USAMRIID labs. "A giant germ factory," mused Coen. Then they drove past the homes of both scientists—Ivins' modest bungalow, Hatfill's empty unit in the Detrick Plaza Apartments—just minutes apart and with views of the top-secret facility's security fence. Finally, they cruised past the funeral home where Bruce Ivins' remains awaited their final disbursement. The journalists drove some moments contemplating this latest anthrax grave. "Dead men tell no tales . . ." noted Nadler. "Unless he left e-mails." Coen nodded. He was thinking that Ivins was just the latest in a procession of germ war scientists who knew some awful truths about secret knowledge and died under mysterious circumstances. "The body count is rising," said Coen.

CHAPTER TWO

Enter Stephen Dresch

THE SCOURGE OF BIOPORT

Coen and Nadler would not be where they were in the autumn of 2008—knee-deep in declassified documents, forensic reports, scribbled notes and interview transcripts; on deadline with a dark film and book about the international biowarfare underworld that encompassed years of globe-trotting, lab-sniffing, interview-begging and dirty-tricks witnessing; on edge about every new underreported anthrax-related revelation; and far more comfortable with bacterial bombshells than they would perhaps care to be—without the work of Stephen Dresch.

Dresch was an independent investigator—a sleuth-for-hire whose constant quarry were corruption, incompetence, professional negligence and government turpitude. He was an intellectual—a former college dean with an Ivy League doctorate in economics who never rid his speech of academe, even when lowering the boom on mobsters or reading the riot act to high-ranked public servants. A Republican-leaning Libertarian from the notoriously independent-minded Upper Peninsula of Michigan—which he represented in the state legislature for two years in the '90s before being ousted, he always claimed, by Karl Rove's operatives—Dresch wore the physical trappings of an iconoclast. By the time he entered Coen and Nadler's realm, age had bleached his full beard and long hair; years of chain smoking had stained his fingers and teeth. He looked, many would comment, more like the Unabomber than a tireless crime buster who harried the FBI to catch America's most wanted. But even in the last years of his life there was an unquenchable youthful light in his eyes—a ray of determination to somehow lessen the badness caused by the overwhelming abundance of malefactors.

After receiving a doctorate in economics from Yale in 1975, Dresch went to work at the National Bureau of Economic Research in New York City and then to a think tank in Vienna where he would take frequent research trips behind the Iron Curtain and in the US. His unorthodox career next landed him at Michigan Tech University's Business and Engineering School in 1985. His five-year tenure as dean of the school culminated in the ouster of several senior officials who, at Dresch's instigation, were convicted on criminal charges of corruption. From that point, Dresch's life became one long search for veracity, progressing from easy-game embezzlement into arenas where the truth, if it ever existed, had gone to die. His final investigative obsession, on which he literally expended his last breath, was anthrax.

It would be easy to write off Stephen Dresch, at first blush, as a conspiracy nut. Bob Coen almost did. Any man who knew as much as Dresch did about the comings and goings of Clinton Commerce Secretary Ron Brown, Oklahoma City bomber

Terry Nichols and 1991 World Trade Center terrorist Ramzi Yusuf must be looking for detours between dead ends, he figured. Dresch, Coen would be the first to admit, gave off an aura of mild wackiness. What, after all, is a "high-level forensic economist?" he wondered. And how do you explain the peculiar alter ego Dresch had apparently invented to hang on his website shingle at "Jhêön & Associates"—one Asphasia Quermut Jhêön, who, in addition to being a truth-seeking sidekick, was also, apparently, a bohemian spirit with deep sources in the Bulgarian and Turkish undergrounds. Together, promised the homepage, Dresch and Asphasia represented "an informal association of individuals dedicated to the principles of liberty and devoted to the exposure and extirpation of corruption." Informal indeed—it was Dresch who answered all of Jhêön's e-mails.

But that did not change the fact that Dresch had helped support his wife and four kids by completing assignments for clients spanning from Lloyd's of London to New York wise guys waging war against the Feds' tough RICO-racketeering statutes. He had proven his chops on more than one occasion, and earned a few headlines. It was his legwork, for example, that helped the Brooklyn District Attorney indict FBI Special Agent Lindley DeVecchio for allegedly assisting a 1992 mob hit in Bensonhurst. The sensational charges were later dismissed under unusual circumstances, but not before Dresch's partner Angela Clemente was badly beaten in a parking lot by unknown assailants. And it was his tip that led the FBI to a cache of explosives left by the Oklahoma City bombers, presumably to execute a tenth anniversary attack in 2005. The bureau first denied finding anything, then quickly buried details about the cache, which Terry Nichols, serving time for the 1995 bombing of the Alfred P. Murrah Building, had revealed to a fellow inmate (and Dresch client), along with the news that the explosives were originally provided to Timothy McVeigh's gang during an FBI-sting gone horribly wrong. Dresch pursued proof of the cover-up with nearly as much vigor as he had applied towards preventing a second act of terrorism.

Throughout his gumshoe voyages, Dresch balanced his oddball behavior with a very strict work ethic. For all his talk of "extirpation" and discoveries of "serious mal-, mis- and non-feasance within the system of criminal justice," Dresch was a factfinder, not a brainstormer. He cast a wide net for the dots he would connect, but once he did, Dresch was more intent on drawing subpoenas than conclusions. "I resist becoming an inveterate 'conspiracy theorist,'" he once wrote to Coen, discouraging him from attributing specific motives to one or more players in their anthrax drama. "The answer may be as simple as . . . sloth, indifference, narrow self-interest."

It was a convoluted path that led Dresch from Oklahoma City to Fort Detrick and secret germ labs abroad. But he wasn't surprised when it passed close to his own home. Because what he labeled "the international bioweapons mafia"—a mob he considered the biggest threat to humanity in the twenty-first century—had first come to his attention in the Upper Peninsula Michigan landscape. For Stephen Dresch, the case began with a company called BioPort.

BioPort came into being in 1998, when the state-owned Michigan Biological Products Institute (MBPI) was sold at auction for $24 million. The primary investors and new owners were the Lebanese financier Ibrahim El-Hibri and his son Fuad, an international telecom magnate with German and eventually US citizenship. The El-Hibris were reported to be known as "friendly to American interests" but also, according to dicey websites, "close to the bin-Laden family." It would be a couple more years before Michael Moore's *Fahrenheit 9/11* hammered home the truth that those weren't mutually exclusive, but already, the El-

Hibris were raising many red flags.

What excited the blood of the conspiracy-mongers was the fact that this little-known facility—MBPI—held the exclusive contract to provide the US government with the anthrax vaccine, and that in addition to the physical plant, the Michigan sale included $130 million in contracts with the Department of Defense. That compelled Dresch, among others, to do some due diligence. He learned that the El-Hibris had participated in the privatization of portions of the United Kingdom's leading biodefense facility, Porton Down, a decade earlier. As part owners of the spun-off private holdings Porton International and Porton Products, the family was a key player in the sale and distribution of all UK manufactured anthrax vaccine. This included doses sold to Saudi Arabia in a series of deals approved by the British Ministry of Defense in 1990 at a time when the US refused to sell doses to the Saudis. With the acquisition of the Michigan plant, the family had planted stakes in the only two leading anthrax vaccine producers in the West.

The El-Hibris did not have science backgrounds or biotech business experience before the Porton takeover—but were clearly canny investors. What alarmed Dresch—and he was not alone—was the troubling fact that the sale of MBPI to BioPort had transferred control of a sensitive government program to a network of companies, one of which was headquartered offshore in the Dutch Caribbean. Fuad El-Hibri himself informed Congress in 1999 that the controlling shareholder in BioPort—Intervac LLC—was partly owned by I and F Holdings NV, a Netherlands Antilles investment company owned by his father. No one on the House Committee on Government Reform asked him if El-Hibri senior had any partners in I and F Holdings. So a legitimate question was raised: Who actually owned the largest anthrax vaccine manufacturing plant in the West, if not the world? Who really knew?

Dresch began studying just how Ibrahim and Fuad El-Hibri had managed such a sweet arrangement. His attentions focused on the third key player in the BioPort deal, Admiral William J. Crowe, a former Chairman of the Joint Chiefs of Staff and a 13 percent stakeholder in Intervac, which the El-Hibris used to purchase MBPI and transform it into BioPort. A guy, Dresch surmised, who would have better luck talking the Pentagon into spending money in Michigan than even the most amenable, pro-American Lebanese or German businessmen.

Admiral Crowe, like a disproportionate number of the characters that Dresch collected files on in the 1990s, was born in Oklahoma City. He was a self-styled Anglophile who, after serving as senior military commander under Ronald Reagan and George H.W. Bush, endorsed the "draft-dodging" Bill Clinton for president. Crowe landed the British ambassador's post from the victorious Clinton, which he held for three years before he left government to join the biotech revolution.

The anthrax vaccine peddled by Crowe's new business partners was made mandatory for most soldiers deployed overseas by the Clinton Defense Department in 1998. This new world order earned him and BioPort the tight scrutiny of a vocal and organized lot of veterans convinced that the maladies suffered by soldiers under the catch-all diagnosis of Gulf War Syndrome were directly linked to the Michigan plant's anthrax vaccine, which had been administered to about 150,000 troops (members of the US military) during the 1990 war.

Dr. Meryl Nass, a practitioner based in Maine, emerged as an outspoken advocate for the vets. She reported that the vaccine was linked to multiple sclerosis and lupus as well as illnesses symptomatic of Gulf War Syndrome, like memory loss, muscle and joint pain, severe fatigue and gastrointestinal disorders.

Soon after Crowe testified to Congress in 1999 that he had

"never, repeat never, solicited any official of this administration" to install or promote a mandatory inoculation program, a spokesman told ABC News that the admiral hadn't "invested a penny" in BioPort. Dresch could not resist shooting Crowe a note asking "what services have you provided to your partners ... which warranted their granting to you" a 13 percent interest? He chided the admiral for BioPort's tripling the cost of its vaccine in its latest military contract (from $3.50 to over $10 a dose). The challenge, typed on Jhêön & Associates letterhead, was copied to the Chairman of the House Committee on Government Reform. It was Stephen Dresch's opening thrust in what would become a prolonged battle for transparency in the corporate universe of biodefense. And throughout his later travels and investigations, BioPort remained in his thoughts: especially when Fuad El-Hibri admitted to Congress in 1999 that he jacked the price of a single dose of the vaccine to $40 when he sold 30,000 doses to the Canadian government for its soldiers destined for the Coalition of the Willing.

Dresch already had an anthrax ax to grind. He had been hired to investigate the sudden death of an Oklahoma City associate of US Commerce Secretary Ron Brown (who, thanks to a suspicious airline crash over Croatia, was also dead). Mr. Ron Miller, 53, was up to his eyeballs in an oil and gas scandal involving an associate of President Bill Clinton, an affair that could have reached the Oval Office, when he dropped dead one morning in 1997 due to "natural causes," according to the Oklahoma City medical examiner. But Dresch had determined that the postmortems were consistent with inhalation anthrax poisoning's unique killing mode. On his persistence, the medical examiner officially changed his verdict to "unknown."

With these two anthrax beachfronts taken, Dresch lit an unfiltered Pall Mall and unstrapped his battle helmet for a moment. But just as soon as he stashed his *Bacillus anthracis* files in the back end of his cabinet, did the microbe raise its virulent head once more—in post offices along the eastern seaboard. He joined the fray almost immediately, writing congressional investigators and the FBI about leads he thought they should follow and bulking up his own Internet operations.

Dresch was not prepared to point a finger at a single suspect in the 2001 anthrax attacks. His goal was to get as many fingers pointing into as many secret corners as possible. Dresch was fast concluding that the diabolical powder was the key to a number of as yet unexplained alliances and secret motives. Germ warfare, like politics, he supposed, had made some very strange bedfellows. Every time the news referred to the anthrax letters as an "unprecedented attack on US soil," Dresch sighed. Already, he warned investigators, it may have been used by assassins aligned with a sitting US president. And there were other precedents, he pointed out, less close to home—enough to warrant a broader search by the FBI—broader than US borders, and far beyond Fort Detrick.

When investigators began focusing on a lone domestic culprit, Dresch quickly sent a corrective missive: "In fact, whether of domestic or foreign origin, these anthrax incidents emerge within the rich context of current and historical, foreign and domestic activity involving lethal biological and chemical agents, and the elements comprising this context are interrelated across time and geography." The phrases "rich context," "lethal biological and chemical agents" and "interrelated across time and geography" were all in bold text. The letter was sent to Henry Hyde, chairman of the House Committee on International Relations.

Dresch, of course, suggested that BioPort should be a corporation of interest. In point of fact, Bruce Ivins, working at Fort Detrick, was helping the company out with some technical problems it was having with the vaccine around the time of the attacks.

And even the FBI leaked suggestions that one possible motive Ivins had for mailing killer anthrax was to cause a panic, making his vaccine work more valuable. It took the FBI seven years to concede the corporate connection, when it released Ivins' e-mails detailing some of his frustrations with the vaccine program. It was a rare moment indeed when Stephen Dresch and the FBI were in agreement.

When the FBI introduced Steven Hatfill as a "person of interest" in the anthrax investigation, Dresch was only too willing to look into it. He noted the scientist's work at Fort Detrick, his ongoing mobile germ unit project and the papers he commissioned on anthrax that cast his biowar preparedness credentials in a suspect light. In the weeks following Hatfill's sudden dominance of the 24-hour news cycle, Dresch contacted nearly every reference on Hatfill's eye-popping CV, learning that much of it was bogus.

Dresch was particularly interested in Hatfill's Rhodesian experience. He found himself spending a great deal of time on the website of a Rhodesian Special Forces unit, the Selous Scouts, trying to find someone who could confirm that Hatfill was one of them. That is where Bob Coen, who was asking the same question, found him in December 2001.

When Coen told Nadler that he had met a like-minded soul over the Internet, Nadler logged on too, heading for Dresch's personal website. He ignored the funky portal, with its ghostly charcoal sketch of the author (apparently a scan of a sidewalk portrait done by an Arbat street artist in Moscow) and dove into the website's meat: Dresch was posting not only long memos he wrote to congressional leaders and FBI officials overseeing aspects of the anthrax case, but also some hard-to-find documents he had unearthed relative to the investigation. Dresch was clearly intrigued with the international aspects of the case—roads that Nadler and Coen had not yet connected to Amerithrax in any definite fashion. He was focused on the

South African apartheid state's anthrax activities within its notorious germ warfare program, Project Coast. Perhaps there was a Johannesburg connection to the anthrax attacks?

Dresch was willing to share leads with Coen. His standard MO favored the inclusive, and he regularly traded information with professional and citizen journalists. Dresch talked regularly with writers from the *New York Times*, *Washington Post* and FreeRepublic.com and posted relevant documents on the web as soon as he obtained them.

Both Coen and Nadler liked the fact that he was working the case pro bono and had built up a small international network of other investigators: there was a Russian with KGB connections, a South African investigative journalist and assorted arms dealers living in southern climes who had all signed on to help. Dresch, it seemed, was a full-service operation. And a fearless one at that. His leads linked anthrax to intelligence agencies, multinational corporations and secret military operations. And he would thank all his sources, no matter how sinister the leads they provided, with a calm sign-off—instructions to "Carry on."

Nadler and Coen were particularly impressed with a 1994 memo Dresch promised to share. It was a Top Secret report from the South African Army's surgeon general to South African President Nelson Mandela detailing how the military allegedly dumped the deadly stocks from its notoriously racist germ war program into the South Atlantic Ocean shortly after the fall of apartheid. The actual fate of these so-called legacy stocks had been ambiguous for years. This document, if true, was a nice part of the puzzle. "We've got to meet this guy," Nadler said to Coen. "Ask him if he's heading to New York soon."

That afternoon they called Michigan and invited Dresch to come to Brooklyn for a discussion about a documentary, collaboration and all things germ related. The next day, the detective hopped into his reconverted 1989 Chevy police cruiser and, fueled by black coffee and unfiltered nicotine, drove forty hours for the meeting.

When Dresch walked into their office on a grey winter day in 2003, he was enveloped in smoke and wrapped in a battered grey trench coat—a character straight out of central casting. He was articulate, clear-eyed, sober and just a tad melodramatic. Crossing the office to stand before the picture window overlooking the East River, Dresch peered at the high-rises across the water in Manhattan and shook his shaggy head. "I don't like it," he grumbled. "It's a clear sniper shot from the other side." He kept a straight face for a beat and then allowed the briefest of smiles to escape.

"Now what exactly can I do for you fellows?" he asked.

The three of them talked for hours. Nadler saw in Dresch just what he had hoped for—an American original with no political hang-ups, neither an ideological hardhead at war with the neocons, nor a wild-eyed conspiracy theorist. Nadler sensed Dresch's deep distrust of federal law enforcers. The PI was willing to work with mob-connected clients to bring down bureau bigwigs he considered irreparably tainted by entrenched self-interests.

"The FBI is so acutely politicized, it won't touch anything that smells of Pandora," he told the journalists. "There's too much to lose in this anthrax case. The bureau doesn't even want to know what's in there."

Dresch didn't have much more respect for a lot of the press, which was too easily misdirected in the chaotic post-9/11 news atmosphere.

"To a large degree, it's up to individual citizens on this one, gentlemen," he concluded. Coen and Nadler both guessed that

Dresch had come to the same conclusion time and time again in his career. But they were fine with that.

"I don't see how we could find a better protagonist for our story," Coen told Nadler, as their guest inspected the fire escape. "He's the guy," agreed Nadler. "Our Philip Marlowe."

The meeting proceeded to a bar down the block from the office, where the three lowered their voices and began sharing notes. Dresch painted for Bob and Eric a vision of a tangled, secretive web of unholy alliances, putting the most cataclysmic of weapons in the hands of unscrupulous men. He spoke of proxy wars on the African continent and the Soviet and US bioweapon programs behind them; he told them about the "Shy Fish," a man who had been known to take receipt of North Korean weapons on his private boat in the middle of the Pacific, and who organized the delivery of genetically mutated biological agents smuggled into the US from South Africa in a tube of toothpaste; he told them the story behind the racist gynecologist whose refrigerator of germs forced the evacuation of an entire suburban Los Angeles subdivision; he filled them in on the connections he had drawn between Ron Brown, the Oklahoma City bombing, and the Amerithrax attacks; he reminded them that it was the US that had provided Iraq with biological weapons materials ("You've got Don Rumsfeld sitting over in Baghdad drinking scotch with Saddam Hussein, probably watching porno movies"); he spoke of the mysterious deaths of scores of microbiologists since 2001; and he assured them of the existence of a powerful "international bioweapons mafia" that met clandestinely in the 1980s at a resort in Luxembourg

"Why do I do this? Why do I delve into such dangerous affairs?" he responded to a question about what motivated him. "I'm interested in the nightmare world, and I guess it boils down to my need to know how the world really works and find the thread that unravels all of the mysteries. I've always believed that truth is a powerful disinfectant worth discovering and spreading. There you have it."

Another round of beers and many more incomplete threads later, Coen and Nadler were resolved. They would follow as many of Dresch's leads as possible, with their cameras squarely trained on the smoking detective. They intuited that these would lead to many more graves and to scandals and to the ghosts that would haunt both. They toasted their newfound quest. Excitedly, Coen and Nadler wondered if their film and book might do more than ask questions—they might posit answers. Dresch stamped out his cigarette and lit another.

"Let me tell you guys something," he said, exhaling smoke from his mouth, nose and, it seemed in the amber-lit bar, his ears. "I've always had very modest expectations of the effect of anything that I have done. Ultimately you do what you do because it's interesting. You don't do it because it's important; in the greater scheme of things, nothing ultimately is important."

There was a long minute of silence as the three men deferred to this existential dismissal. Then Dresch brought the team back to the real world and announced the next step in the investigation. He had long thought it crucial to meet a man who knew more secrets about the dark world of biological warfare than anyone. That man was David Kelly, one-time head of the UK's microbiology department at Porton Down, their equivalent of Fort Detrick. It was Kelly who led the UN's bioinspections in Iraq and who had crossed political lines and national borders to learn from germ warriors in the Soviet Union, South Africa and Iraq. And Dresch had learned from a reliable source that Kelly was "privy to some highly sensitive information regarding the Daschle anthrax while visiting the US" and had imparted this to Tony Blair at a briefing. And some people "in certain circles," he was told, were quite unhappy at these revelations.

The trio parted ways and with salutations and specific plans for follow-ups. Dresch was put in charge of forging a liaison to David Kelly. But before long, they learned that Kelly was almost certainly out of their reach. For in late July 2003, it was David Kelly was found dead. Dead in the woods.

CHAPTER THREE

The Ghost of David Kelly

THE DODGY DOSSIER

David Kelly is buried in the gothic quiet of St. Mary's Longworth cemetery in Oxfordshire. From his grave you can see the dense foliage of Harrowdown Hill, where the microbiologist was found dead on the morning of July 18, 2003. Just fifty-eight years old and at the pinnacle of his career, he was, to some, a man who knew too much about the secrets of state biodefense and the germ weapon business. His death was officially ruled as a suicide. In the official narrative, Kelly had slit his left wrist, swallowed twenty-some painkillers—co-proxamol—swiped from his wife's medicine cabinet, and thus, had ended his career before others could end it for him.

Just a short drive from Oxford, the village of Southmoor is nestled alongside the A420 road, sharing pubs and neighbors and favorite walks with the villages of Kingston to the west and Longworth to the north. Kelly was known to take in a game of cribbage at the Hind's Head down the road from his cottage, and he took particular pleasure in walking along the bridle paths and open fields surrounding his home.

But Kelly was most in his element on foreign, even enemy, soil. He was a WMD inspector. His job was to tramp around places where nobody wanted him and to peek behind the scenes into places they wanted him even less. He was exceptionally good at it, and colleagues said he enjoyed the work. Three years prying open the secret germ weapons factories of Siberia, followed by three dozen trips to Iraq to assess Saddam Hussein's potential as a biological warrior had made Kelly an unusually well-known character in an intentionally low-profile business. As far as bacteriologists go, David Kelly, senior adviser to the UN weapons inspections team, was almost famous.

And then in May 2003, Kelly supposedly went off message in a big way. He is said to have talked to journalists about what he knew and what he didn't know about Iraq's biological weapons program. What he may have said threatened to bring down the government. Instead, it brought down David Kelly. And what he did or didn't know informed US Secretary of State Colin Powell's performance with an anthrax vial at the United Nations, who reminded the world that the small container of powder he held generated mass fear in the US and beyond during the anthrax attacks before going on to warn that Saddam had vats full of the stuff and could launch a horrible biowar in 45 minutes. This was an effective pitch—arguably the most effective primal rationale for going to war against Iraq.

The Kelly affair actually had less to do with anthrax and Iraq than it did with public trust and a high-stakes row between the government and the media. It centered around allegations that Prime Minister Tony Blair and his top advisers had ordered intelligence agencies to bolster the case for war against Iraq by exaggerating the existing data on Saddam Hussein's secret weapons programs. Kelly, among many Defense Ministry experts, was uncomfortable with some of the language found in the dossier prepared in September of 2002. He implied as much to a reporter, Andrew Gilligan of the BBC.

"It was 'sexed up,'" paraphrased Gilligan from that now infamous encounter.

The sobriquet was catnip for the press and a public relations disaster for a prime minister skating on the thin edge of infamy.

It had been ten years since Kelly stepped down as head of microbiology at the government's top weapons research facility, Porton Down, but his salary as a weapons consultant and adviser on arms control was still paid by the Ministry of Defense. His expertise was increasingly sought after and widely shared. He was often seconded by the Foreign Office in issues of intelligence and by the United Nations arms control watchdog agencies. Technically (and significantly, in the case of the Iraq dossier), Kelly was a civilian with unusually broad access to military secrets and a mandate to provide background material for the press. For twenty years, Kelly navigated the sensitive shoals of his work with a foot in both circles—intelligence and media. But in the late spring of 2003, he tripped . . . or was tripped.

Kelly corresponded regularly with a number of journalists—Judith Miller of the *New York Times* and James Bone of *The Times of London* relied on his input in reporting issues related to weapons programs, biowarfare and rogue regimes. But these were background conversations, nearly always off-the-record. Some reporters figured Kelly was a convenient way for MI5, the British military intelligence agency, to leak information to the press. Others considered him a straight-shooting expert who kept beat journalists on track. More than one insider would say point blank that Kelly was a spy.

Andrew Gilligan was not on Kelly's list of close media acquaintances, but as Gilligan had recently returned from assignment in Baghdad, the scientist agreed to meet with him to hear the reporter's impression of how things were going in Iraq, since he had not been there in some time. In return, Gilligan wanted to get Kelly's view of the fact that no weapons of mass destruction had as yet been found. When their informal conversation turned away from Baghdad and towards 10 Downing Street, Gilligan began to take notes. Based partly on those notes, one week later he went live on the air to talk about how the failure of the coalition in Iraq to find Saddam Hussein's much-touted weapons of mass destruction had damaged the reputation of the Blair government, saying:

A week before the publication date of the Iraq dossier, it was actually rather a bland production. It didn't—the draft prepared for Mr. Blair by the intelligence agencies actually didn't say very much more than was public knowledge already, and Downing Street, our source says, ordered a week before publication, ordered it to be sexed up, to be made more exciting, and ordered more facts to be discovered.

It was a shocking revelation. The media immediately pounced upon Gilligan's phrase "sexed up." Downing Street, on the other hand, homed in on his reference to "our source," and particularly, to its singularity.

David Kelly, in the hullabaloo that followed the BBC broadcast, did not even recognize Gilligan's "senior official in charge of drawing up the dossier" as himself—or so he testified some months later. His role in the dossier was hardly central; he had been asked to provide historical background about the Iraqi chemical and biological weapons program—not to analyze the current intelligence. But Gilligan in his Parliamentary testimony on June 13, 2003, characterized his source as "a civil servant in the non-secret part of the Civil Service as distinct from the secret part." This was a more accurate description of David Kelly.

Kelly had indeed voiced concerns, particularly with the report's conclusion that Iraq possessed a "vast arsenal." The regime, he insisted during a March 2002 seminar at London's University College, possessed only the potential to build an arsenal. It was a subtlety that the government preferred not to respect. There was also the matter of the dossier's alarming claim that Iraq could launch a full-scale germ attack on forty-five minutes' notice. He also mentioned to Gilligan—and in the days after the initial story, to other BBC reporters—that the pressure to make the report more urgent in tone had come from the "No. 10 press office."

At the time of the "sexed-up" affair, the press office of No. 10 Downing Street was, for all intents and purposes, one man—Alastair Campbell. A combative personality with a wide streak of excess, Campbell was closely aligned to the prime minister, professionally, politically and personally. He started his career as a journalist, writing for tabloids and men's magazines and then as the political correspondent for the *Daily Mirror*. An alcoholic, ambitious, unapologetic left-winger, Campbell flew high in the '80s. It landed him in a psych ward where he spent several days recovering from his crack-up. Dried out and medicated, Campbell began his recovery, which was soon given a kick-start with the acquaintance of Tony Blair, a fresh-faced candidate for Labour Party leader. In 1994, Campbell left journalism for politics and then married the two on Blair's succession to the prime ministership. The Blair press office of No. 10 Downing Street, created and controlled by the still addictive personality of the pugnacious, bagpipe-playing Scot, was considered the most powerful in Britain's history.

Campbell didn't lose a minute in responding to the Gilligan charge, demanding a retraction and even an apology. The BBC demurred. Within days, the dispute had escalated into all-out war, with both sides willing to sacrifice a great deal rather than back down. Campbell, who had once punched out a fellow reporter, was oil on the fire, calling the BBC reporting, "a fundamental attack upon the integrity of the government, the prime minister, the intelligence agencies, let alone . . . the evil spin doctors in the dark who do their dirty works in the minds of the journalists." Disregarding years of experience at London's legendarily hype-driving tabloids, Campbell asserted in an interview, "I think the public are probably bored rigid with all this." They were wishful words, ones which his interviewer Jon Snow did not miss as disingenuous, offering that the public would likely stay tuned as long as Campbell himself continued with his "extraordinary intemperate language." (He had twice accused the BBC of "weasel words.")

With his boss on the line and his own name implicated, Campbell pursued his relentless attack. The battle continued through the end of June, with the media apparently winning: Polls showed a government deeply distrusted by its constituents; newspapers protracted the scandal with headlines like "Lie Another Day." Even the staid *Economist* magazine piled on, with a close-up shot of the prime minister's concerned face on the cover and the single-word caption "BLIAR."

But by July, the tide was turning. Gilligan had told his editors that his source was Kelly; Kelly had also informed his own higher-ups of the May interview. In Parliament, Campbell was absolved of improperly influencing the content of the so-called dodgy dossier, upping the stakes in the feud between Downing Street and the BBC. It was at this moment, perhaps the hottest in the super-charged event, that the Ministry of Defense chose to drop Kelly into the firing line by naming him publicly as Gilligan's source. The Ministry of Defense press office called Kelly and told him to leave town, as a baying pack of press hounds was headed for his door. Kelly and his wife fled to

Cornwall. They returned to London some days later, when the renowned scientist was summoned before Parliament for questioning. As denouement of an unprecedented drama, it did not disappoint.

There, before an inquiry panel of ten, sat a man who had held his own against Iraqi thugs and Soviet generals. Kelly was known as an extremely tough negotiator—a man said to have bullied a woman to tears while in the interrogator's seat. (Iraq's anthrax expert, "Dr. Germ," would never regain her tough-as-nails reputation.) It was, by all accounts, a humiliating moment for Kelly, who was forced to split hairs and defer humbly. The hearing room was thick with discomfort. Kelly's questioners repeatedly asked him to speak up over the noise of the fans. Kelly apologized for his "soft voice."

Under oath, Kelly denied being the source of Gilligan's story, denied having expressed disbelief in the September dossier and denied having told a reporter that the government had been "obsessed with finding intelligence to justify an immediate Iraqi threat"—a comment that wound up on the evening news soon after Gilligan's report and was attributed to "a senior official intimately involved with the process of pulling together the original September dossier."

Throughout the forty-five minute hearing, Kelly enjoyed little dignity from his questioners, some of whom exhibited an unattractive mixture of displaced sympathy and mocking impatience: "Your Ministers, then, are responsible for treating you uniquely as a civil servant in highly publicizing you before going to the Intelligence and Security Committee . . . why did you go along with it, Dr. Kelly?" asked Sir John Stanley, inferring that Kelly was willingly taking heat for his Ministry of Defense employers. "You were being exploited were you not? Why did you feel it was incumbent upon you to go along with the request that clearly had been made to you to be thrown to the wolves?"

Kelly deferred to the Ministry to answer that. But he would soon hear it again from Andrew Mackinlay: "I reckon you are chaff; you have been thrown up to deflect our probing. Have you ever felt like a fall guy? You have been set up, have you not?"

At one point the chairman of the panel actually asked the preeminent scientist "what lessons [he had] learned" from the affair, to which Kelly replied, "Never to talk to a journalist again, I think." It was the first ounce of cheek he had mustered all day.

This public rebuke would have been a tough nut to swallow for a man whose job was to suss out fabrication and corral slippery weapons officials to the straight and narrow. He might have felt that his reputation, if not his honor, had been irreparably damaged. Moreover, the negative publicity, he might have feared, could have a deleterious effect on his work—even, perhaps putting him at risk of censure or demotion. His daughter and his wife said that the whole episode had affected him tremendously. They spoke of a man diminished, demoralized and betrayed, "a man with a broken heart." But others would refute that characterization. He had joked with colleagues that the grilling was not much tougher than an oral dissertation defense. He wrote to another that now "the worst is behind me" and that he looked forward to an imminent trip to Iraq for some "real work." Also forthcoming—a daughter's wedding, and the possibility of Knighthood from the Queen, hinted at before the dossier disaster. "Cheerio," was the last thing reportedly heard from David Kelly as he continued on his walk that summer day, after a spot of chat with a neighbor on the road. "Cheerio?" From a man carrying his own death in his pocket?

The notion persisted that the eminent scientist was undone by his public grilling; that he had become hopelessly implicated by the scandal; that Kelly had read his outing by the Defense Ministry as a sour herald of his future; that a man who had concerned himself previously with the safeguarding of humanity against chemical and biological Armageddon was now preoccupied with the safety of his pension.

His last day alive was spent alone in his office, followed by a wordless lunch with his wife. She went up for a nap and he went out for a walk. After his body was found on Harrowdown Hill the next morning, Kelly's family publicly accepted the cause of death as suicide, despite still unexplained forensic and chronological discrepancies. They have been turning away journalists ever since.

WHAT HAPPENED ON HARROWDOWN HILL?

If David Kelly had presented a headache for the Blair government while alive, he proved to be an even larger one dead. News from Harrowdown Hill reached the Prime Minister en route to Tokyo. He immediately and somberly ordered an inquiry and ignored a blunt shout during a press conference that day with the Japanese prime minister: "Prime Minister—do you have blood on your hands?"

The man tasked with conducting the official inquiry was Lord Brian Hutton, an appeals court judge and former chief justice of Northern Ireland. He had already proven his reliability in sensitive state matters when he cleared the British army of any responsibility in the infamous 1972 Bloody Sunday massacre in which twenty-seven civil rights protesters on the wrong end of UK military bullets died in Derry. His mandate now from the Ministry of Justice was "urgently to conduct an investigation into the circumstances surrounding the death of Dr. Kelly." The unspoken mandate was not to rock the boat again. And he delivered.

In just twenty-two days, Hutton heard testimony of seventy-four witnesses—none of them under oath. Much of the questioning tracked the accusations, incriminations, insinuations and insults flying like so many acrobats in a media circus. Hutton's inquiry aimed for the far bar of culpability: Did the government, in particular Downing Street, and in particular Campbell, bear responsibility for Kelly's death by persecution? Did they hound the man to take his own life? It did not explore, indeed stridently ignored, the possibility of a far more direct responsibility. The urgency with which Lord Hutton drew up his conclusions on the "circumstances surrounding" Kelly's death did not translate into careful consideration of the cause of death. In the Hutton Report, Kelly was a suicide until proven otherwise. The burden of proof—well, there was no burden of proof. The coroner's official inquest was pending; any further problems could be worked out then.

To avoid the question of foul play, Hutton and his senior counsel needed to keep their eyes wide shut to a number of glaring inconsistencies among witnesses. They eschewed cross-examination, and relied solely on postmortem pathology reports provided by well-wired experts assigned by the Home Office. This willful lack of curiosity was largely enabled by the fact that Hutton's inquiry lacked subpoena power and an independent jury. No one was on trial. No charges were brought. The formal inquest, which would have brought such authorities, was suspended, and with it much evidence and eyewitness testimony sworn upon a bible. Nobody, observed Dresch, played the game smoother than the British.

On the evening before the release of Hutton's conclusion, Tony Blair spoke out again about the serious nature of Kelly's death, admitting that his job was "at risk" should the report prove critical of the government's handling of the affair. For all his vulnerable sincerity, the prime minister must have known that his job was safe. It would have been a brazen affront to traditional courtesy had Hutton not given Blair a heads-up of any imminent bad news. Indeed, the next day he exonerated the Blair government of overestimating Saddam Hussein's WMDs and of underestimating David Kelly's hurt feelings. The Hutton report concluded that no third party could be held responsible for Kelly's suicide. Lord Hutton insisted that he was "satisfied that Dr. Kelly had taken his own life by cutting his left wrist."

Dresch phoned Coen to say that he, for one, wasn't buying it.

"Do you know what Kelly said before the invasion?" asked Dresch. "He said that if we went into Iraq, he would end up 'dead in the woods.' I'm not kidding. Those were his words."

Even without this eerie prophecy (and Kelly's spooky last e-mail sent to Judith Miller of the *New York Times* referencing "many dark forces playing games") the Harrowdown Hill tragedy was ripe for conspiracy theory. Virtually every aspect of the case, codenamed "Operation Mason" by the Thames Valley Police, invited questions. Amateur sleuths familiar with some of the police accounts wondered why it was local volunteer searchers who found Kelly's body close to mid-morning, and not the police who had been on the case since the night before (or indeed, the heat-seeking helicopter that passed over the wooded promontory in the wee hours after his death). They questioned why those volunteers found the body in one position while the first detectives on the scene reported it in another; why the bottled water, knife and wristwatch reportedly found near the body by the same detectives were not observed by said searchers; why medical experts describe a death by arterial hemorrhage as a decidedly bloody affair, but the paramedics on the scene saw just a few patches of dried blood; why one of those paramedics missed seeing a wound altogether on David Kelly's left wrist; why Kelly's dental records disappeared for two days.

It was the medicine above all that proved most troublesome for the skeptics. Shortly after the Hutton report was released, three doctors—David Halpin, C. Stephen Frost and Searle Sennett—went to the press with their professional opinions that an incision to the left wrist such as the one found on Kelly could not result in a substantial enough loss of blood to cause death. They noted that even—indeed, especially—had the ulnar artery been opened completely, it was highly unlikely to result in fatal blood loss. Moreover, after studying official toxicology reports, they disputed the postmortem's attribution of co-proxamol as potentially fatal.

In Brooklyn, Coen and Nadler added more and more inexplicable rumors to the Kelly file, culled from the Internet: a forty-five-foot antenna in the middle of Kelly's yard, erected by MI5 agents in the middle of the night; a mysterious boating party on the Thames below Harrowdown Hill; a silent "Third Man" in the company of the first detectives on scene, whose identity was never given or alluded to in testimony; eight computers removed from Kelly's home and offices by MI6 agents.

They created a special file for the reports of one Rowena Thursby, a self-proclaimed "Truthseeker," who had taken on the thankless role of preeminent bee in Hutton's bonnet. Thursby wrote prolifically on the inconclusive evidence from Harrowdown Hill and on the apparent unwillingness of authorities to consider scenarios in which Kelly's death was made to look like a suicide. The fact that Thursby was the bedridden author of four different blogs (including one called "Beyond Belief," consisting of a single posting pondering how best to "escape the matrix of belief systems") did not radically damage her credibility among more earthbound rejecters of the government case. She was a tireless collector of discrepancies and nonsequiters. When, three years after the scandal, the BBC produced an hour-long program about Kelly's death on their *Conspiracy Theory* program, Thursby was prominently featured.

Despite her eccentricities, Thursby's argument for giving Kelly a fair shake was well written and focused. Moreover, she had managed to coalesce a unified advocates group of credible medical experts, scholars and lawyers which she named the Kelly Investigation Group and which had a great deal of success in keeping the story alive in the media. So into Coen and Nadler's file went "The New Alchemy: Turning Murder into Suicide." (Page 6 of her report was devoted to "abrasions," "bruises" and her derisive response to Lord Hutton's apparent willingness to accept the three fresh cuts on Kelly's scalp as the result of "contact with the underbrush." *Are we supposed to believe this cool scientist . . . had been hitting his head repeatedly on the ground?* read Thursby's scornful annotation.)

Meanwhile Dresch, Nadler and Coen were weighing motives. Downing Street, they agreed, had much to hide, but an assassination? There were other players, just as Kelly had intimated—"dark actors playing games."

"You've got to understand," Dresch told Coen one night by phone. "Kelly was at the very center. MI5, MI6, CIA and who knows who else, okay? He was basically recruited. He knows all the secrets. And it wasn't just weapons of mass destruction he knew." Dresch again painted for the journalists a portrait of a man who had crossed well over the border of weapons inspector into the shadowy territory of an international mafia dealing in biological arms. Kelly, insisted Dresch, knew more than just the secrets he had been tasked with exposing as a UN weapons inspector; he knew secrets that he had never revealed. For too many people far from Downing Street, David Kelly was a man who knew too much.

The next day Coen booked flights to England for himself and Dresch. He was determined to take a closer look at what happened on Harrowdown Hill and why.

Dresch and Coen landed in England on March 15, 2004, the day before Oxfordshire Coroner Nicholas Gardiner was to hold a hearing on reopening the formal inquest into David Kelly's death that had been superseded by the Hutton Inquiry eight months earlier. The persistent concerns about Hutton's narrow focus and the fact that none of the testimony was under oath provided a firm foundation for the possibility that the inquest, with its powers of subpoena, might be resumed. Even the Inquiry's primary source for postmortem evidence, the Home Office pathologist Nicholas Hunt was now saying that he would "feel more comfortable with a full coroner's inquest." Clearly there was more to reveal than had come to light in the environs of Court 76 at the Royal Courts of Justice.

Early the next morning in the blustery, slate grey English weather, they stood outside the Oxford coroner's court along with a gaggle of news hacks, TV reporters and satellite trucks. "So, this is what a British media circus looks like," Dresch said. Coen talked to various members of the scrum: A man with a boxer hat from Rowena Thursby's Kelly Investigation Group was handing out flyers detailing the cover-up, engaging anyone who would listen to him. The many reporters regarded him with raised eyebrows until one among them crossed over to let him know that his zipper was undone. Meanwhile, an attorney well known for representing intelligence whistle-blowers stepped into the fray. Soon after followed a fellow who identified himself as a "gentleman pig farmer," replete with tweed suit, galoshes and pipe; lastly a bearded youth who had tin foil wrapped around the inside of his scarf and protruding from his socks in order to deflect the radio waves. Dresch and Coen gave each of them a moment to speak about what they were about to witness.

Both Dresch and Coen had hoped that Gardiner's status as a simple county coroner would make him less subject to the political considerations that held court during the Hutton Inquiry. So they were disappointed when the hearing ended ten minutes after it began with Nicholas Gardiner's announcement that he would not be reopening the inquest, citing a lack of fresh evidence. He said Kelly's family was satisfied with the ruling of suicide and he saw "no exceptional reasons" to keep the matter open: "The Lord Chancellor's belief in the adequacy of the inquiry was well founded," the coroner concluded, dismissing lingering public questions about the case. Dresch said this was unconscionable: "He has responded to the doctors and Thursby and the Kelly Group by saying they aren't 'properly interested parties.' This is wrong-headed and just downright un-civic. Isn't it the job of a public coroner to allay the concerns of the public?"

"He is deferring to the family," mused Coen. "He says that their wishes should be protected."

Meanwhile, the TV reporters did their stand-ups. A gentleman in a smart suit did the rounds, making sure he was interviewed by every journalist on the scene. He was Michael Shrimpton, a barrister best known for his campaign to oppose Britain's entry into the European Union. Now he was claiming that French intelligence agents had murdered Kelly in an elaborate plot. Shrimpton had insinuated himself into Thursby's Kelly Investigation Group.

"Who's he working for?" wondered Dresch, who observed that Shrimpton had all the markings of a classic agent provocateur, sent to infiltrate the opposition and muddy the waters. As Rowena's group handed out press releases asking about incon-

as lying flat on his back—was the fact that Coen and Dresch were the first journalists to seek her out.

Before leaving, Dresch asked Holmes to draw him a map of Harrowdown Hill where she and Chapman had discovered Kelly, marking the way she entered the thicket of trees and brambles at the summit and the location of the tree where the body was found. He went over it slowly with her several times to make sure he understood it clearly. Dresch put the map in his pocket.

From there, they headed for the headquarters of the Thames Valley Police, a compound of low-slung buildings in the town of Addington. The Thames Valley Police is the largest suburban Home Office force in Britain, with over 4,000 police officers on staff. Of special interest was Detective Constable Graham Coe, the officer who had run into Holmes and Brock as they came away from Harrowdown Hill. It was Coe, according to Holmes, who was accompanied by two plainclothes detectives, and Coe who told the Inquiry that he was in the company of only one other detective. It was Coe who discovered the knife and the watch that Holmes hadn't seen, and Coe who reported that David Kelly's body was lying horizontally, with his head on the ground.

Coen had contacted the Thames Valley Police before leaving Brooklyn to try and set up an appointment. He had been pleasantly surprised by the friendly voice of press officer Nikky Malin, who was clearly used to handling the media requests. Malin said they would help in any way they could. Coen followed up with a letter asking for quite specific information, at which point Malin grew less helpful. When Dresch and Coen arrived in person, she was nowhere to be found. Nor was there a single officer involved in the Kelly case available to speak with the Americans.

"Time to visit the Bahá'ís," said Dresch when they returned, frustrated, to the car.

It was another odd detail of the David Kelly story: that the

sistencies, the press faded away, except for Coen and D
who continued to film for a while after the media had gor

That evening in the pubs packed with Saint Patrick
revelers, Dresch and Coen sat drinking pints while the T
announcers solemnly declared, "The official debate is o
David Kelly committed suicide."

The next day they met with Dr. John Scurr, a vascular su
some renown, in his Lister Hospital office. Scurr had jo
public criticism of the Hutton report but at first was a
vous about doing an interview. But Dresch insisted, re
him that "your particular expertise makes you emine
fied to explain why you believe the suicide verdict to b
sible." Scurr relented. He hunted about for a pruning
demonstrated the awkwardness of a right-handed m
the artery that runs from his left pinky finger from
towards the inside. Scurr said that he had looked in
and found that there had not been a single reporte
ulnar artery severance reported that year except fo
microbiologist PhD David Kelly. "Bit of a girl's w
things, anyway," he concluded.

The next day as a gale swept across the Oxford
they tracked down Louise Holmes, a member of th
and-rescue team who, along with her dog Brock, a
found Kelly's body. They called her from a villag
nervously told them that she had been warned by
to speak to the media. They quickly drove off to
tage. She reluctantly let them in.

She told them exactly what she had told the Hu
that the dead man she found that morning was
ground, but propped against the tree, and that h
back in a funny position. Stranger than Holmes
clearly contrary to the police report in which Ke

cool-headed, life-long agnostic scientist had been converted before his death to this Middle Eastern faith, shepherded into the flock by a US military intelligence officer. This begged for investigation.

The US agent's name was Mai Pederson. She was a linguist for the US Air Force Intelligence Service whom Kelly met in 1998 while in Iraq looking for weapons. Pederson was his translator. She also knew how to use a gun, fight hand-to-hand combat and, according to the *Daily Mail*, was "an accomplished belly dancer."

Soon after meeting Pederson, Kelly began making occasional appearances in Monterey, California for studies at the US Army's Defense Language Institute, where he took active measures to indoctrinate himself in the Bahá'í Faith. Pederson, his sponsor, lived nearby.

Coen and Nadler eventually confirmed Kelly's "conversion" themselves, in an interview with the Monterey chapter head, a senior citizen named Marilyn Vonberg. She was pleased to have them come talk to her, and just vaguely apologetic that a third party, one Lee Steinmetz, a more media-savvy member of the local Bahá'í, community, had insisted that he be present as well.

"How did you get to know David Kelly?" Coen began. But no sooner had Ms. Vonberg started her answer, saying, "Well, we had a close Bahá'í friend," than Steinmetz interrupted: "Cut. Cut. Cut. I really think it would be better to talk about Dr. Kelly coming to your home and just leave it at that. Ask her again."

So Coen asked Marilyn again how she got to know Kelly . . . and Mai Pederson remained elusive.

What Marilyn and Lee told the journalists was that Dr. David Kelly, after several visits to Monterey, had indeed joined the faith by signing a Bahá'í declaration card.

"It's an important thing to all Bahá'ís when someone says, 'I want to declare.' So we have a card that they sign, and it's quite exciting when someone signs their card. It means you believe in the teachings of the Bahá'í Faith, which is the unity of all religions."

Some five or six million people around the world have embraced the Bahá'í Faith, a monotheistic religion with a strong emphasis on peace, harmony and the unity of all global faiths. Their central mission is to bring peace to the world and unite people of different religions and races. The faith calls for full equality among the sexes and an end to extremes of wealth and poverty. It is a church made for a UN weapons inspector like Kelly. It held regularly scheduled services conducted in the UN's Turtle Bay neighborhood in New York. A liturgy embraced by a goodly percentage of Blue Helmets, Bahá'ísm was granted a consultative status with half a dozen UN agencies. Among its tenets is the assertion that God is too great for humans to comprehend. Though Kelly had never been much of a joiner, nor a religious man, his wife Janice confirmed her husband's apparent conversion to the Hutton Inquiry, adding that she did not know much more about the religion.

In the wake of Kelly's death, US Air Force Sgt. Pederson answered a few polite police inquiries and then quickly took a powder. She refused summonses to resurface for Lord Hutton, but did share her thoughts later, in 2008, with Sharon Churcher, a veteran Fleet Streeter. In essence, Pederson told Churcher that David Kelly had not committed suicide. Kelly and she were "like brother and sister." Kelly believed his mother had taken her life and he had an aversion to suicide. Suicide was against Bahá'í teachings, she said. Kelly had received death threats based on his work in Iraq. Kelly had an aversion to swallowing tablets. Kelly couldn't use his right hand with any force, said Pederson.

She said she was in Alabama and that she had hired a lawyer.

At this, USAF Sgt. Mai Pederson again disappeared.

The day after the coroner's aborted inquest hearing, Coen called up the local Bahá'í chapter and asked for their address. "What is this regarding?" asked the woman on the phone. Coen said it was a personal matter. "Oh I do understand," she said sympathetically. She gave him the address and told him to come by any time.

The next call was to Oneworld Publications, a small press in Oxford that was reportedly in a book deal with David Kelly when he died. Coen and Dresch had seen the correspondence posted on the Internet from Oneworld editor Victoria Roddam to the scientist dating from April 2003, just as the whistle blew on the dossier and all hell broke loose on Downing Street: "I think the time is ripe now more than ever for a title which addresses the relationship between government, policy and war," she had written.

On the phone, Coen said he wanted a catalogue and asked for the address to come pick one up. He jotted it down and hung up. "You're not going to believe this," he told Dresch. "It's the same place."

The Victorian townhouse shared by the Oxford chapter of the Bahá'í and Oneworld was the shabbiest house on the block. The windows appeared empty, the limestone crumbling. A rusted bicycle was padlocked near the front door. There was no visible indication, from the exterior, of any professional offices of any kind. Though it was midday, the heavy curtains in the window were drawn. It had an eerie, almost haunted feeling.

"Very strange indeed," noted Dresch.

A young man answered the door. Told that they had come to see Victoria Roddam, he asked the visitors to wait at the door. He returned after a few minutes and invited Dresch and Coen to a comfortable office on the first floor where they were asked what their business with Roddam was. They decided to come clean and explained that they were investigating the Kelly connection, at which point they were ushered into an adjoining waiting room full of Bahá'ís and Oneworld books, told to make themselves comfortable on couches and offered tea. The young man kept disappearing and could be heard speaking to someone in hushed tones over the phone.

Coen was well into his second cup of tea and Dresch was leafing through a copy of "An Introduction the Principles of Bahá'í," when a middle aged woman entered the room, introducing herself as Juliet Mabey, the director of Oneworld. Mabey explained that Roddam had been so upset about the whole affair that she could not bring herself to speak about it. Yes, she said, Kelly had been involved in very preliminary discussions with Oneworld about a book on his work. But she would not provide any further details because the deal had not gone any further. With a gentle smile and offerings of books, she showed the pair to the door.

Had Kelly had a crisis of faith and decided to write a tell-all book about the germ weapons world? Coen asked Mabey on the doorstep.

"Thank you for your interest," she said. And the doors were shut.

The storm clouds blowing across Oxfordshire seemed even more ominous the next day as the two Americans ventured to Southmoor, to drive by the house where Kelly had lived with his wife, Janice. They easily found the two-story Tudor on one of the village's main roads. While Coen filmed the home and hearth, trying to keep the lens clear of raindrops, Dresch stood back, smoking pensively.

The encroaching dark felt to Dresch like a curtain on all the dead ends of Oxfordshire. Wiping his glasses, he announced with certainty, "It's time to go up Harrowdown Hill."

And so it was. Driving through the tiny medieval village of

Longworth and its adjoining farm pastures, they parked their car at the bottom of the tractor track and began the thirty-minute walk to the summit that led up to the copse of trees where David Kelly took his last breath.

The cloud cover was clearing away and a fresh wind had picked up. Dresch seemed reenergized. He marched up the muddy track with new determination, like a hound on the scent. Finding a gap in the thicket Dresch pushed through, and using the map provided by Louise Holmes found what appeared to be the tree where Kelly's body had been discovered. The pair stood a few moments in meditation before Dresch looked up to the mosaic of bare branches silhouetted against the sky. "I wonder what his last image was," he said quietly.

By the time they returned to the bottom of Harrowdown Hill, the sky was already turning to an inky magenta and Coen watched the flocks of birds flying in and out of the trees. There was time for the last film shot of the day and two men drove quickly across the valley to St. Mary's Church in Longworth. In the fading light, Coen thought that the twelfth-century church steeple was a perfect gothic scene for a twenty-first-century germ war epic, with the squawking blackbirds, the tombstones in the church cemetery and eerie light.

Dresch called out, "I've found it . . . the flowers are remarkably fresh for March." There, standing at the grave of David Kelly, as ravens greeted the twilight, for a long time Dresch was still, smoking and staring out at the darkening horizon. He then pointed out a forested outcrop across the valley. "You can see the place of his death from his grave," he said.

CHAPTER FOUR

The Ghost of Frank Olson

OPERATION ANTLER

One day in the late 1990s, the story goes, a 56-year-old British army veteran named Michael Roche chained himself to the fence at Porton Down and refused to leave. He wanted answers. Maybe also reparations. At the very least, an apology. Roche believed himself to be one among hundreds of British servicemen and women subjected to harmful, even lethal, experiments in the name of their country—an estimated 20,000 "human guinea pigs" used at the army's chemical and biological weapons research base, Porton Down.

This super-secret facility, located in southeast England not far from Stonehenge and the cathedral town of Salisbury, was set up in 1916 as the "experimental ground" for the War Department, which at the time was fighting the Kaiser's Germany—an army with chlorine, phosgene and mustard gas at its disposal. The fate of Great Britain's soldiers, it was asserted, rested on the findings of the two small laboratory huts at the compound. That's when human testing—the gravest bogeyman of biological and chemical warfare—became a reality just as entrenched as Porton Down's top-secret shroud. In the aftermath of World War II, it was incumbent upon the Allies to demonstrate a moral, as well as military, victory over Hitler's Third Reich. They were offered up easy fodder for this argument in the unspeakable doings of Dr. Mengele and his diabolical pack of Nazi doctors. In occupied Berlin, Allied armies discovered stockpiles of unknown, highly toxic agents and documents detailing experiments. Liberating the death camps, they saw raw, brutal evidence of some of the most unspeakable human testing operations in modern history. The Allies were compelled to put the Nazi physicians on trial at Nuremberg and pledged to abide by the subsequent "Nuremberg Code" outlining the parameters, responsibilities and ethical guidelines for human scientific experiments. Adherence to this code, it seems, became a very delicate dance during the coming Cold War exigencies both at Porton Down and at the biological and chemical weapons base of England's triumphant American "cousins" at Fort Detrick.

After V-E Day, the Western victors forged a new alliance against the Communists behind the Iron Curtain. A tripartite agreement between Canada, the United States and Britain was signed to govern Western military research and development throughout the Cold War.

By 1945, Porton Down had expanded significantly from its origins as a few cottages and outbuildings on the Salisbury Plain. Even as it maintained its mission statement to ensure that "the British armed forces were provided with effective protective measures against the threat that chemical and biological weapons may be used against them," Porton Down was allowing masked doctors in top-secret labs to usher enlisted men into mustard gas showers. Such were the unsavory methodologies and irresponsible recruitment strategies that finally emerged for public discussion in the late 1990s. For a period following Mr. Roche's initial charge, the papers were full of stories of atrocities allegedly committed by British authorities over the years: Reports of Indian soldiers serving under the British Raj used as guinea pigs to test the effects of mustard gas during World War II; tales of elderly patients euthanized; and charges that terminally sick individuals with leukemia were injected with a "Monkey Disease" virus around 1968. The Indians and the geriatrics, whether gassed or not, never got a chance to protest. The servicemen, too, were forced to sign a vow of secrecy before taking part in the experiments, many of which were described as a search for the common cold. But in 1999, decades of silence were broken when a former guinea pig, Airman Gordon Bell, filed a criminal complaint prompting local detectives of the Wiltshire Constabulary to launch an inquiry into the management and methods of the human testing program at Porton Down from 1939 to 1989. Notices in local newspapers and veterans boards encouraged all participants to come forward, resulting in the largest investigation ever undertaken by the county force. The Home Office, prodded by Parliament, even provided £870,000 (the cost was to eventually rise to more than £2 million) to foot the bill for additional investigators from special branches of the Armed Forces. This relatively large probe—an unusual public x-ray of national security state secrets—was codenamed "Operation Antler." Police investigated charges of alleged criminal activity at Porton Down that included murder and manslaughter.

Three years of legwork by Antler's twenty-five-man investigatory team revealed not just the extensiveness of the testing (some 700 servicemen came forward to bear witness), but also the government's recklessness in allowing trials of substances known to be highly toxic to proceed without the informed consent of the subjects. In some instances, this complicity came in the guise of willful neglect; the defense minister from 1964 to 1970, Lord Healey, acknowledged to the *Telegraph* newspaper that he did not merely turn a blind eye—he had asked for blinders: "I was aware that testing on soldiers was ongoing at Porton Down, but I did not know the details. Even I, as minister, did not want to know all secrets at the MoD and only wished to be told on a 'need to know' basis. The great problem with this is that I was only given information that civil servants wanted to tell me."

By 2003, Operation Antler had amassed enough evidence of untoward activity at Porton Down for police authorities to recommend that criminal charges—including assault and "administering of noxious substances"—be brought against at least three former scientists. Veterans and their supporters in Parliament hoped the criminal proceedings would shine a light on high-ranking Ministry of Defense officials who had knowledge of the dark experiments. They were especially heartened by official Wiltshire police "update letters" and leaks indicating there were documents proving this. It appeared that there would not be a large enough rug to sweep this one under. It seemed certain dark secrets and black marks on Great Britain's Cold War record were finally going to come to light.

This was not to be. In July 2003, Operation Antler was suddenly, quietly dropped by Crown Prosecutor Kate Leonard. Leonard had previously given the veterans' kin hope when she called Antler an "extensive" probe, entailing "a wide range of enquiries." But in the end, she advised against prosecution, citing "insufficient evidence." Appalled, a lawyer representing many of the servicemen's families declared that "an embarrassment of monumental proportions is being buried."

And buried it was. Even the press, which had been closely covering Operation Antler since its launch, shuffled the anticlimactic denouement beyond the front page. But there was a reason for the demotion. The cases were dropped on July 7, 2003, the day before the Ministry of the Defense—to big fanfare—hung out to dry their most prestigious scientist, the former superintendent of microbiology research at Porton Down, Dr. David Kelly.

In all these details, Dresch, Nadler and Coen smelled a rat. They suspected that the same forces at work trying to keep the Kelly case cold had had a hand in the deep-sixing of Operation Antler. Kelly, after all, had been a top official for the last five years of the probe's period of investigation. Had Kelly been a witness to Michael Roche's one-man protest? If so—was he concerned? Was he ashamed? Was he supportive? Would Kelly have been a target? A witness? If he were a direct target for criminal charges, could he have been a bigger threat to other parties? Might he have been ready to tell more than even the investigators had known? Particularly if, as some of his acquaintances had suggested, he was growing "resentful" of his employers?

To answer this, Coen went to see Alan Care, the personal injury lawyer who represented the Porton Down veterans of Operation Antler in a civil suit. On his way to Care's office, Coen had a last-minute sense that they should talk out in the open somewhere. A park maybe. When the attorney, a man with a gaunt face and a world-weary smile, met him at his office door and immediately donned a pair of sunglasses, Coen, looking for MI5 wires molded smoothly into the door frame, realized he had the same idea.

"Let's take a walk and talk somewhere else," said Care. "There's a nice park around the corner."

Care, though involved in many of the chemical war cases detailed in Operation Antler, didn't have access to the brief on biological experiments that would have taken place in the division that David Kelly inherited.

"I think he must've had some idea," he said. "What I don't understand is why the Hutton Inquiry did not reach out to the Antler case when the two were going on side by side. You basically have thirty detectives who are investigating the goings on at Porton Down in terms of criminal behavior; you have Kelly's death; and the two were never put together. It seems very odd. It seems as though it just dropped behind the filing cabinet."

There were other aspects of Operation Antler that Care could not legally discuss. The Official Secrets Act—a uniquely British restriction and the scourge of truth seekers probing the Empire for years—had insinuated its censoring head into the investigation. A number of the documents Care had unearthed on the veteran guinea pigs fell under this sweeping arc of protection, which covered anyone "working" for any branch of Her Majesty's Government—including these, the most lowly of subjects.

What Care could speak about plainly were the Strangelovian excesses endured by many of his clients: the man who was put in a gas chamber with dozens of rabbits, all of which died; the eye drops causing chronic conjunctivitis; the mustard gas, lewisite and CS gas used for riot control; the biological agent pyrexial; "basically any substance you think would be useful in chemical warfare," each clearly pushing the boundaries defined at Nuremberg. He described the compensations offered to volunteers: two shillings and forty-eight-hour leave. And he disputed the term "volunteer."

"Some of them were told they were going in for research on the common cold," said Care. Private Ronald Maddison, a twenty-year-old Royal Air Force engineer, checked in at Porton Down on May 6, 1953, to do his part in "curing the common cold." A Porton technical officer dripped 200 mg of GB sarin—the deadly nerve agent invented by German scientists in the 1930s and used by the Nazis for their ugly war aims—onto a patch of uniform taped to his bare arm. About twenty minutes later, sweating profusely, Maddison reported that he couldn't hear anything and "felt queer." He experienced seizures and spewed from the mouth. "Frog spawn or tapioca," recalled one traumatized witness. "I saw his skin turning blue. It started from the ankle and started spreading up his leg." Three hours and several injections, respirations and resuscitations later, Maddison was dead. An official inquest, held behind closed doors, in 1953 ruled it a death by "misadventure."

Care's legal efforts on behalf of Maddison and other Porton Down volunteers paid off. In the wake of Operation Antler, Maddison became the first Porton Down volunteer to be vindicated, when, fifty years after his agonizing death, a new inquest jury ruled that the volunteer was "unlawfully killed." His survivors were eventually awarded a £100,000 settlement in 2006. Two years later, 350 other veterans were paid £3 million in compensation and an apology was given in the UK parliament by the Minister for Defense.

As Coen and Care walked away from their bench, the lawyer gave the journalist a tip. He told him to remember that Porton Down was just one leg of a tortured triangle. There was a tripartite agreement during the Cold War arms race, a liaison between Great Britain, Canada and the United States providing for a division of labor as well as a steady share of research and development. "The process of cross-information went on between the three countries during the entire time the experiments took place," he said.

That is why, Care explained, the coroner in the Antler investigation traveled to Washington to retrieve Pentagon documents on the Porton Down experiments, which were eventually released to UK authorities on the condition they be kept secret from the public.

"I've heard reports that there was a US Army scientist present at Porton Down during Maddison's ill-fated experiment, a man who threatened to compromise the very premise of the Allies' post-war security. His name was Frank Olson. Did he see what happened that day?" said Care.

With that, he shook Coen's hand and excused himself.

Frank Olson, it turned out, was connected to much more than just human experiments at Porton Down. At their office on the East River, Coen and Nadler trolled the Internet and learned that the case of Frank Olson was an underground legend linked with one of the CIA's most notorious covert Cold War programs—MK-ULTRA.

In the official narrative, Olson was an Army scientist who leaped to his death from the thirteenth floor window of a Manhattan hotel in 1953. Years later, in 1976, a variation on the legend was manufactured in response to post-Watergate hearings into "intelligence abuses" by the agency. In the new version, Olson's death was precipitated by a dose of LSD slipped to him at a party in a CIA mind-control experiment gone wrong. President Gerald Ford even offered an unprecedented public apology to the Olson family at a White House ceremony, and promised "appropriate compensation." Then-CIA chief William Colby voiced contrition on behalf of the spy agency. And Congress eventually paid the family $750,000. The cash came with an agreement that the settlement would absolve the government from any further legal claims by the Olsons.

Eric Olson was nine when his father died. He was sixty-three when Nadler and Coen came across his elaborate website entitled "The Frank Olson Legacy Project." In between, he had crossed the country by bicycle at the tender age of 16, finished a doctorate in psychology at Harvard mentored by the Yale Professor Robert Jay Lifton, and for decades was haunted by the questions of why and how his father died.

When the journalists contacted Eric Olson and explained their ongoing interest in germ programs and dead scientists, a common bond was found. Olson took the train to New York and walked across the Brooklyn Bridge to meet with them. He was intrigued by the information they had uncovered about his father's connection with Operation Antler. The moment he laid eyes on the elaborate and chaotic flow chart that dominated one of the office walls detailing the inter-connections of their germ war investigations, Olson sat down on the couch and revealed a new rabbit hole. This one deep in Fort Detrick's most hidden corners. "My father worked in the far north corner of Fort Detrick," he explained. "The Special Operations Division."

Olson explained to Coen and Nadler that day that his father was a Fort Detrick specialist with both Army and CIA mandates. He was working on delivery systems for biological agents—including anthrax—but he had gotten himself mixed up with a particularly unpleasant covert operation. It was a super secret project combining mind-control and experimental drugs for maximal interrogation results. "Crazy?" asked Olson. "Yes. Cold War? Most definitely." But a goof-up it was not. Special Operations was where Frank Olson decided he wanted out . . . but instead it was the end of the road.

If Porton Down's human trials were concentrated on matching the Nazis' gifts for chemistry, Olson's Special Operations Division was taking a page from the Japanese army's dirty book. The Japanese, after all, were giving the Germans a run for their money on the atrocity front throughout the war.

In fact, the Nazi experiments, for all their hideousness, were not germ-related. It was the Japanese, headed by an army doctor named Shiro Ishii, who set the standard for criminal use of bacteria. Ishii interpreted the 1925 Geneva Convention outlawing the use of poisonous gas as an opportunity for Japan to corner an illicit market. He began Japan's bioweapons program in 1931 and cheered heartily the following year when the Japanese army presented him with occupied Manchuria as a massive testing ground. During the interwar period, Ishii recruited hundreds of scientists to work in research camps like the infamous Ping

Fan, where thousands of Chinese men, women and children would live, on average, three weeks before succumbing to their experimental diet. By the outbreak of World War II, Japan was in possession of a true biological arsenal, which it used with little discretion throughout the war. Ishii and his infamous Unit 731 received special commendations for their work in spreading plague, cholera and typhoid throughout the Pacific theater. They were also sending payloads by hot air balloon across the ocean, but there is no evidence that any biological agent made landfall in the US.

After V-J day, the US found itself in possession of a number of Japanese scientists who revealed the extent not only of the Japanese Imperial Army's use of bioweapons, but also its affinity for mind control as a weapon of war. Knowing that the Soviets had seized control not just of Japanese scientists but also of the labs, torture chambers and anatomy theaters they left throughout Manchuria, the Americans were wary of putting the defeated doctors on trial as they had in Nuremberg. Why advertise to the Soviets the capacity of the facilities they had inherited, US intelligence officials asked. Much more prudent, it was thought, was to tap the captured scientists for information that the US could use to counter any future Kremlin-directed malevolence. And Fort Detrick, already the largest purchaser of guinea pigs in the world, got into the human testing spirit just like its counterpart on Salisbury Plain. Between 1954 and 1973, Army authorities recruited 2,200 US soldiers to participate in biological weapons testing for "defensive" purposes only. And then the Army doctors busted out of their labs, embarking on a spate of mad-scientist urban drills to demonstrate the nation's vulnerability and document the weak links of preparedness: They sprayed non-fatal germs, but some which could make people ill: *Bacillus subtilis variant niger* in the New York City subway; they piped *Serratia marcescens* through the Pentagon's air conditioning vents; they aerated the Pacific coast from the deck of a Navy vessel so that "nearly every one of the 800,000 people in San Francisco exposed to the cloud . . . inhaled 5,000 fluorescent particles." People went to the hospital in droves. Eleven people were ultimately infected with the *Serratia* germ. One died.

Frank Olson had been part of many of the clandestine tests—including the aresolization of anthrax—that the US conducted in the early 1950s. His son still remembers his father returning from his trips to the vast Dugway Proving Ground with stories of the desert skies over Utah; young Eric would have dreams on those nights of a mythical wilderness where his father had something to prove.

It was in this climate of concern about the need to achieve parity with what the Soviets had possibly already incorporated into their arsenal, that military and intelligence officers embraced ever-more extreme notions of what constituted a "weapon." In 1953, the year of Ronald Maddison's death at Porton Down, CIA director Allen Dulles declared it was mind control that would turn the tide of the arms race. The communists, he insisted, were already practicing it on American POWs in Korea. With that, a whole wave of psychics and experts on mind-altering substances were welcomed to Fort Detrick, where the top-secret Special Operations Division was set up to study the effect of various drugs, chemicals, and persuasive techniques on GI Joe and his counterparts abroad. Frank Olson, who had been recruited at then Camp Detrick in 1943, was eventually assigned to the top-secret Special Operations Division in 1950, and there his moral doubts intensified.

Olson traveled a lot on assignment. He made frequent trips to Porton Down, where his colleagues were also experimenting with psychoactive drugs. In July 1953, Olson took a business trip through Europe. He made several stops in Germany, the UK and Morocco. According to Eric Olson, it was on this trip that something happened that shook him profoundly. He believes that it may have been seeing an innovative torture method practiced on an ex-Nazi, or the administration of an untried truth serum on a captured Soviet agent. It may have been a successful operation, technically, or a botch of disturbing proportions such as was the case with Private Maddison. What was certain, his son believed with all his heart, was that Frank Olson had witnessed something to make him question the work he was involved in.

"I mean at nine years old you don't discuss your father's attitude toward biological warfare or anything else, but I remember, I remember he was very upset." That's how Eric Olson remembered his father's state of mind when he returned home from that trip in July 1953. Shortly thereafter, Olson attended a two-day work-related retreat, with fellow members of Special Operations. He returned even more withdrawn. It was at the retreat, Olson's family was later told, that Olson and four other colleagues had been slipped LSD in their brandy.

That weekend, after the retreat, Olson told his wife Alice he had made a "terrible mistake" and promised to explain later what he meant by this. He never did. He did tell her that he was quitting his Army job to become a dentist. But the next morning at the office when he tendered his resignation his colleagues persuaded him to see a psychiatrist in New York. They insisted that they all leave "immediately," even though it was the day before the Thanksgiving holiday weekend. Three days later, Frank Olson was dead, a smashed man on the sidewalk below his thirteenth floor room in the Hotel Statler in the heart of midtown Manhattan.

Eric Olson drank tea as he laid out his story for Coen and Nadler. He had told it many times before.

He recalled the closed casket draped with the American flag that his father was buried in. His family was told that his face was too badly injured to see. The funeral register contained the signatures of Fort Detrick colleagues in attendance, including the head of MK-ULTRA, the notorious Dr. Sidney Gottlieb.

For more than twenty years, despite great anxiety and lurking suspicions that something didn't add up, no family member nor anyone else publicly questioned Frank Olson's death until a front-page *Washington Post* article appeared on June 11, 1975, detailing the CIA wrongdoings revealed during the Rockefeller Commission Hearings. The Watergate scandal and Nixon's impeachment had opened a brief but important window on the agency's dirtiest secrets. One of the headlines read "Suicide Revealed" and alleged that an unnamed Army scientist had been given LSD without his knowledge before jumping out a window to his death. The Olsons suspected immediately that this was their "suicide." This was then confirmed to them by Col. Vincent Ruwet, who had been Frank Olson's superior in Special Operations based at Fort Detrick. The story was publicly revealed by a *New York Times* journalist who had several scoops related to the CIA's role in the Watergate scandal and had prompted Congress to investigate. The reporter was Seymour Hersh, who had already written the book that blew the lid off of secret US military programs. His *Chemical and Biological Warfare: America's Hidden Arsenal*, published in 1968, was an instant classic.

Hersh's front page story appeared the day the Olson family held a well-attended press conference in the garden of their Frederick, Maryland home, in which they claimed that the US government was responsible for Frank Olson's death. By then, the family's lawyers were in the midst of preparing a lawsuit against the government. Just ten days after this press conference, the Olsons were in the White House for the historic apology from President Ford. Three days later, the family was invited back to Washington, this time to CIA headquarters for a lunch with Director William Colby, who turned over a dossier to the Olson family. Eric remembers Colby as being extremely nervous. With good reason—Colby was under fire from agency veterans for taking seriously the post-Watergate directive to expose excesses by compiling a file on the activities of his predecessors as CIA chief. Written documentation of twenty-five years of agency misdeeds may have been what an invigorated Congress wanted—but none of the senior spooks did. Two decades later, Colby died in a mysterious canoeing accident.

After a year of negotiations, the Olson family agreed to $1.25 million in government compensation. By the time the settlement was approved by Congress, the amount had been slashed to a $750,000 award that would prevent the Olsons from making further monetary claims.

For years, Frank Olson's oldest son considered this settlement a "personal, political and moral affront." "I waited and waited and studied matters further," Olson told Coen and Nadler, as his tea got cold. Olson admitted that he became relentless—even obsessed—in his efforts to uncover the truth. He tracked down documents, journalists, and former colleagues. He even confronted Dr. Sidney Gottlieb, the father of the CIA's MK-ULTRA's excesses and a man who once tried to assassinate the Congo's Prime Minister Patrice Lumumba with the CIA's secret stash of anthrax. No one gave Olson a satisfactory explanation. Even the documents Colby had given them long ago, he told the journalists, were "a cover story."

After his mother, who never really recovered from her husband's death, instead succumbing to alcoholism, died in 1994, Eric Olson decided upon a dramatic maneuver. He recruited the help of one of the country's leading pathologists, James Starrs, from George Mason University, and had his father's body exhumed. Olson watched from yards away as an earthmover excavated the grave. The coffin was retrieved and opened to reveal a well-preserved cadaver. Olson remembered marveling at how "clean—perfect, almost" the embalmed face appeared more than forty years later. There was no evidence of the cuts, lacerations or disfigurement that the government honchos had claimed marred his features. After studying X-rays of the skull, Dr. Starrs determined that Olson's fatal head wound was caused by something other than an asphalt landing. He called it "blunt force trauma to the front of the head before falling to the ground."

The forensic evidence uncovered in the exhumation and Olson's subsequent bird-dogging was enough to convince the Manhattan District Attorney's Office in 1996 to reopen the Frank Olson case as a possible homicide. Working with the DA's investigators, Eric Olson amassed a bewildering amount of additional data, including evidence that the Olson case was cited as an example of a perfectly disguised assassination in a manual used by Israel's intelligence agency Mossad. Another tantalizing piece of evidence was that a British psychiatrist and member of the MK-ULTRA network at Porton Down had overheard Frank Olson talking about how upset he had become by the interrogation experiments he had been witnessing, and that he had warned higher ups that Olson was a potential security risk.

Five years later, in a noteable foreshadowing of the sudden denoument of "Operation Antler" in England, the Manhattan DA's office suddenly dropped the case after informing Olson it didn't have enough evidence to proceed. It offered no further explanation. But still Olson wouldn't stop pressing the New York prosecutors. His next move came soon after he obtained a 1975 memo unearthed by University of California, Davis historian Kathryn Olmstead within the Gerald Ford Presidential Library in 2001. The memo was from a White House aide to President Ford's chief of staff warning that a lawsuit brought by the Olson family risked disclosing "highly classified national security information." The aide was Dick Cheney; the chief of staff, Donald Rumsfeld.

"It was a smoking gun that proved they bought us off cheaply, and we could argue the original settlement with my family was pure fraud," said Olson, whose attorney said he should sue the government for $100 million. Olson brought the memo to the Manhattan District Attorney's office, thinking it would re-energize its investigation, which had languished for a year. But it ultimately didn't.

Olson was silent for a long time. It was late afternoon: The wind had picked up. The memoryof the phone call he received on September 12, 2001, still stung. His lawyer had called to say he did not want to be part of any lawsuit against the US government. He was no longer comfortable serving subpoenas to Cheney and Rumsfeld to grill them about Frank Olson.

Several weeks later, Nadler, Coen and Olson continued the conversation in the same house that Frank Olson left fifty years earlier in the midst of his career crisis. The talk quickly turned spiritual. Eric Olson, a big man whose relaxed eloquence belies the obsessive energy that has fueled his search for the truth, was describing the religious nature of his father's change of heart. Frank Olson was a Lutheran and Martin Luther's message, his son explained, was a response to the Catholic assertion that in a battle against the devil, all is forgiven however sinful or evil it may appear.

"Well, that's the story of the CIA," he exclaimed, "We can do whatever we want because we're fighting the Soviet Union." This is key, said Olson, because two nights before his departure for New York, Frank Olson took his wife to the movies. They saw a new film about the life of Martin Luther. The climactic scene shows the theologian vowing to stand up against the corrupted church.

"It's the whole Western notion of conscience," continued Olson. "That you can't hide behind an institution, you have to take responsibility for yourself. And my father sees this, Luther goes in to nail his theses to the door of the church. My father, the very next day goes in and resigns, says, 'I'm leaving.'"

But instead they took him to New York.

Eric Olson has spent thirty years digging for the truth behind his father's death. He has determined that Frank Olson was murdered in that hotel room in New York to keep him from talking about what he knew. And some of what he knew dealt with weaponizing anthrax. Coen and Nadler kept in touch with Eric Olson as their investigation continued. When the news of Bruce Ivins' suicide was still fresh, and the still growing tally of dead scientists in government service at Fort Detrick hung heavy, they reconnected. They even went to Bruce Ivins' memorial service in Frederick together.

After the short services, Eric Olson let off some steam: "I mean how many murders? How many secret state assassinations? How many National Security homicides?" he asked warily. "What's striking to me is you were bound to get situations during the Cold War, where certain scientists, certain policy makers, certain administrators, certain military people knew what was going on, and said, 'You know we're not doing this. This is not what the United States should be doing.' The question is, what were you going to do with such people? You couldn't put them on trial, you couldn't even put them on military trial. Because in many cases, the stuff they were doing had such a level of secrecy attached to it that you couldn't even deny it. I mean you couldn't even speak about it at all. And my father was probably the epitome of that. Of this"—Olson searched for the word—"this boundary between biological warfare and covert operations represented by the CIA. You know people have gotten this sort of cynical general view. They say, 'Oh we know the CIA kills people.' And I always say: 'Yeah, who do you know they killed? Give me the phone numbers of their family so

I can send my condolences, you know.'"

Olson shook his head and stretched his long legs. In the distance a siren wailed.

"How many murders?" he repeated. "I know one. And if there was one . . . there certainly was more than one. But one is all I know."

After their talk, the three men took a drive around Fort Detrick, Ground Zero of so many troubled germ dreams. It was here that both Frank Olson and Bruce Ivins raised their families and went to work with an assumption that their job contributed to the safety of the nation. Olson was developing a perfect delivery system for anthrax as a weapon. Fifty years later, Ivins hoped to design a perfect vaccine for anthrax. Their spirits were palpable on the suburban residential force field around Fort Detrick's secret labs.

Coen was driving, and he came to a stop outside Bruce Ivins' house. For a long time the three men sat parked across the street, talking about the dead man's eccentricities, mental distress and security clearance.

"Well that's really the question isn't it," said Eric Olson. "I mean this has nothing to do with conspiracy. It has to do with what kind of a leash you are going to keep these scientists on."

Olson was beginning to get antsy as they drove around the fort's perimeter. He didn't like being so near Fort Detrick. Though he lived just a few miles away from its fences, he generally avoided this immediate neighborhood. Coen and Nadler were able to convince him to drive by the fortified compound so they could film, and as they did so, they noticed a small group of people gathered with banners outside the gate, including an elderly Japanese couple. It was late on a Saturday afternoon, August 9—the anniversary of the A-bombing of Nagasaki. Here were actual survivors of that original WMD horror, standing in front of Fort Detrick, banners unfurled with the slogans "Never Again" and "End All Germ War Research!"

One of the demonstrators, an intense local attorney who spied Coen's camera came straight up to the car. Pointing to the high gates of Fort Detrick's campus, he yelled, "This place is about destroying and killing!" It was almost too much for Olson, who asked to please go home. After returning him to the Olson family home, Coen and Nadler went alone to the nearby cemetery. Standing at the grave of Frank Olson, Nadler repeated something he had heard his son say: "*That's the problem you have. There's a fundamental issue between the military and the scientists who they need to do their research for them.*"

And for about the hundredth time that day, Bob Coen thought of the growing ranks of the dead in this story—Frank Olson, Bruce Ivins and David Kelly: anthrax scientists needed by the powers that be.

Until they didn't need them anymore.

CHAPTER FIVE

The Ghosts of Sverdlovsk

AN ERRATIC GUIDE

By 1953 (the year in which Olson and Maddison's hushed funerals were joined by the grandiose spectacle of the Soviet Union mourning its leader, Joseph Stalin), the generals in charge of Fort Detrick and Porton Down were beginning to recognize that anthrax would not replace artillery and that tularemia was not the new landmine. The ascendancy of the atomic age quickly eclipsed the stockpiling of anthrax. Nonetheless, offensive US biological military programs flourished for another fifteen years—in the military-industrial zones outside DC, in the American Southwest—in a race against the dark labs on the other side of "Checkpoint Charlie." The biological arms race went very hot during the Cold War.

Dresch had always believed that answers could be found by exploring the Cold War germ war legacy in Russia. For while the West labored on its germ weapons, the Soviets were whipping their own lab rats into shape. In particular, Dresch wanted the journalists to follow up on leads found in evidence recently released by the FBI Amerithrax investigators—tips that smelled, to Dresch, like old Soviet anthrax maneuvers. He wanted them to look into Strain 836, the USSR's most powerful weapons-grade anthrax, four times more deadly than its predecessor. Made operational in 1987, Anthrax 836 is an extremely fine, silky, greyish brown powder that can drift invisibly for miles. Dresch suggested that the Amerithrax case was Oswald 2.0—another Moscow connection to an historic American crime moment. Coen thought it was worth some probing. So, at Dresch's suggestion, he reached out to a Russian contact, a shadowy operative Dresch called "K," who may or may not have ever worked for the KGB. What he did know for certain was that some years earlier K had made himself a target of Britain's MI6 when he helped the former MI6 agent Peter Wright publish his explosive memoir in Russia. *Spycatcher* directly defied the Official Secrets Act, earning K an investigation by Scotland Yard, a permanent file in British intelligence and a card in Dresch's Rolodex.

In December 2007, Nadler and Coen traveled to Moscow and rendezvoused with K.

He was a veritable bear of a man, in his thirties, with thick brown hair tied back in a ponytail and a hard-eyed smirk. Not exactly your stereotypical KGB man, thought Nadler as they exchanged greetings. It was cold in Moscow, yet K wore only a heavy woolen shirt as an outer garment. It would be his uniform for the next twelve days.

Over lunch at an American-styled diner off Mayakovsky Square that featured a Coke Float Extraordinaire and blintzes with sour cream, K took notes in a tiny book and snapped pictures from an even smaller camera.

"Is just for friends, for friends only," he laughed loudly, when Coen asked what he was doing. "Nothing to worry about." Coen and Nadler ate with gritted teeth, but what could they do? Dresch had said he was okay, and Dresch had not been wrong yet.

Eventually, the journalists would come to respect K's indisputable abilities; he lined up solid interviews and produced great background information, just as Dresch had promised. But K's strengths did not include psychological assurances. Which is why, after several days together, Coen and Nadler were suddenly joined in their hotel by Dylan Verrechia, the cameraman who was supposed to share an adjoining room with their fixer. "He's pacing," said Verrechia by way of explanation. "And muttering about how it's hard to be a killer." Verrechia slept on the floor of their room that night. K showed up for work as usual the next morning, with no hard feelings.

The first important Russian germ war hot zone to visit was a drab industrial city of three million—a city now called Yekaterinburg, but known in Soviet times as Sverdlovsk. It was a three-hour flight north by northeast of Moscow into the Ural Mountains.

It is tempting to give Sverdlovsk the dubious honor of being home to Russia's darkest secret, dirtiest cover-up, gravest accident or most tragic state neglect. Unfortunately there are far too many contenders. The former Soviet Union is strung with a multi-chained necklace of black marks: There are cities hidden from the outside world, cities populated by the banished innocent, cities built by slave labor, cities built for slave labor and cities poisoned by their own products. There is for example, the Ukranian city of Chernobyl, site of a massive explosion and the worst nuclear accident in history. The human error that occurred there claimed fewer immediate deaths than what occurred at Sverdlovsk, though the eventual indirect death toll from radiation would be far higher. The disaster and subsequent cover-up at Chernobyl would contribute to the fall of the Communist Party and demise of the Soviet Union; the Sverdlovsk "incident" five years earlier showed that the two cities shared more than latitudinal coordinates.

Sverdlovsk is one of the most haunted zones of Soviet rule. "Bad commie karma down there." said Nadler as they flew east. "Let's not forget its pedigree, after all. This is where the Bolsheviks put the whole Romanov family before a firing squad, then boiled the bones in an acid bath and buried them in a fire pit in the woods outside town." Nadler snapped shut the guidebook and settled back to watch the darkening landscape below. A flash against the window told him that K was taking his picture . . . again.

It was the middle of the night when they arrived at the Sverdlovsk airport. Theirs was the last plane to arrive. The parking lot, like the frozen landscape they had landed in, was deserted save for their driver, who helped load their stuff into a Mercedes minivan with tinted windows. They checked into a hotel where some former officers of the local KGB bureau were holding a vodka-fueled reunion. The revelers did not take it kindly when Verrechia decided to grab some footage of the ex-spies deep in their cups singing old fight songs. He persuaded them not to pulverize his camera and then they went to bed with a battle song about the Russo-Japanese war of 1907 pounding in their ears—apparently the sailors all went down with the ship . . . again and again until dawn.

In 1940, with the Germans menacing Russia's border, Joseph Stalin ordered that the Soviet military-industrial complex move east to the Urals. Sverdlovsk, as a gateway to the new wartime heartland, housed many of the relocated factories as well as technical institutions and government agencies. One of them was the Ministry of Defense's Institute of Military Technical Problems, otherwise known as Compound 19. During the Cold War, the primary problem concerning Compound 19 was anthrax.

Compound 19 was not one of the so-called secret cities, those iconic children of Stalin's rabidly paranoid premise of progress. There were about three dozen such cities—entirely self-contained "closed administrative-territorial formations" known only by postal code, invisible on Soviet maps. There's a Sverdlovsk-44 and a Sverdlovsk-45, where for fifty years some 150,000 citizens lived in complete isolation from the rest of the world. They have made it onto the map in the twenty-first century, but remain closed cities even today. Compound 19 was located in the industrial beltway on the outskirts of Sverdlovsk—a secret city in everything but name. Inside, the residents and workers enjoyed high salaries, luxury goods, elite schools, sports clubs and their own KGB outpost. Foreigners were barred from visiting Sverdlovsk because of its industrial importance. In fact it was so secret that it became the locus of one of the key incidents of the Cold War, when in 1959,the American U-2 spy plane piloted by Francis Gary Powers was shot down as it flew over the city, taking images with the most sophisticated equipment Eastman Kodak could provide the war against communism.

Within Sverdlovsk, Soviet citizens were barred from visiting Compound 19. The secrecy prevailed not only for the usual Soviet reasons but also because technicians there were messing with a virulent strain of anthrax: This fact became less of a secret in April 1979.

SIBERIAN ULCER

In Russia, as everywhere, the scientific name for anthrax is *Bacillus anthracis*. The laymen's term however, is translated literally as *Siberian ulcer*. Indeed, the most common form of anthrax infection in Siberia and everywhere is the cutaneous form, a topical infection that is treatable with antibiotics and rarely fatal. A natural pathogen in grazing animals, anthrax was known to affect people working with skins, wool and raw meat. Before 1979, Sverdlovsk health clinics regularly administered anthrax vaccine to about fifty people a year, men and women who worked with animal hides or in the meat processing plants. But no one had ever seen anything like what was attacking the people of Sverdlovsk in April 1979. It was pulmonary anthrax, caused by the inhalation of thousands of spores.

The lethal cloud of aerosolized anthrax escaped from a ventilator in Compound 19 sometime within the first four days of April. The first human victims arrived at the hospital two days later. Doctors were initially confounded and reported the deaths as flu or pneumonia. But as the death toll mounted, a retired pathologist named Faina Abramova was called in to assist. When she examined her first corpse and found the brain permeated with blood she pronounced her startling opinion. *Sibirskaya yazva*, Siberian ulcer. Her colleagues were crestfallen.

Nearly a week passed before the extent of the outbreak was realized outside the hospitals. Lev Grinberg, a junior practitioner at Hospital No. 24, heard about the diagnosis from Abramova. His small flat in a typical Kruschev-era apartment block was Coen and Nadler's first stop.

Grinberg ushered the journalists into his comfortable study, which was lined with various Jewish talismans—a mezuzah on the doorframe, a Hanukah menorah in the breakfront and a silver hand to ward off the evil eye, all of which he asked them not to film. He served tea with sugar and began the story he had told many times before.

The news of the strange cluster of deaths, he recalled, initially failed to resonate. Because on April 10, 1979, as the city of Sverdlovsk was bracing for an unprecedented epidemic, the Society of Pathologist-Anatomists was throwing a party. "Dr. Abramova and I were dancing together and she told me 'Leva, today I diagnosed anthrax,'" he recalled.

Grinberg was one of Abramova's students. In 1979, he was just a young doctor, a soon-to-be father and a good-natured colleague. "I forgot about it. It was festive," he shrugged. But the next day he was called to another hospital where several deaths had left the staff short of pathologists. "It should be said I wasn't in top form following this party," he noted. Grinberg performed an autopsy on one of the dead without precautionary clothing or masks, wondering all the while whether the city was besieged by plague or by a biological attack. Afterwards he went home and locked himself in the bathroom away from his pregnant wife until the examiner from the bacteriology department called with the results.

"What I did, well, I smoked cigarettes one after another, sitting on, pardon me, a crapper with a phone in my hands," he recalled.

By then, General Yefim Smirnov, the regional bio-commander, had already knocked heads in Sverdlovsk. He reportedly met early on with the regional Communist Party boss, a burly reformer-in-waiting named Boris Yeltsin. What he told him remains unsubstantiated, but thereafter, all public discussion of the mysterious deaths and the surreptitious disposal of bodies in the city would be kept at a minimum. Smirnov reportedly then visited the body of the only Compound 19 employee known to have perished from the anthrax leak. He and the Deputy Minister of Health of the USSR, General P.N. Burgasov, had a drink over the corpse and agreed that the outbreak would have to be explained somehow. And so Burgasov spent the next week ensuring that every television, radio station and regional paper issued warnings about eating "tainted meat" from the non-state markets. The people of Sverdlovsk, he announced, had been poisoned with gastrointestinal anthrax. The official line was "watch what you eat, comrades."

Now people were truly frightened. They hadn't bought the party line for years. Rumors were rife. Families refused to pick up the bodies of their loved ones from the hospital. After all, the victims of the outbreak were all downwind of Compound 19. The people who lived and were now dying in its shadow may not have known what exactly went on behind the gates, but they knew that the residents inside, with their special compensations and well-stocked stores, were not buying bad meat on the open market. In town there was an immediate and visceral reaction to the notion of poisoned meat. A quarter of a century later, survivors would recall butchers and shopgirls berated by angry mobs and trash bins full of suspect meat.

And still people were dying.

After the second week of April, the state response began to quicken. The stricken were all confined to the infection ward at Hospital No. 40. Vaccination rounds began, and by April 26, 57,000 people had been dosed. The illnesses ebbed. But then a second wave came, just after the May 1 holiday. Victory Day (in commemoration of Hitler's defeat) was traditionally celebrated with a citywide clean-up. Some observers have hypothesized that the brooms of patriotism might have stirred up dormant spores. At any rate, another dozen would die in May.

"All in all we autopsied around one hundred cases," Grinberg told the journalists. "From these, forty-two were positively diagnosed with anthrax. With those autopsied before, there were sixty-six altogether." That number—two-thirds of the devil's address—fittingly became the official death toll. Grinberg and Abramova's final report provided a medically conclusive and damning pathology of the outbreak.

News of the poisoning of Sverdlovsk leaked at a time when things were particularly bad between Moscow and the West: there was the provocative invasion of Afghanistan, the ensuing Olympic boycott and stalled talks on nuclear disarmament. With President Ronald Reagan preparing a case against an Evil Empire, the West widely expected disinformation from the Kremlin in 1980. But even the liberal crowd acknowledged that the obfuscation surrounding a serious biological event was cause for real concern—even if it was a huge propaganda victory for Smiley's People. If the Compound 19 rumors were true, then the Russians clearly had never intended to comply with the Biological Weapons Convention (BWC). Détente was definitely dead, and it was Moscow's fault.

Throughout the 1980s, Western scientists argued among themselves over the Soviet capability for biowarfare. At heart was a disagreement about the motivations for a ban on such programs in the first place. When Richard Nixon vowed in 1969 to "renounce the use of any form of deadly biological weapons that either kill or incapacitate," there was widespread relief that both parties to the Cold War had recognized a human cataclysm in the making. The BWC, in that regard, was seen as part of the ongoing effort to stem the proliferation of all weapons of mass destruction. And when the Soviet Union signed up, it was proof that the prayers of that 1980s uber-rockstar with a conscience, Sting, seemed to ring true: the Russians love their children too.

But a more cynical view of the treaty interpreted it as a recognition on the part of the superpowers that biological pathogens could become the poor man's WMD; that Third World states with ambitions but not the means to invest in enriched uranium could be inspired by the innovative potentials of anthrax, plague and tularemia. As long as there was state-sanctioned biological weapons research, every two-bit dictator could develop a lethal threat rivaling the industrialized world. To nip that threat in the bud, the international ban—pledged by Nixon and his realpolitik consigliere Henry Kissinger—went further than previous arms treaties, by outlawing not just the use of biological agents, but also the "development, production, stockpiling and transfer of [such agents] . . . whatever their origin or method of production." Perhaps the superpowers were not sincere in their renunciation of bioweapons, but merely used the treaty to stop lesser nations from moving forward with theirs.

Interest in the real politics behind the BWC was reanimated, as it were, by the sloppy work ethics of the night shift at Compound 19.

Harvard biology professor Matthew Meselson played an important role in the aftermath of the Sverdlovsk incident. No stranger to geo-political intrigue, Meselson had spent portions of his five-decade career whispering into the ears of high-ranking US policy-makers. Early on, he advised Harvard colleague Arthur Schlesinger during John F. Kennedy's thousand days. Later, he reached out to a former mate in Cambridge, Massachusetts, Dr. Henry Kissinger, and helped convince President Nixon to officially end the US germ weapons effort. So when the Sverdlovsk anthrax deaths hit the wires, Meselson went into action.

At first he fought the Reagan crowd, arguing that attention should be paid to the Soviet line that the anthrax deaths were caused by tainted meat. For this he was attacked by the Gipper's team. And there it stood until the hopeful days of post-perestroika when the former party boss of Sverdlovsk, Boris Yeltsin, climbed up on a tank in front of the Parliament in Moscow and anointed a new era in Russian history. The words he said up there, it should be remembered, were directed towards the soldiers and the generals. But maybe too, he was thinking of lab technicians: "The clouds of terror . . . are gathering over the whole country," he boomed. "They must not be allowed to bring eternal night." Meselson seized the moment as an opportunity to investigate the scene of the incident personally.

Toward that end, Meselson took Yeltsin's special adviser on the environment and public health, Alexei Yablokov, to a Washington, DC, nightclub when the guy hit US shores.

"He says, 'Well, you could go to Sverdlovsk, but you won't find anything, it's . . . years ago and why take the ghost out of the closet?'" Meselson said when he was interviewed by Coen and Nadler in the fall of 2007 up at Harvard. But Yablokov eventually gave Meselson his blessing.

"Pretty soon I get a telex from the rector of the local university . . . saying essentially, 'The city is yours.'"

Meselson and a small team of international scientists including his wife Jeanne Guillemin, a respected sociologist, were welcomed to Sverdlovsk and given guides—professors of chemistry and physics. "These were wonderful guys. They knew how to do everything, from fixing a carburetor to fixing the KGB and everything in between," he recalled. One of them introduced Meselson to the brave pathologist Dr. Faina Abramova, a feisty sixty-seven-year-old, who gave him a list of almost six dozen names with dates of birth, dates of death and the addresses where they were living at the time of their death—April 1979. The Americans recruited two local women,

English professors at the university, and together with Professor Guillemin these three ladies knocked on the doors of every house on the list. "They'd say they were studying their health . . . studying this epidemic. We understand you lost your husband or a son or just, 'may we talk to you.' And in every case except one, they were invited in," continued Meselson. "I would be sitting outside in the car waiting and waiting and waiting, and then they come out. A few times they came out crying."

By now, Meselson had also seen the tissue samples safeguarded by Grinberg and Abramova. He conceded that no form of gastrointestinal anthrax was capable of the extensive brain hemorrhaging seen in the distinctive blood-red "cardinal's cap" on these slides. On a map of the Sverdlovsk region, Meselson marked the villages where animals as well as people were reported to have contracted anthrax. They were in a straight line. The line led right to Compound 19.

"Bad meat doesn't travel in straight lines out to 50 kilometers south of the city," Meselson told Nadler and Coen during their interview a decade later. He was convinced that the anthrax had been delivered by a direct air current and not by a queue of sick cows. Sverdlovsk had been the site of a pulmonary anthrax outbreak. The gastrointestinal theory pushed by the Soviets was a sham. Anthrax powder—deadly, invisible and eager for hosts to infect—was in the air of Sverdlovsk for hours that terrible night and day in 1979. And Professor Meselson—who once tended toward the cover story—now had the data to prove it.

Coen and Nadler and their cameraman Verrechia spent the morning after interviewing Lev Grinberg wandering in search of the section of the city's cemetery where the Sverdlovsk anthrax victims had been buried in special state-ordered lead-lined caskets. It was bitterly cold, making the tricky hunt for the anthrax victims' graves all the more arduous. Adding to their growing dismay, K and their driver, who had been keeping warm in the van, drove off without warning, leaving the Americans knee-deep in snow, mouths agape, hands-on-earmuffs like Munch's screamer. They stood for a moment in baffled silence, without money or passports, and with only the dead for company. Then they broke the silence of the cemetery to loudly curse the apparent treachery of K and the gullibility of hapless bed-ridden Dresch.

Much, if not all, was forgiven a half hour later when the van returned just as suddenly as it had departed. K asserted that he needed cigarettes and laughed at the cosmic humor of it all. There could also have been Ural Vodka involved. At any rate, it was time to "carry on."

The next stop was the ceramic factory where many of the 1979 anthrax victims—workers on the night shift—had been infected. While Verecchia set up cameras and filmed the gates of the factory, located off a main boulevard on the outskirts of the city, Coen eyed an old woman in a headscarf trudging along the icy pavement. He asked K to ask her if she remembered the outbreak.

"What took you so long to ask me?" said Tatiana Mikhailovna. "I've been waiting thirty years." Thereupon she entered into a lengthy conversation with Coen, whom she claimed to have recognized from a meeting several years previously. Coen (who had never been in Russia before) listened courteously, as K translated. "People are still sick today," she complained, in a toothless grimace. "It's the children who suffer, always the children." Coen assured her that though he couldn't remember their last meeting, he would never forget this one. With that, Tatiana Mikhailovna shuffled away.

Then it was time to hop back in the van and, with only tinted windows and tenuous American political connections as protection, the team went on to film what they could of Compound 19—one of the least media-friendly spots in the world.

As the Mercedes minivan glided along the highway outside of Sverdlovsk, Coen was quiet. Both he and Nadler were understandably on edge. Verrechia and K betrayed no such unsettlement, laughing easily at bad jokes, oblivious to the severe military espionage the team was about to commit. It was one thing to hound congressional staffers online and sniff around the gates of Fort Detrick, where security guards might run out for coffee to the nearby Dunkin Donuts. It was quite another to be foreigners on tourist visas heading with professional cameras to investigate a germ lab designed by the architects of General Shiro Ishii's infamous Unit 731 and built by prisoners from the gulag—particularly a facility whose purpose was being strenuously denied by the current bosses of the Kremlin.

No foreign journalists had ever gained entry into the compound. And just one other US crew, led by ABC's Diane Sawyer, had managed to film the exterior. But she saw it in 1991, when Boris Yeltsin, gripped with perestroika fever, was admitting that the compound was a military facility and that anthrax used in germ weapons had leaked. Now, eighteen years later, Coen and Nadler were operating in a new bad-old era—Vladimir Putin had rewritten history: "Terrorists" had caused the outbreak.

The vehicle took the exit, and there it was—Compound 19. The van glided around the high razor-wire topped walls and Verrechia got the shot through the tinted glass. "Slower, slower," he hissed as the driver worked the pedals. "Okay?" asked Coen, agitated. "Okay?"

"I think we got it," said Verrechia.

"Let's do it again?" K suggested.

"No," barked Nadler. "We got it. Let's get the hell out of here." And the van sped back to Sverdlovsk.

As the team collected their thoughts, Coen took a moment to

reflect upon the nature of the secrecy surrounding anthrax and on something that Lev Grinberg had been troubled by when they met. The pathologist was fascinated and disturbed when no one from the States had contacted him in the wake of the US anthrax attacks. After all, he had done autopsies on more inhalation anthrax victims than anyone alive. He had given a lecture tour in America in the '90s and collaborated with US anthrax specialists back then. He had watched the unfolding Amerithrax investigation with concern. "During Soviet times, I could understand such secrecy, but in the US, why the same thing?" he had asked Coen. "What are they trying to hide?"

Coen watched the walls of Compound 19 retreat into the distance and it became clear to him that the walls went up wherever anthrax was found, and that no one really wanted you to look behind them. Those that did, did so at their own peril.

CHAPTER SIX

The Ghost of Vladimir Pasechnik

BIOPREPARAT

If Sverdlovsk was the poster city for the dangers of anthrax production and a presage of the US's own anthrax murder mysteries, then Vladimir Pasechnik was Bruce Ivins on Russian anabolic steroids—a far more significant figure in the chronicles of the Anthrax Wars, and one who also turned up dead under mysterious circumstances.

Comrade Pasechnik had been head of the Institute of Ultra Pure Biochemical Preparations in Leningrad for a decade when, in 1989, he took a business trip to France, eluded his KGB minders, and asked for asylum at the British Embassy. He was received and transported to England, where he was debriefed by David Kelly and other top scientists at Porton Down. Pasechnik told the British that in Russia he had supervised a team of 400 scientists in developing an aerosolized, nonresistant "superplague." He said the Institute in its entirety employed 3,500 people and that it could produce 200 kilograms of weaponized material a week. Pasechnik said it had only recently come to his attention that this work in fact violated an international treaty.

Prefaced by years of heightened speculation in the West, Pasechnik's defection fully revealed the depths of the Soviet Union's deceit. The Red Army's bioweapons program, he said, was hidden not just from Western intelligence, but also from its own scientists. An elaborate "front"—a massive civilian pharmaceutical network called Biopreparat, employing as many as 40,000 people in forty compounds across the country—covered as much as half of the Soviet program. The other half, strictly military, was even less penetrable. Pasechnik revealed that Biopreparat was a multidisciplinary program, directed by secret divisions in the Ministries of Health and Agriculture as well as the Academy of Sciences. It operated in mammoth hinterland complexes and in small testing chambers hidden tidily behind the unassuming walls of a downtown Leningrad street. It stockpiled hundreds of tons of pathological agents, spending as much as 1.5 billion rubles to operate. Its purpose was to develop large-scale strategic bioweapons, and it had been underway since 1973—two years before the Soviet Union ratified the Biological Weapons Convention.

Pasechnik guessed that only about a dozen high-ranking managers had a full picture of Biopreparat's functioning schema. Even fewer knew what was happening in the companion Ministry of Defense program, which ran parallel to but separately from Biopreparat. The system's technocrats and scientists, explained Pasechnik, worked within the "legend" arrangement—in which every assignment came with a cover story to be learned by rote. The alibi system, the scientists were told, was as important as the scientific methods it covered.

Pasechnik's information, which would not be publicized until 1994, boiled down to an astounding revelation: The Soviet germ program was the largest and most sophisticated offensive biological warfare program ever operated. It was ten times the size of anything created within the framework of the Western tripartite bioweapons research in the years after World War II and perhaps one hundred times the size of the fledgling germ program in Iraq, with which David Kelly and his team of international inspectors would soon become preoccupied.

Kelly went to intelligence officials with the information in 1989, and before a month was up, Margaret Thatcher had Mikhail Gorbachev's arm behind his back as George H.W. Bush bent his ear. The Soviet premier acquiesced to inspections to verify that the USSR was in compliance with the BWC. Vladimir Pasechnik's name and photograph were scrupulously removed from every document in Leningrad's Ultra Pure facility.

But his career was not over—not yet. Based on his undeniable qualifications and experience, David Kelly made Pasechnik an offer: to set up shop on Porton Down grounds and continue his work. Not, of course, for a sinister state-sanctioned plan to make a viral bomb or aerosolized plague. Pasechnik's research would be purely pacific. He would help the British develop an anti-anthrax phage program—an antibody response based on bacteria-specialized viruses called lytic bacteriophages. These microbes, found in abundance in nature, were the Soviet's preferred variant to antibiotics but were considered "alternative" in the West, where antibiotics have long reigned supreme. But by the late-twentieth century there was a growing concern that the overzealous use of antibiotics had in fact weakened the human immune system while strengthening certain bacteria into new resistant forms. Phage therapy, in which the phage attacks a host bacterium and injects it with its own DNA, was not only viable, but a promising and extremely profitable scientific solution in the post-antibiotic age. Especially when it came to anthrax. The 2001 anthrax attacks in the United States would soon turn anti-anthrax phages into a billion dollar business; but at the turn of the millennium, governments were not yet throwing money at the problem. Still, it appeared that some people could see the cash on the horizon. Pasechnik was one of them.

In January 2000, Pasechnik entered the private sector by founding Regma Bio Technologies, which opened on Porton Down's campus in May of that year. The firm's principal research was built on the significant groundwork done in the anti-anthrax phage field in the Soviet Union.

Regma, Coen and Nadler learned, had eventually signed contracts with the US Navy for its phage labors. That made Pasechnik a major germ war player on the radar of at least three superpowers, presumably more, at the time of his sudden death, which occurred in November 2001—at the apex of hysteria surrounding the anthrax attacks in the US. His death was not reported in the international press until two days after he passed away. The *New York Times* obituary reported the cause as a stroke. Most of the details found in the obituary were attributed to Christopher Davis, one of Pasechnik's British intelligence handlers from years earlier.

In Russia, Tass News Agency reported, according to K's translation sent to Dresch: "The chief developer (while in Soviet Union) of the military-grade plague as well as several successful types of binary weapons died, according to the *New York Times* obituary, from the stroke. Although the fact that the newspaper quotes a former member of British intelligence rather than the doctor, makes people to believe in the other versions of the death of the person who knew too much." K's translation was rough, but as far as Coen and Nadler were concerned, Tass was on the right track.

It remains unclear what postmortem maneuvers actually took place. There is no proof that an autopsy was ever done, nor, indeed, any independent exam. Pasechnik's wife, a top scientist herself who followed her husband to the West and became a Regma partner, refused all interviews. Pasechnik's business partners got very, very antsy.

Gordon Thomas, who knew David Kelly well and is the author of some fifty books on intelligence matters informed by two generations of MI6 sources, told Coen that the failure to do a full inquest was highly negligent and a harbinger of significant events. "I think there has been an urgent need for some time for us to look again at the death of Mr. Pasechnik because what happened to him was perhaps a forerunner of what would happen to Kelly," he said bluntly.

Nadler and Coen decided to take a closer look at Regma. They learned that it was a Kelly-brokered arrangement with seed money from a Canadian multi-millionaire named Caisey Harlingten, a far-sighted fellow who had invested heavily in post-Soviet phage therapies, even bankrolling the world-class Phage Institute in Tbilisi, Georgia.

He was also, it turned out, highly wary of inquisitive reporters.

"What do you want to know, who are you and why are you asking these questions?" Harlingten demanded of Coen when the journalist got him on the phone. Once he calmed down and Coen explained the nature of his inquiry, he answered that he was just "on the business end of things" at Regma. "Vlad was the scientist."

Coen pressed for a meeting with Harlingten, in person. "No way," said Harlingten. "My wife would kill me. She wants me to get out of this stuff." But after a second call Harlingten agreed to give the journalist an hour. He told him to meet him at Westminster Abbey.

"I don't know why the hell I'm doing this," he added. "Get over here quick."

Coen scrambled into a cab, rushing the driver to get to Westminster as fast as he could. He searched the crowds of tourists for a man he thought could be wearing Savile Row and called Harlingten's cell. He answered, "I'm directly in front of you." Coen looked up and saw someone resembling an aging rock star in faded jeans, with shoulder-length grey hair.

Harlingten immediately launched into a story about Pasechnik's health shortly before his death: "We were walking on the streets here one day. And I kept hurrying him. But he said he had to rest. So not too much later, he went in for a heart bypass. He seemed to bounce back from that just fine. And then he worked like a dog, because we were working like hell. And all along he was doing whatever he was doing—all that other stuff on the side."

"What stuff?" Coen broke in.

"Yeah, he was still working for THEM. Advising, doing consulting and whatever voodoo they do—all that biowar stuff is going on," Harlingten answered. "The only thing suspicious about his death was when Vlad called me right before and said, 'I won't be coming in to the office for a few days [because] I'm not feeling well.' He said 'a few days.' I just thought that was a little weird because when people are feeling sick they usually don't know if it's going to be for a few days."

The sudden demise of Pasechnik at a key moment in the anthrax timeline—coupled two years later with David Kelly's—spawned a unique Internet sensation monitored by Coen and Nadler, who came to believe along with many others that there were grains of truth within this phenomenon. Analysts from around the globe began compiling lists featuring the rather mysterious—often quite bizarre—deaths of scores of microbiologists since the anthrax attack:

- East Anglia University Professor Ian Langford, age 40, found naked from the waist up and wedged under a chair in a ransacked and blood-spattered room (dead of natural causes, said the authorities);
- Harvard microbiologist Don Wiley, 57, "accidentally" blown off a bridge in Memphis late at night;
- Kelly's successor at Porton Down, Paul Norman, killed in a light-plane crash;
- Professor Robert Schwartz, 57, an expert in DNA sequencing, slashed with a samurai sword in his Virginia home, reportedly by a pagan cult;
- University of Miami researcher Benito Que, 52, found comatose on a Miami street after a beating by four men—one with a baseball bat, according to witnesses. Death ruled "natural" by officialdom.

More inflammatory lists or conspiracy websites would include more than three dozen names. But even cautious and respected sources were alarmed. John Eldridge, the editor of the prestigious Jane's Nuclear, Biological and Chemical Defence Weekly, was quoted in the *News of the World* saying, "If I were a microbiologist, I would be worried." Eldridge refused to elaborate when a British MP investigating David Kelly's death, Norman Baker, called him at home. Instead the WMD expert exercised his own caution by barking, "How did you get this number?" and slamming down the phone. Eventually, the *New York Times Magazine* was moved to publish a feature article titled "The Odds of That," analyzing the statistical probability of the number of dead scientists. The paper concluded the numbers of the fallen were within statistical norms.

After his meeting with Harlingten, Coen took a two-hour drive to visit Pasechnik's grave in a small old churchyard in Shrewton, not far from the legendary Stonehenge. Vladimir

Pasechnik's Russian name on the headstone seemed quite out of place there, lonely almost, looming over an untended grave overgrown with grass and wildflowers. Sudden shrieks of blackbirds punctuated the silence at the defector's final resting place, just as they had at David Kelly's grave. It was a fitting epitaph to a career that clung closer to the clandestine than most.

Pasechnik's real legacy was in his debriefing years earlier. By exposing Biopreparat, he essentially revealed a global CV on behalf of a whole generation of highly skilled biologists who, once their life's work was abandoned at home, became much in demand abroad. Whether Vladimir Pasechnik died of natural or mysterious causes, the last years of his life had an enormous impact globally. His shadow haunts all corners of the earth—for in its shade toil the doctors of Biopreparat and their apprentices; and it is impossible to accurately foretell what they have wrought. For in reality Vladimir Pasechnik was one of the godfathers of what some came to see as a new global germ war mob, and it was almost time to hit the mattresses.

What Pasechnik described to his debriefer David Kelly in the early 1990s redefined the pathological armory: Suddenly it was possible to speak nostalgically of "conventional biological weapons"—those classical agents like tularemia, cyanide, mustard gas and anthrax, which had long defined systematic weaponization. In comparison, such advanced biotechnologies as genetically engineered plague, synthesized viruses, and designer pathogenic "chimeras" that would induce symptoms as yet unknown in their victims, raised the chill of non-conventional capabilities to a whole new level. The Soviets, Pasechnik claimed, had created these things.

"I wonder how much fun Zappa had writing ballads to the new chimeras," said Coen one day as he was reading over the Pasechnik research materials. He had been thinking recently, yet again, of the book that had opened his eyes just a decade ago to the relative insanity of science's potential to destroy humankind in the microscopic splicing of two organisms. It was Frank Zappa's 1994 memoir, *The Real Frank Zappa Book*, which *Vanity Fair* called a "primer of the sonic avant-garde." Zappa himself explained, in chapter one, that he wrote the book thinking that "somebody, somewhere, is interested in who I am, how I got that way, and what the fuck I'm talking about." Bob Coen, one of those somebodies, was particularly intrigued by Zappa's reference to the 1969 congressional testimony by the directors of the Defense Advanced Research Project Agency (DARPA) which predicted that, given current funding, modern molecular biology would see, in the next "five to ten years" a new synthetic biological virus that will be "refractory to the immune system," meaning resistant to treatment. Coen was so curious about this hearing, which took place just months before Richard Nixon's unilateral dismissal of the biological weapons program, that he made a trip to the Library of Congress to look it up. In the transcript, a Dr. Donald Macarthur encouraged funding up to $10 million to develop synthetic biological agents, lest the US come out on the short end of the mutant germ gap.

But there was even more devastating news from Pasechnik: Not only had the DARPA folks' worst fears come true, the Soviets were indeed working on mutants "refractory to the immune system," they had also succeeded in getting them onto a warhead of an intercontinental cruise ballistic missile—"an incredible achievement," according to one of the British scientists who was the first to learn of the capability.

"You have to be able to make sure that this tiny microorganism, when it finally lands on the unfortunate individual, is alive and kicking, will get into the body, multiply, injure and kill them," Christopher Davis of the UK's Defense Intelligence

Staff told journalists in 1998. "Now if they have to go through the process of being grown up, harvested, stored, put in various machines, then put on warheads, and then passed through the atmosphere and then brought back and then released you have an enormous trip this little organism has taken which it doesn't normally do in a hostile environment. All the aspects to bring together, to make it right, is an enormous achievement."

As Professor Malcolm Dando of the University of Bradford, a Peace Studies academic who has spent much time studying the Soviets' germ war efforts, observed to Coen and Nadler: "It was staggering. Huge numbers of people. Very highly qualified people doing very advanced work on not just the old classical agents but trying to develop new agents in very diverse ways. And producing massive amounts of weaponized biological material. The size of the program and the diversity of what was being attempted and the scale of the production was really very shocking."

Shocking enough for the West to demand that the Soviet Union come clean. A little over a year after Pasechnik's arrival in England, thirteen American and British inspectors were granted extraordinary Glasnost-moment permission to tour the corridors of his old workplace as well as three other facilities: the Institute of Immunology in Chekhov, the Institute of Microbiology in Obolensk, and the Institute of Molecular Biology in Koltsovo, otherwise known as Vector. The sites were selected from dozens of potential targets by David Kelly through a series of negotiations with Soviet officials. The inspectors were hunting for telltale signs of an operational offensive program: explosion chambers, maximum security labs, a military presence within civilian sites. This historic first inspection fell short of heralding a new era of transparency. For starters, one of the American inspectors was instructed not to disclose his destination even to his wife. In conclusion, the inspection was significant as much for the things the team did not see than what they did see. "The visits did not go without incident," dryly noted David Kelly many years later. "Candid and credible accounts of many of the activities at these facilities were not provided."

They were barred from many areas including the test chambers and plague labs at the massive Obolensk facility (which to the shock of the inspection team, appeared to be ten times the size of Fort Detrick) and the containment lab at Koltsovo's Vector, where some 10,000 exotic strains of viruses were kept in the world's largest pathogen bank. Also at Koltsovo, chaperoning officials contradicted the staff at the facility. At Pasechnik's Ultra Pure in Leningrad, the inspectors were told that the milling machines were for grinding salt. At one point a scuffle even broke out when Christopher Davis, impatient with yet another darkened unit and lame apologies for the lack of light bulbs, pulled out a flashlight and was promptly tackled by his minder. Later after asking pointed questions about smallpox research, Davis and Kelly both were detained in a small office for an hour.

Daily schedules, already tight, were deliberately made tighter with leisurely meals, lengthy briefings devoid of content and frequent bus delays. British author Tom Mangold, who would later push himself as a Kelly confidant, described a plan in which "the hell of boredom would be assuaged by the heaven of post-briefing cognac and vodkas—large ones."

At no point during the four-day visit did the director of Biopreparat make himself available to the team. Instead, his deputy Kanatjan Alibekov would accompany the inspectors, with express orders to obfuscate. He accomplished this task well and still managed to impress the scientists. Just forty years old at the time, Alibekov had already designed a research lab in Siberia and run a germ factory in Kazakhstan that was said to be able to produce 300 pounds of killer anthrax in short order—a task taken over from Compound 19 after the Sverdlovsk disaster. The soft-spoken young Kazakh with a doctorate in microbiology impressed the Americans and British as perhaps the most knowledgeable and reasonable of all the officials they met. He was a top candidate on the list to ask for more courtesies—an opportunity realized a year later when he too jumped the sinking Biopreparat ship for the West.

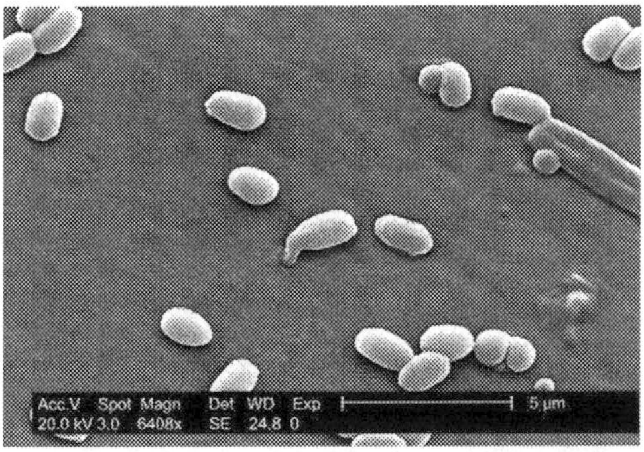

Anthrax spores. *Bacillus anthracis* bacteria is naturally occurring. When "weaponized," the spores are refined so that they can be inhaled. The result is almost always fatal. Worldwide panic ensued just after 9/11 when anthrax powder was sent to media offices and the US Capitol.

Bruce Ivins, the US Army microbiologist who worked at the military's biodefense center at Fort Detrick in Maryland. Ivins killed himself in July 2008, just as the FBI was about to charge him as the culprit in the 2001 anthrax attacks. The bureau insists he was the sole criminal involved, but many of his coworkers and independent scientists disagree. They say that if he was involved at all, he could not have acted alone.

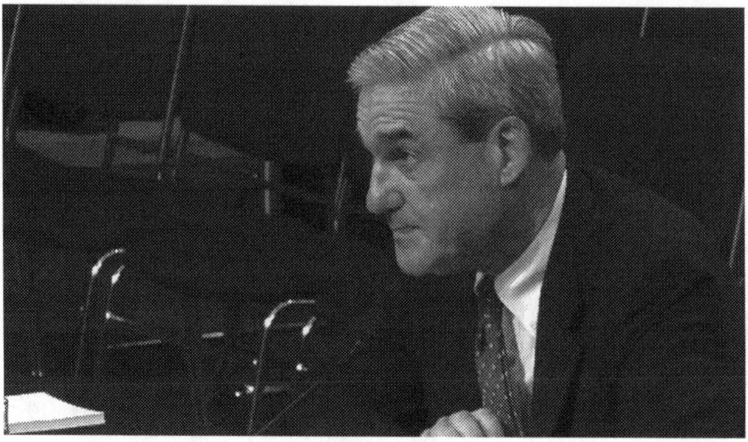

FBI Director Robert Mueller testifying before the Senate Judiciary Committee on Capitol Hill in September 2008. Mueller defended the FBI's anthrax investigation but withheld the public release of classified information identifying which US laboratories make "weaponized" anthrax.

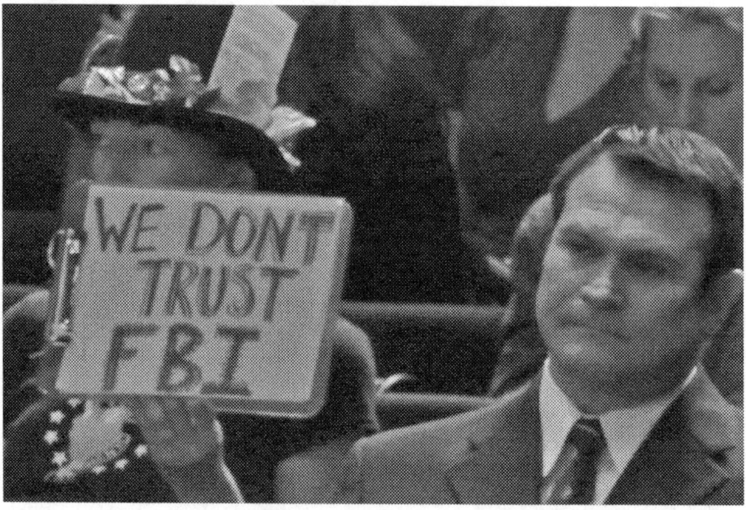

Steven Hatfill, who was named as a "person of interest" by the FBI shortly after the 2001 anthrax attacks and before they identified Ivins as the perpetrator six years later. Hatfill successfully sued the government and collected $5.8 million from the US Justice Department, which cleared him of any guilt.

Stephen Dresch (above and below), a private investigator and former state legislator from Michigan, followed anthrax leads for years and dismissed the FBI's "lone actor" theory as simplistic and indicative of the federal government's reluctance to probe too deeply into the "international bioweapons mafia."

FI^{2}

Forensic Intelligence International, LLC
the Kauth house, 318 Cooper Avenue, Hancock, Michigan 49930
151 Moore Street SE, Crawfordville, Georgia 30631
Tel. 906-482-4899 (MI), 706-456-2696 (GA), 706-294-9993 (cellular)
Fax & Voice Mail 603-452-8208 | E-mail: sdresch@forensic-intelligence.org

Monday, December 10, 2001

The Honorable Henry J. Hyde, Chairman
Committee on International Relations
U.S. House of Representatives

Re: Investigation into Responsibility for Recent Anthrax Incidents

Dear Chairman Hyde:

While I was able to monitor only a portion of the Committee's hearings of Wednesday, December 5, 2001 (as broadcast by C-SPAN), at which Messrs. Spertzel and Alibek and Ms. Harris testified concerning responsibility for the recent anthrax incidents, I was struck by the absence of references by the witnesses and by members of the Committee to certain matters of potential significance. Interestingly, these appear also to have been ignored in course of law-enforcement and related investigations of these incidents and by the news media.

Two fundamental lacunae of inquiries into the recent anthrax incidents can be identified:

First, the recent incidents are assumed to be without historical precedent. Yet, such an assumption is **false logic**. Because there is a lack of documented cases does not mean there have been no incidents.

Second, the institutional or historical context of these events has been largely ignored. In fact, whether of domestic or foreign origin, these anthrax incidents emerge within the **rich context** of current and historical, foreign and domestic activity involving **lethal biological and chemical agents**, and the elements comprising this context are **interrelated across time and geography**.

Because of these lacunae, traditional law enforcement methods of "investigating crimes" is dangerously inadequate.

Having devoted substantial attention to this nexus of issues over the past two years,[1] I take the liberty of outlining briefly specific matters which the Committee and other bodies with oversight and law-enforcement responsibility should consider.

Ill-founded presumption of the uniqueness of recent events – Official public pronouncements and media commentaries have repeatedly stated that the recent incidents of inhalational-anthrax-initiated illness and death represent the first to be observed in the United State since 1976.[2]

That the last *officially-recognized* case of inhalational-anthrax infection occurred in 1976 cannot be interpreted to mean that no cases of inhalational-anthrax infection have occurred in the interim. Rather,

1 At the outset I should indicate that my interest in this subject emerged from the serendipitous intersection of two initially independent lines of inquiry. One originated in my role as an economic consultant to a major national law firm defending a client in litigation initiated in the aftermath of an airplane crash, which eventually led to an inquiry into the nominally unrelated (and unexplained) death of a businessman in Oklahoma (requiring intensive study of its possible causes, including inhalational anthrax). The second, which I was motivated to pursue, initially, as a former member of the Michigan House of Representatives, involved the privatization of the state's Biological Products Laboratory, the sole U.S. manufacturer of anthrax vaccine. I have been assisted in these increasingly intertwined inquiries by a Russian investigator.

2 See, e.g., J. Jernigan et al., "Bioterrorism-Related Inhalation Anthrax: The First 10 Cases Reported in the United States," **Emerging Infectious Diseases** (U.S. Centers for Disease Control and Prevention), vol. 7, no. 6 (Nov.-Dec. 2001), http://www.cdc.gov/ncidod/EID/vol7no6/jernigan.htm.

Dresch's letter to Rep. Henry Hyde, sent just weeks after the anthrax attacks. Dresch warned that "traditional law enforcement methods of investigating crimes" is "dangerously inadequate" and urged lawmakers to broaden their investigation. He offered leads "interrelated across time and geography" that included corporations, the CIA and the secret biological programs of the former Soviet Union and apartheid-era South Africa.

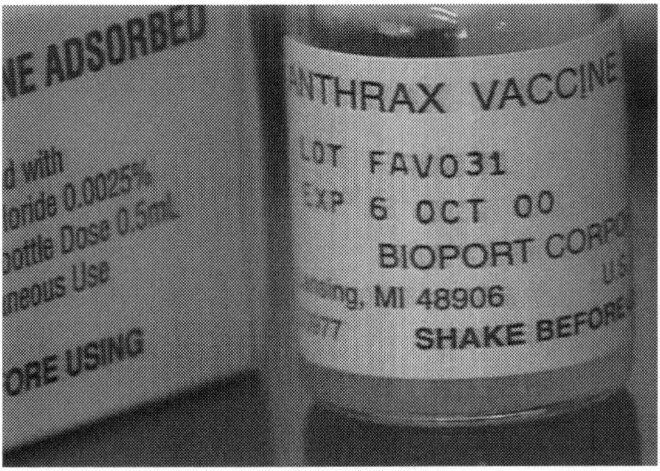

BioPort's anthrax vaccine. Dresch's interest in anthrax began when BioPort, a corporation with links of ownership offshore in the Dutch Caribbean, took control of the manufacture and distribution of an anthrax vaccine in the US and received hundreds of millions of dollars of government contracts.

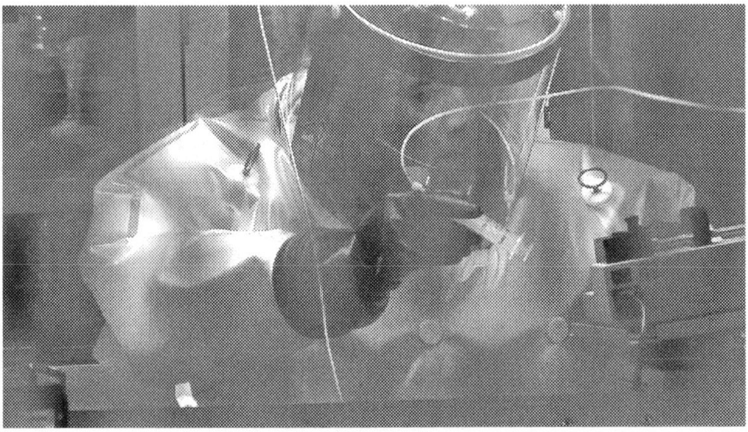

A scientist working in a high-containment germ lab. Biodefense became big business in the aftermath of the 2001 anthrax attacks. Fear of "bioterrorism" has allowed the US government to budget more than $50 billion to combat this new threat. What used to be the work of a handful of government labs is now in large part a private sector cash cow. Hundreds of labs in the United States are now approved to handle deadly pathogens.

British microbiologist and UN weapons inspector Dr. David Kelly, whose mysterious "suicide" in July 2003 was an international sensation. His demise almost brought down the government of Tony Blair, but many think the official probe into his death was a whitewash. One member of Parliament, who wrote a book on the matter, says he is certain Kelly was murdered. "Who did it?" remains a hot topic of conjecture.

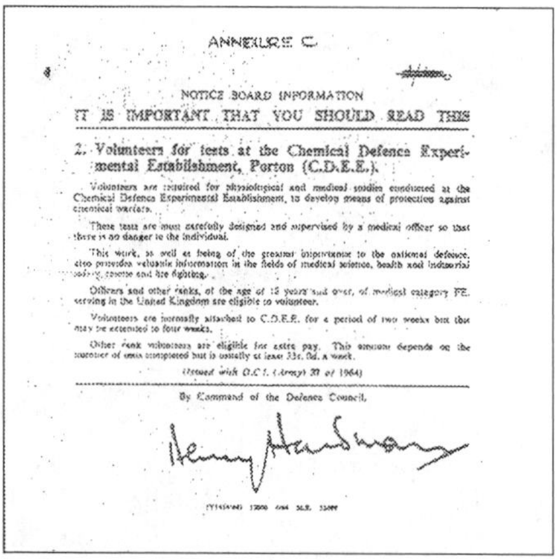

ANNEXURE C

NOTICE BOARD INFORMATION

IT IS IMPORTANT THAT YOU SHOULD READ THIS

2. Volunteers for tests at the Chemical Defence Experimental Establishment, Porton (C.D.E.E.).

Volunteers are required for physiological and medical studies conducted at the Chemical Defence Experimental Establishment, to develop means of protection against chemical warfare.

These tests are most carefully designed and supervised by a medical officer so that there is no danger to the individual.

This work, as well as being of the greatest importance to the national defence, also provides valuable information in the fields of medical science, health and industrial safety, [illegible] and fire fighting.

Officers and other ranks, of the age of 18 years and over, of medical category FE. serving in the United Kingdom are eligible to volunteer.

Volunteers are normally attached to C.D.E.E. for a period of two weeks but this may be extended to four weeks.

Other rank volunteers are eligible for extra pay. This amount depends on the number of tests completed but is usually at least 33s. 0d. a week.

(Issued with O.C.I. (Army) 30 of 1964)

By Command of the Defence Council,

A 1964 notice recruiting volunteer British servicemen for chemical and biological agents testing at the UK's top-secret Porton Down research facility. In 2000, Porton Down was the target of an unprecedented criminal investigation into illegal human experimentation spanning more than four decades. In the 1980s, Kelly headed the facility's microbiology department, and days before he died, British authorities killed the case. Did Kelly know too much?

Frank Olson, the US Army scientist who worked on weaponizing anthrax at Fort Detrick during the height of the Cold War. Following a disturbing trip he took to Porton Down, he told his family he wanted to quit the military. Several days later, in November 1953, he was dead from a fall out of a thirteenth-floor window of a New York hotel. His death was officially ruled "an accident."

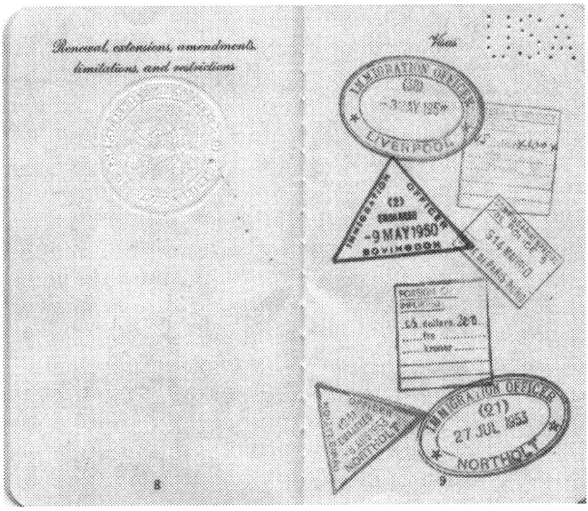

Frank Olson's passport, showing entry stamps to the UK in July 1953, the last trip he would make before his death a few months later.

Eric Olson, pictured as a child with his father and mother. Olson came to believe the official story surrounding Frank Olson's death was a lie. He eventually had his father's body exhumed and unearthed evidence that his father was murdered.

Left to right: Nadler, Coen, K, and Verrechia shiver in Yekaterinburg, Russia, formerly Sverdlovsk, the site of a horrible 1979 accident in which anthrax leaked from a secret Soviet military germ lab and killed sixty-six citizens. Today, the Russian government says the incident was caused by "terrorists," and many suspect the biowarfare program continues at "Compound 19" on the outskirts of the city.

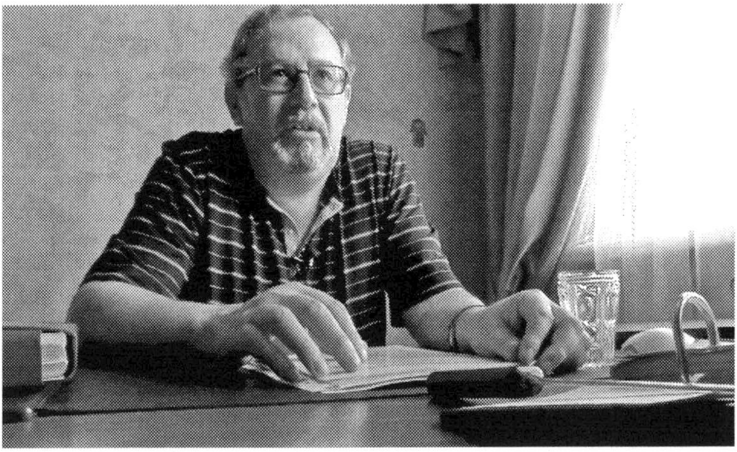

Lev Grinberg was a state pathologist who examined the tissues of the Sverdlovsk anthrax victims in 1979 and found evidence that they died from inhaling anthrax spores, not from eating tainted meat, as authorities claimed. The brave doctor, who has conducted more post-mortems on anthrax victims than anyone else in the world, waited for his American contacts to seek his expertise after the 2001 attacks. The call never came.

Tatiana Mikhailovna, a survivor of the anthrax leak in Sverdlovsk. She remembers the ensuing panic and says that people continue to suffer health problems to this day.

Vladimir Pasechnik, a senior scientist in the secret Soviet bioweapons program for decades. His defection to the West in 1989 and his revelations about the extent of the program stunned experts. Among other things, he claimed the Soviets had the ability to arm intercontinental ballistic missiles with bubonic plague. His sudden death in November 2001—at the height of the anthrax attacks panic—prompted suspicions that a stroke was not the real cause of his demise.

(WO/2003/010316) BACTERIOPHAGE-MEDIATED LYSIS ANTHRAX BACTERIA

Latest bibliographic data on file with the International Bureau

Publication Number: WO/2003/010316 **International Application No.:** PCT/GB2002/003384
Publication Date: 06.02.2003 **International Filing Date:** 24.07.2002

Int. Class.: *A61K 35/76* (2006.01), *C07K 16/12* (2006.01), *C12N 15/10* (2006.01), *C12N 7/00* (2006.01)

Applicants: **PHAGE GENOMICS INC.** [US/GB]; P.O. Box 27740, Las Vegas, NV 89126 (US) *(All Except US)*.
POLYANSKAYA, Natasha [GB/GB]; 1 Copper Beech Close, Shrewton, Salisbury, Wiltshire SP3 4HU (GB) *(US Only)*.
WEST, David [GB/GB]; 29 Anwood Road, Salisbury, Wiltshire SP1 3PR (GB) *(US Only)*
BIFANI, Juan, Pablo [IT/GB]; 26 Fernshaw Road, London SW10 0TF (GB) *(US Only)*.

Inventors: **PASECHNIK, Vladimir.**
WEST, David [GB/GB]; 29 Anwood Road, Salisbury, Wiltshire SP1 3PR (GB).
BIFANI, Juan, Pablo [IT/GB]; 26 Fernshaw Road, London SW10 0TF (GB)

Agent: **CRUMP, Julian, Richard, John**; 3 Cleveland, 40-43 Chancery Lane, London WC2A 1JQ (GB).

Priority Data: 0118009.0 24.07.2001 GB

Title: BACTERIOPHAGE-MEDIATED LYSIS ANTHRAX BACTERIA

Abstract: The present invention provides a recombinant lytic bacteriophage, said bacteriophage being adapted to express at least one non-structural protein which is adapted to cause lysis of anthrax bacteria and at least one non-structural protein which is adapted to inhibit anthrax toxin activity ; a pharmaceutical composition including such a bacteriophage ; and a method for the treatment of anthrax in a host, comprising the step of administering to said host a recombinant bacteriophage in accordance with the invention, which bacteriophage is lytic to at least one strain or to a mixture of strains of bacteria within said host.

Designated States: AE, AG, AL, AM, AT, AU, AZ, BA, BB, BG, BR, BY, BZ, CA, CH, CN, CO, CR, CU, CZ, DE, DK, DM, DZ, EC, EE, ES, FI, GB, GD, GE, GH, GM, HR, HU, ID, IL, IN, IS, JP, KE, KG, KP, KR, KZ, LC, LK, LR, LS, LT, LU, LV, MA, MD, MG, MK, MN, MW, MX, MZ, NO, NZ, OM, PH, PL, PT, RO, RU, SD, SE, SG, SI, SK, SL, TJ, TM, TN, TR, TT, TZ, UA, UG, US, UZ, VN, YU, ZA, ZM, ZW.
African Regional Intellectual Property Org. (ARIPO) (GH, GM, KE, LS, MW, MZ, SD, SL, SZ, TZ, UG, ZM, ZW)
Eurasian Patent Organization (EAPO) (AM, AZ, BY, KG, KZ, MD, RU, TJ, TM)
European Patent Office (EPO) (AT, BE, BG, CH, CY, CZ, DE, DK, EE, ES, FI, FR, GB, GR, IE, IT, LU, MC, NL, PT, SE, SK, TR)
African Intellectual Property Organization (OAPI) (BF, BJ, CF, CG, CI, CM, GA, GN, GQ, GW, ML, MR, NE, SN, TD, TG).

Publication Language: English (EN)

Filing Language: English (EN)

Patent application for an anti-anthrax phage therapy, invented in part by Pasechnik. After his defection, Pasechnik was debriefed by David Kelly and allowed to set up a private biotech company within Porton Down. The company went on to receive a contract from the US Navy to develop new therapies against anthrax.

Ken Alibek (Kanatjan Alibekov), a senior Soviet army scientist and Vladimir Pasechnik's number-two. His subsequent defection to the US transformed him into a valuable asset for US intelligence. His congressional testimony helped to highlight the "threat" of bioterrorism and was useful in the run-up to the war in Iraq. Alibek went on to consult for the US government and private corporations on biodefense before setting up a biotech company in Kiev, Ukraine.

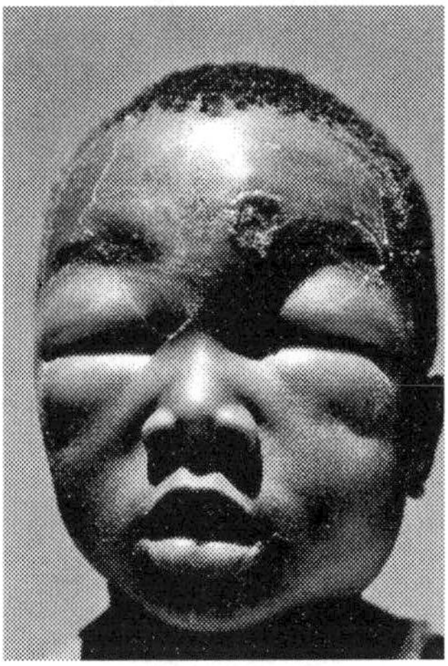

A child victim of the anthrax outbreak that ravaged Zimbabwe between 1978 and 1980, killing 182 and infecting more than 10,000. It has long been suspected that this largest outbreak of anthrax in modern history was the result of biological warfare conducted by the Rhodesian Army special forces unit, the Selous Scouts, against the black population during the country's liberation war.

Jim Parker, a former member of the crack Rhodesian Army counter-insurgency unit the Selous Scouts. He is the first Scout to come forward and confirm the unit's use of anthrax as a weapon against blacks in Zimbabwe's battle for independence in the late 1970s.

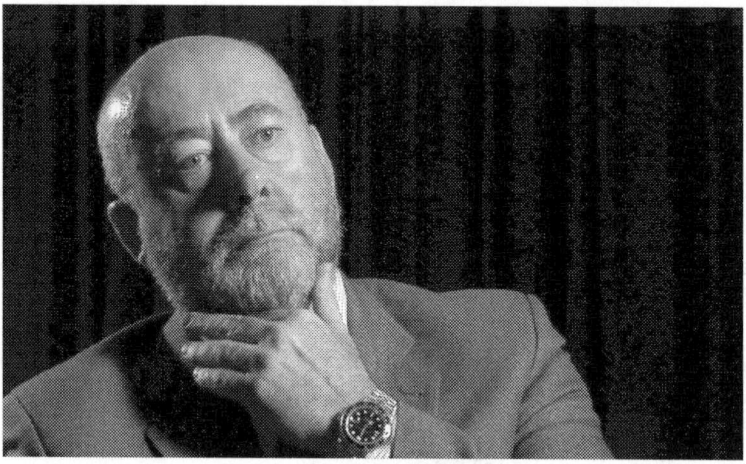

Wouter Basson, dubbed "Doctor Death," the South African medical officer who headed the apartheid state's notorious Project Coast biological weapons program in the 1980s. The program used anthrax and cholera as assassination weapons and worked on a vaccine that could sterilize the black population without their knowledge. Basson traveled the world gathering information about germ-war weapons from institutions and scientists in the West including, he claims, Dr. David Kelly.

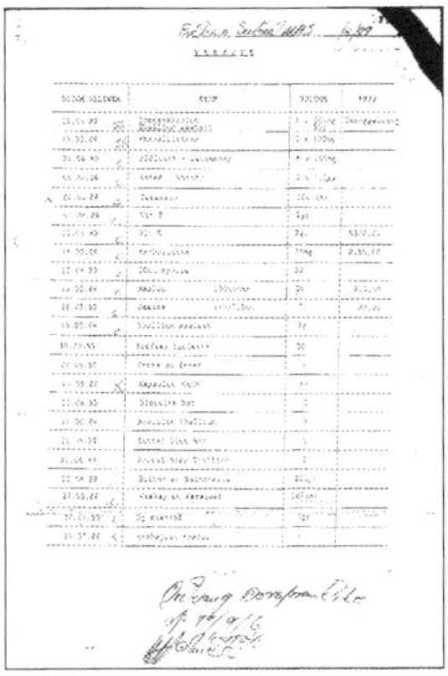

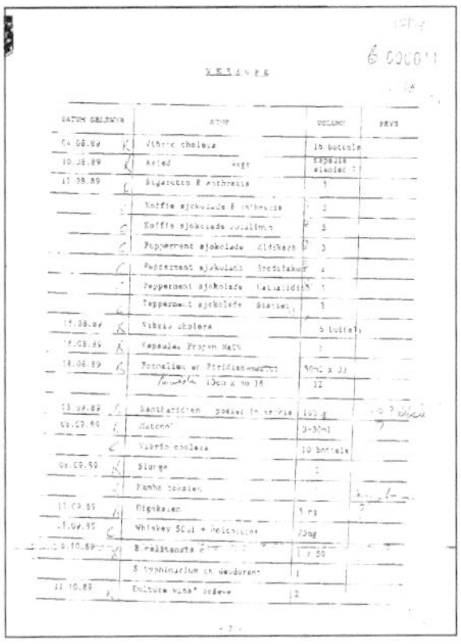

DATUM GELEWER	STOF	VOLUME	PRYS
04.08.89	Vibrio cholera	16 bottels	
10.08.89	[illegible]	[illegible]	
11.08.89	Sigarette B anthracis	5	
	Koffie sjokolade B anthracis	3	
	Koffie sjokolade botulinum	3	
	Peppermint sjokolade Aldikarb	3	
	Peppermint sjokolade [illegible]	[illegible]	
	Peppermint sjokolade [illegible]	[illegible]	
	Peppermint sjokolade [illegible]	3	
15.08.89	Vibrio cholera	5 bottels	
[illegible]	Kapsules [illegible]	[illegible]	
18.08.89	Formalien en [illegible]	[illegible]	
	[illegible]	[illegible]	
[illegible]	[illegible]	[illegible]	
[illegible]	[illegible]	[illegible]	
	Vibrio cholera	10 bottels	
[illegible]	[illegible]	[illegible]	
	Mamba toksien		
[illegible]	[illegible]	[illegible]	
[illegible]	Whiskey [illegible]	[illegible]	
[illegible]	[illegible]	[illegible]	
	S. typhimurium in deodorant	1	
[illegible]	[illegible]	[illegible]	

A Project Coast document listing germs and toxins, including vials of cholera and anthrax-laced cigarettes, supplied to the apartheid state's security agents. It was entered as evidence by prosecutors during Wouter Basson's lengthy criminal trial. Basson was acquitted of all charges and remains on the South African military payroll.

Larry Ford, the California gynecologist whose patients included Hollywood stars. Ford moonlighted by supplying deadly biological agents to Project Coast and allegedly had links to the CIA. After he committed suicide in March 2000, police discovered a trove of deadly germs in the refrigerator of his million-dollar Irvine home. The neighborhood was evacuated for a week as the cleanup progressed.

TOP SECRET

000211

GENEESHEER-GENERAAL
SURGEON GENERAL

GG/UG/302/6/J1282/5

Telephone: 671-5431

SAMS Headquarters
Private Bag X102
Hennopsmeer
0046
August 1994

BRIEFING TO PRESIDENT MANDELA ON THE DEFENSIVE CHEMICAL AND BIOLOGICAL WARFARE PROGRAMME OF THE SADF AND THE RSA'S POSITION WRT THE CWC AND BWC

BACKGROUND

1. Towards the end of the 70's it became clear to the military intelligence community that the buildup of Russian and Cuban surrogate forces in Angola (and the rest of Southern Africa) which included access to advanced weapon technology, could pose a definite conventional threat to the RSA. In particular their ability to use chemical weapons against Unita or SADF forces were seen to be of major importance as neither Unita nor the SADF had any defensive and/or offensive chemical capability.

2. Increasing rumours about the use of chemical agents against Unita as well as the capture of defensive chemical equipment eg Decontamination vehicles, Chemical agent detection apparatus, Protective clothing and masks and medical treatment regimes, gave impetus to an urgent meeting of the CSADF, a small group of the DCC and the Minister of Defence during 1980. At this meeting it was decided that a member of the SAMS with the necessary scientific and military background should be sent overseas to determine covertly what the status and capabilities of the Western allies were with reference to Chemical and Biological Warfare and their defensive measures against it. At the same time contact was to be made with

TOP SECRET

A top-secret briefing document prepared in 1994 for newly elected South African president Nelson Mandela from Army Surgeon General Niel Knobel, unearthed by Steven Dresch. It outlines the activities of the apartheid-era Project Coast program and certifies that all stocks of agents and toxins were destroyed—dumped in the south Atlantic Ocean. But were they? Questions over the true fate of the germ stocks persist to this day.

Niel Knobel, the former South African Army surgeon general who collaborated with Larry Ford during the Project Coast years and later oversaw the supposed destruction of its germ stocks. Knobel suspects that Larry Ford was working with the CIA and may have been murdered.

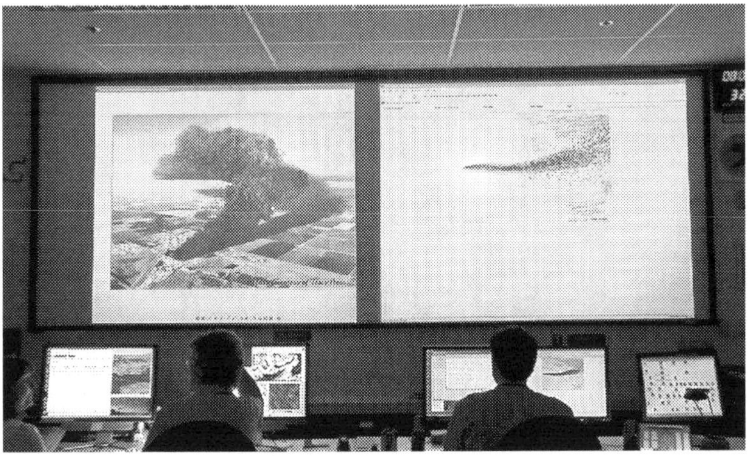

Control room in the National Atmospheric Release Advisory Center at Lawrence Livermore National Laboratory, which monitors the release of biological agents worldwide and works closely with the Department of Defense.

Steve Erickson (left), a citizen activist, monitors activities outside the US Army's vast Dugway Proving Ground in Utah, the military's main biological weapons testing site. It is also a place where anthrax is weaponized ostensibly for "defensive" purposes. Erickson sees disturbing signs that the US military may be gearing up for "offensive" maneuvers. "There's plenty of space here to keep a secret," he told Coen (center) as cameraman Dylan Verrechia (right) films.

University of Illinois law professor Francis Boyle, who was responsible for drafting the Biological Weapons Anti-Terrorism Act of 1989, which makes it a criminal offense to violate the international treaty banning germ weapon research and development. He believes that scores of university, corporate and government researchers should be indicted today for the work they are performing under the rubric of "biodefense." He argues that the US military is making plans for biological war.

ALIBEK

Less than a year after the first US/UK inspection trip to Russia, the Soviet Union was a thing of the past. An attempted coup during Gorbachev's summer vacation was thwarted by the combined forces of an outraged citizenry, unsupportive armed forces and a powerfully persuasive demagogue—Boris Yeltsin, president of the Russian Soviet Federative Socialist Republic. Mikhail Gorbachev was rescued from his Crimean captivity but not from political obsolescence. Four months later, Boris Yeltsin officially disbanded the Soviet Union.

As the communist state imploded, it took the Party's fantasy economy with it. Funding for research, not to mention the tens of thousands of researchers, was in jeopardy. The facilities of Biopreparat faced the same fate as any other factory in the Soviet Union—unpaid wages, civilian conversion and closure. The vaunted Soviet military industrial complex was reduced to making coffins, not centrifuges. The munitions factory would put missiles up for sale as "scarecrows."

Yeltsin's public disavowal of the biological program further clouded the horizon. In 1992, the Russian president banned all biological weapons-related activities, ordered stockpiles destroyed and agreed to admit a second team of British and American inspectors into the closed facilities—visits that revealed to the Western team further evidence of large-scale biological activity. The open-ended invitation was reciprocal and was formalized in an agreement between the US, Britain and the Russian Federation, but in reality, the logistics of reciprocal inspections, compliance documentation and verification procedures proved elusive in the realignment of post-Soviet power structures.

"This was a complex political environment in which to investigate an illicit Soviet BW programme," was Kelly's characteristically understated annotation in the "Verification Yearbook" of 2002.

The British and American inspectors assumed that the Russian bioweapons program was in retrenchment. It had to be, given the economic collapse and a significant brain drain. But there remained real obstacles to verification: With political uncertainty, job insecurity, and the systems' hard-wired secrecy all working against them, the inspectors needed all the help they could get.

Re-enter, Kanatjan Alibekov.

The deputy director of Biopreparat had been assiduously courted since the first inspection. He was the senior Soviet official to take part in a December 1991 junket across the US, during which American scientists hoped to set a model of bioweapon compliance for their Russian counterparts. The tour had the desired effect. Convinced by the derelict remnants at the Pine Bluff, Arkansas testing facility that the Americans had actually followed through on their promise to quit bioweapons, Alibekov said he now realized that "The System" was predicated on a bogus premise: The USSR did not need to either develop biological weapons or perish. So, he too, went west.

Alibekov's defection to Washington, DC in 1992 marked the beginning of a new career path. Alibekov's few Western contacts were forged during the 1991 reciprocal inspections. Charles Bailey, deputy director of Fort Detrick's USAMRIID and the closest thing to Alibekov's counterpart, was one of them. Bailey called his predecessor, William Patrick, who had worked in Fort Detrick during the era when the US still ran a biological weapons program, to debrief the Kazakh scientist. Patrick circled the Beltway twice with an eye in the rearview mirror before he discreetly pulled into the suburban safe house where Alibekov greeted him at the door. Patrick handed over his business card, embossed with a skull and crossbones. Alibekov burst out laughing. His English was not good enough to tell Patrick what he was thinking: At USAMRIID, there were three full-time anthrax researchers. There were 2,000 in the USSR. But if any one of them ever flourished a business card reading "Bioweapons expert," he'd certainly be out of a job. When he emerged publicly from his makeover in 1998 Kanatjan Alibekov had become Ken Alibek, a committed "life scientist" who told the US Senate that his "personal and professional goal has been to make the greatest contribution . . . to eliminating the danger of biological weapons." He would start with his former fiefdom.

"I am 100 percent sure that Russia is still interested in researching and developing biological weapons," he told US lawmakers at a congressional hearing in 2000. Biopreparat may have been shut down, he informed the House Armed Services Committee, but the Defense Ministry's Fifteenth Directorate was still operating four facilities for biological weapons research and development.

As the former director of Ultra Pure, Vladimir Pasechnik, retreated from the limelight to spend more of his time in the lab with his phages, Alibek gladly took on the role of Russia's bioweapon whistle-blower. And he blew hard. Among his most alarming proclamations was the assertion that Russia's favorite biological agents were those that had no cure. Cocktails of Ebola and plague, for instance, or the ectromelia virus spliced with Venezuelan equine encephalitis.

There were other agents requiring no manipulation to achieve their perfect awfulness that were fair game in Biopreparat's universe. More than any other nightmare scenario, Alibek enjoyed telling the story of Nikolai Ustinov, whose gruesome death, if not utterly clandestine, would have merited the Order of Lenin and made the scientist a Hero of Soviet Science. Ustinov was a Biopreparat scientist working in the Vector virology center at Koltsovo who accidentally injected himself with a strain of Marburg virus from an unknown source. Knowing he would die, he chose to keep a journal of that death. For several weeks Ustinov chronicled the pain and the hemorrhaging. He also noted the psychological effects of dying in quarantine surrounded by peers in biohazard suits. The final pages of his extraordinary diary were smeared with blood, written as the author bled from his pores. Afterwards, Ustinov's colleagues extracted his liver, spleen and much blood. They isolated the virus, a Class A pathogen, and named it Variant U in honor of its host. Then they cultured it, dried it and aerosolized it. Alibek said that Marburg Variant U was one of the Vector products he was at greatest pains to hide from the first team of inspectors. It had been on the verge of becoming operational, ready to be manufactured in large quantities and loaded into warheads. Dr. Ustinov had become a weapon of mass destruction. And he still menaces this earth, Alibek would conclude, like the teller of a fiendish ghost story. Because hundreds of scientists and technicians have left the top-secret confines of the Vector compound, and any one of them could have taken a few ounces of Marburg Variant U with them.

Alibek's testimony scared the bejeezus out of the US military intelligentsia. It wasn't that they didn't know that biological weapons were a rising threat. There were plenty of signals—Russia was not alone in abandoning its scientists to the kindness of strangers; there were plenty of Iraqi biologists defecting west too. They, too, brought tales of fully operational germ factories. This intelligence had not fallen on deaf ears—in the twilight of the old millennium, moribund programs stirred, and risk assessments shifted from the conventional arms race to the lesser-known evils of twenty-first century terrorism. For anyone listening, there was alarm to be registered, covert transfers to be monitored, and protestations to be heard and seconded. But perhaps most importantly, there was money to be made. Biodefense, once the lonely task of government technicians, was becoming a lucrative business for the private sector. Big Pharma swept aside its weight loss stimulants and took a hard look at the vaccine industry, a new generation of antibiotics and, of course, phages. Soon enough, it wasn't just the giants of the pharmaceutical industry but every venture capitalist with biologist acquaintances getting in on the action. Biodefense was the new growth industry. The $10 million envisioned by Dr. Macarthur back in 1969 would be a drop in the bucket. By 2003, the Bush administration was promising $5.6 billion to purchase "next generation countermeasures against anthrax and smallpox as well as other . . . agents." Project BioShield—a trough for the big biotech horses—was launched in the name of the War on Terror.

Alibek was this new biowar's Cassandra. He regularly opined on the ease with which small terrorist groups or even individuals might produce crude weapons. He would become particularly emphatic on the subject in the run up to war with Iraq in 2003, when his persistent assurances that Saddam Hussein had biological weapons of mass destruction were touted by the Bush administration. But it would be just as simple, he noted, for a rogue collective to steal some vials collecting dust in Siberia. And let's not forget the Biopreparat scientists—a small army of expertise. For every Pasechnik or Alibek toiling for freedom and democracy, he suggested, there were a dozen less repentant bioweaponeers for whom currencies varied only in quantity, not quality. The brain drain from Russia, he warned, was arming the Third World.

"We knew that some of them tried to sell some knowledge to China," Alibek told lawmakers and reporters. "Some traveled to

North Korea. There was a huge event in 1995 in Iran, and about 100 scientists with the knowledge how to develop biological weapons came to Iran in 1995. Some, of course the great majority of them, came back, but we know that some of them are still working in Iraq doing some research work. In my opinion, it is very difficult to find any trace of these people."

Worst of all, to hear Alibek tell it, was the West's complete unpreparedness for the coming threats. "Since the US stopped all offensive biological weapons research in 1969 and significantly curtailed its defensive research until 1994 . . . US knowledge of biological weapons is obsolete in many respects," he told a worried Congress in 1998. Alibek made it clear he was happy to rectify the ignorance. It was a curious, but thorough, transformation—from Kanatjan Alibekov, the man who had calmly and assuredly provided Western inspectors with comfortable blinders and lies about the lethal Soviet labs they stood in . . . to Ken Alibek in America hollering at the same men not to be so permissive of the pathologically-minded terrorists and despots.

For months, Coen and Nadler were preoccupied with these Russian matters paying special attention to the possible links between Pasechnik's sudden death and that of Kelly, his intelligence minder. They paid close attention to the rather groundbreaking work of Norman Baker, a British Member of Parliament who had published a thorough investigation of Kelly's death, in a 2007 book called *The Strange Death of David Kelly*, which was serialized in front-page exclusives for a full week by the *Daily Mail*. Despite the inconvenience of having had the hard drive of his office computer mysteriously wiped clean one evening, and his assistant having been repeatedly intimidated, the MP's dossier was impressively researched and his outrage palpable. Baker was unequivocal: David Kelly was murdered, as any reasonable examination of the forensics was forced to conclude. An especially telling and sensational detail was the Thames Valley coppers' admission to MP Baker that they found no fingerprints on the knife Dr. Kelly allegedly used to slit his wrist. But who did the deed and why? For all his labors, Baker could only guess. His best shot—an Iraqi hit squad mad at the UN weapons inspector and a subsequent police cover-up dictated by geo-political worries—landed with a thud on the Internet. Coen and Nadler performed a close parsing of the pages of this unusual book, which was short-listed for Channel 4's political book of the year. At first, they were looking for a Russian angle, one perhaps given credence by their favorite theory of the moment—a big money dispute involving Vladimir Pasechnik's profitable anti-anthrax phage maneuvers.

Instead, Coen found himself repeatedly drawn to the pages where Baker questioned David Kelly's relationship with a gang on his radar: the South African military men behind the apartheid regime's horrific "Project Coast," a very nasty germ war effort in the late 1980s. For years, Dresch had been pushing the South African angle to all who would listen—the FBI, Congress, the press.

Coen rang up another British MP, Andrew Mackinlay, who as member of the Foreign Affairs Committee had hauled Kelly before Parliament shortly before the scientist's death to quiz him about the road to war in Iraq. After the scientist died, Mackinlay was blamed for humiliating Kelly to the point of suicide. The MP began looking into Kelly's work and after discovering a Porton Down–South Africa connection, started asking questions in the House of Lords about Kelly's relationship with these bad actors in Pretoria, even making inquiries about South African links to Pasechnik's Regma firm. It was a piece of the Kelly affair that no one mentioned. After Kelly's death, Mackinlay obtained documents from the government revealing that his Kelly–South African inquiries—including one query about links between

Pasechnik's company at Porton Down and the apartheid state—had caused the convening of an extraordinary "handling strategy meeting" involving thirteen officials from different government agencies. But any and all information about UK–South African germ work was withheld from the MP.

"This is one of the most closely guarded secrets of the British government," Mackinlay told Nadler and Coen late one evening in a darkened chamber in the Westminster Palace House of Parliament.

During a later meet, Mackinlay would actually drive Coen to a "safehouse" near the M4 motorway, well placed between two international airports where the Afrikaner germ doctors stayed while on a reconnaissance and funding mission years earlier. (Coen was later told by someone he tended to believe that their drive was closely monitored by MI5.) Once at the house, an English cottage dwarfed by an adjoining barn the size of an airplane hanger, Coen got out of the car and shot some film. He had a strange vibe—the place looked like southern Africa. "What the heck were they doing in that barn?" Coen asked himself. And he felt quite certain that the quest for answers would soon lead him back home.

CHAPTER SEVEN

The Ghosts of Africa

THE POISON FIELDS

Stephen Dresch was sick. The years of chain smoking had taken their toll, leaving a cancer that no truth might disinfect. The doctors gave him months to live and Dresch refused treatment. The terminal diagnosis made the Michigan muckraker's Midwestern voice ring all the louder in Bob Coen's head, and when Dresch rang him up one morning in Brooklyn to confirm the primacy of the Dark Continent angle in the anthrax wars, Coen was heartened.

"Are you ready to finally deal with the demons of Project Coast?" Dresch asked the journalists over the speakerphone.

Ever since the beginning of their investigation four years earlier, Coen and Nadler had known that the secrets of the apartheid regime's clandestine biowar program were keys to a much larger puzzle. Since then, their African files had grown to fill an entire bulging drawer of the cabinet. On their dense wall flow chart—the visual tool they used to help make sense of the connections—South Africa loomed large.

Yes, they told Dresch, they were ready to carry on.

That very day Nadler booked flights to Johannesburg and Coen started making calls to set up interviews with the witnesses to one of the most distasteful episodes of bio-weaponry ever recorded. This was delicate territory; it was not easy to convince people-in-the-know to share information on a one-to-one basis. Getting them to talk on camera for a film was a bigger problem. It was clear that they would have more persuading to do once they hit the ground. But the game was afoot. Nadler stayed back at the headquarters on the East River, which they had nicknamed "Mission Control," to organize future legs of the probe, and Coen prepared to take flight.

A week later, Coen looked down from an aircraft over his birthplace. He studied the landscape of today's Zimbabwe—a patchwork of farm fields and rolling savannas. Embattled and desperate, squeezed and starved by a former freedom fighter turned dictator, Robert Mugabe, and by an unforgiving international community determined to drive him out, Zimbabwe was now a failed state. Coen gazed down on the sad shadow of the young independent nation that produced model health and education systems in the late-twentieth century but could claim only violence, disease and a civic collapse in the twenty-first.

Everything that went on below conspired to make Zimbabwe the butt of the global media: sensational images of Mugabe, the "black devil," who starved his people; mind-boggling inflation; and a cholera outbreak in which thousands would die simply because the water treatment facilities could no longer afford the chemicals. All sadly true, but Coen believed that the world had forgotten the very deep wounds that still scarred the whole of southern Africa, wounds first inflicted by African imperialist Cecil Rhodes' private army as it overran ancient Africa kingdoms to gain control of a land rich in minerals and ripe for agriculture. Rhodes' legions fought in the name of Queen Victoria for years. Later, in the 1960s and 1970s, the descendants of these private militias would fight in the bush wars of independence, refusing to cede to the "winds of change" blowing across the rest of the continent. Hundreds of thousands were killed, millions displaced, and scars still ran very deep. Coen had spent twenty-five years covering the region—as a documentary filmmaker and then as a correspondent for CNN. He could not forget this troubled past. But in the West, memories were shorter. In the West, Nelson Mandela, could be branded a "notorious terrorist" by Ronald Reagan and then win the Nobel Peace Prize and become the patron saint of rock stars. To Western minds, Africa's liberation was a closed chapter, and no one bothered to ask why Mandela's former comrade in the liberation struggle, Robert Mugabe, had become reviled in the eyes of the world community. Coen thought it had something to do with anthrax.

One of the darkest chapters of the continent's recent past—the secret use of biological weapons on its unsuspecting population—was something that Coen probably knew more than was good for his mental health. As a reporter in the mid '80s, he had stumbled upon the little known fact that at the height of its liberation war, the largest and still unexplained outbreak of anthrax in recorded history had ravaged Zimbabwe. At the time, the anthrax story was just one in a string of similar frightening stories Coen heard about: the use of chemical and biological agents in the civil wars of Mozambique and Angola; the epidemics of virulent hemorrhagic Marburg and Ebola viruses; and secret jungle labs in the Congo that experimented with polio and other viruses. Most damning of all, to Coen's mind, were the unsatisfactory answers he got from sources who could not really explain why it was southern Africa that bore the brunt of HIV/AIDS epidemics, with infection rates as high as 55 percent in some rural areas. Zimbabwe was one of those worst affected. He was fascinated with the stories told by former schoolmates serving with Rhodesian Army special forces who had been ordered to bring back sick guerillas after raids on rebel camps for special medical procedures and then to subsequently bury them, no questions asked. But while the possible origins of Africa's AIDS epidemic nagged at Coen and some of his fellow reporters, they were more certain about the source of the infections that were sporadically killing innocent farmers.

In 1978 and 1979, Zimbabwe erupted in a massive outbreak of anthrax that decimated the country's cattle population and filled the hospitals with unprecedented numbers of human cases. Since then, every year brought a handful of new infections as the soil ceded virulent pathogens in-waiting. But in 2008, with the country convulsed in racial tension, land seizures and political violence, there was scant attention to the legacy of anthrax. Coen sighed as he gazed down from the plane, knowing that the poison fields of his homeland below were still toxic. Even though he had a hard time with the concept of "white Africans" and considered it an accident of history that he had grown up there, he still considered Zimbabwe the place where he felt most at home. The rainy season, he knew, would add disease to the current crisis—for anthrax spores were some of nature's hardiest bacteria, capable of lying dormant for fifty years, buried in the earth waiting for the right combination of conditions to be regenerated. And every year like clockwork, the summer rains heralded not just the beginning of the planting season but also new anthrax outbreaks across Zimbabwe, the spores quenched back to deadly life after baking under the African sun during the long dry season.

Since he began investigating the role of germ weapons in Africa's liberation struggles in the early 1990s, Coen had kept in touch with rank and file conscripts who had found themselves on the front lines of a nasty war. In particular, he developed contacts within the former ranks of the Rhodesian military's legendary counter-insurgency unit—the notorious Selous Scouts, many of whose members had left the country with the collapse of Ian Smith's white government in 1980. They had moved south across the Limpopo River to South Africa, the last bastion of white rule on the continent, where their expertise became crucial building blocks for some of the apartheid regime's most ruthless units: 32 Battalion, Koevoet "the crowbar" and the Orwellian-named Civil Cooperation Bureau. The dirty tricks conducted by these groups both inside South Africa and against rebels in the neighboring frontline were well known to Coen.

Project Coast—the dirtiest of them all—was the reason he was coming back.

Landing in Johannesburg, Coen sized up the new South Africa—a "Rainbow Nation" where sharply dressed black executives on cell phones drove BMWs and Mercedes and tossed around terms like "black empowerment" as the icing on big deals. The past was not readily alluded to; the sins of apartheid seemed a long way away. But as he drove along the main N1 motorway past the familiar industrial sprawl peppered with the logos of multinational corporations that had once propped up the apartheid regime, the past came back to Coen with a vengeance, and he braced for the days ahead.

He was heading for Pretoria where he rented rooms in a private guesthouse in the hills of the affluent suburbs. He hoped it would be the perfect headquarters for the task at hand—gaining the trust of the white minority to open up about the worst of past sins. It was still a mostly white city Coen saw as he drove down suburban avenues lined with jacaranda trees and mansions hidden behind high walls topped with razor wire and reinforced by high voltage fencing. Signs with prominent skull and crossbones logos reading PROTECTED BY ARMED RESPONSE were posted on nearly every home. It reminded Coen of the white suburbs of Rhodesia where he had grown up.

One of Coen's first calls was to Jim Parker—a former Selous Scout intelligence officer who had recently come forward to talk openly about the "dirty tricks" campaign adopted by the Scouts in the waning days of the Rhodesian war.

Parker had initially become a successful farmer in Zimbabwe after independence. As one of the 4,000 whites that still controlled a quarter of the country's most fertile farmland, he amassed a small fortune. Zimbabwe's white farmers were the backbone of the economy, exporting some of the world's finest tobacco and flowers to the European market and food to the whole of southern Africa. As they prospered, so did Zimbabwe, despite the fact that many farmworkers continued to live in feudal conditions. But all that changed when the boom times waned in the late 1990s. The white farmers got back into politics, bankrolling the Movement for Democratic Change opposition party and prompting Mugabe's violent campaign of land seizures. Parker lost it all—he left Zimbabwe and was now working as a farm manager in an estate near Pretoria.

An imposing figure with steely blue eyes and a formidable beer belly, he didn't seem to be doing too badly as he welcomed Coen, a fellow "Rhodie." As they sat at the home bar, the most important place in any Rhodesian's home, Jim Parker discussed how and why he had come to write an insider's account of the dirty war, *Assignment Selous Scouts*. The project, he said, was sparked by a spiritual conversion.

"I became a religious man and my first confession was seven hours," he said. But he was only just beginning, and Parker didn't end until he had told Coen about a slew of secret Selous operations and those of the equally secretive Special Air Service unit involving chemical and biological agents used to wipe out enemies individually and en masse. His book detailed how the Scouts released cholera among guerillas based in neighboring Mozambique; how they injected the heavy metal thallium, one of the most toxic substances known, into corned beef tins distributed by the World Health Organization; how they had brokered the sale of clothes impregnated with chemicals to local villagers; how they planned at least eleven aborted plots to kill Mugabe, including one in which Prince Charles would be written off as "collateral damage." His public revelations earned him the disdain of his former brothers-in-arms, as well as a few death threats.

"I was proud to be in Rhodesia," he said. "I was proud to fight for my country, and I was proud of what I did at the time, because I believed in it so much. When I found out what the effects were, well, I'm not too proud of some of those things, but I felt I had to disclose." Parker rifled the pages of his book as he seemed to make up his mind about just how much pride he was willing to abandon. "It's our duty to insure that the next generation doesn't make the same stupid mistakes we made. Killing people with chemicals is madness, absolute bloody madness, and it shouldn't be happening anywhere. The reason why I published was to, hopefully, stop the next idiot repeating the mistake."

Parker joined the Scouts in 1977, about four years after the unit had been formed. He abandoned his farmland to fight for his country, he recalled a little ruefully. He was young and, yes, "so brainwashed." His goal, and that of all the Scouts, was simple, he said. "We refused to hand over Rhodesia to black majority rule. And there was a reason behind it; it wasn't just a straight racist thing, no. We'd seen the collapse from Uganda through to Ghana . . . every British state that was handed over collapsed to absolute anarchy. And we vowed that would not happen to Rhodesia."

The reported father of the Rhodesian military's experiments with biological agents, Robert Symington was an anatomy professor at the University of Salisbury with close ties to the Rhodesian military. From his academic office, under an agreement with the Central Intelligence Organization, Symington recruited the country's brightest medical students to develop toxins. Their products were tested on detainees under the supervision of the CIO's "Terrorist Desk" on at least one documented occasion in 1975. In all likelihood they were carried out on undocumented others. Among the students at the school where Symington taught was the Amerithrax suspect-to-be Steven Hatfill. According to the memoir *No Mean Soldier*, written by a British mercenary named Peter McAleese, Hatfill also turned up at that time in Bindura, a small town where the Selous Scouts allegedly prepared for many of their chemical and biological operations.

Of all the agents of biowarfare employed by the Scouts and the Rhodesian elite forces to cripple the insurgency and defend its buckling border against the ZANLA and ZIPRA rebel groups, it was anthrax that would have the most lasting effect . . . and remain the war's most controversial weapon. The anthrax outbreak that began in 1978 and didn't wane until 1980 sickened 10,000 blacks with cutaneous and gastrointestinal symptoms. All told, this was a 30-fold increase in the total number of fatal anthrax cases in humans seen in Rhodesia during the previous three decades combined. Because the bacterium is endemic in Zimbabwe and thrives particularly well in its mineral-rich soil, some observers have long claimed that the outbreak was a natural occurrence—that cows and sheep had contracted it while grazing and the humans who handled, transported or ate the animals had been infected as a result.

But some of the scientific evidence shows a different pattern.

Dr. Meryl Nass, the American scientist critical of the US anthrax vaccine, is also a leading expert on this Rhodesian outbreak. She points to the geographic distribution of cases as she examined them in 1992, which, she says, paints a clear picture of a man-made epidemic. Where anthrax infections in animals are usually contained to the initial point of outbreak, in Rhodesia they spread over time from a single province in the south, until six out of eight provinces were affected. Moreover, Nass found that it was primarily the African-owned cattle in the Tribal Trust Lands that were stricken, while those of white farmers were left mostly unaffected. In her analysis Nass ruled out spread of the disease by insect or by transport of infected meat. Instead, the evidence indicated that "Zimbabwe's anthrax epizootic is most consistent with a new introduction of the organism by some means into Zimbabwe."

Coen had met Nass in Brooklyn soon after the 2001 anthrax attacks. She had been steeped in the controversy for years and had a few very mysterious stories to tell. Soil samples she had brought back from Zimbabwe had been inexplicably lost by the lab she had sent it to for analysis, thwarting her attempts to determine the anthrax's type and origins. Some years later, her home in Maine was gutted in a blaze that one expert recognized as having hallmarks of arson.

Dr. Nass raised the blood pressure of some in the field. Gary Matsumoto, who studied Nass' work while writing his book *Vaccine A*, denigrated her research as "anecdotal," and Hatfill's one-time spokesman Pat Clawson said she "totally lacks any credibility" and "so would any report that included her as a reliable authority." Nass took such criticism in stride and Nadler observed that one had to consider the source when dealing with Clawson. His point of view had been honed in a lifetime at the right-of-center, including a stint as an executive at Oliver North's radio show. His problem with Nass seemed more ideological than empirical.

Early in his investigation, Coen had planned to return to Zimbabwe with Nass to collect new samples, but by the time he was ready to go, Zimbabwe's unstable political situation had made that impossible.

Nass told Coen to look up Dr. James Watt, a Canadian doctor with the Salvation Army who at the time of the outbreak was stationed in Howard Mission in Chiweshe, a Tribal Trust Land bordering a particularly rich white farming district frequently targeted by guerillas during the war. Though operating with the official permission of the white government, the Salvation Army missionaries had been sympathetic to the black nationalist cause. When some of the earliest victims of the anthrax outbreak came to his clinic, Watt diagnosed and documented the cases and sent photographs and samples to the Ministry of Health. He told the authorities that the patients' illnesses followed sightings of low-flying aircraft over the region. His reports were ignored.

For decades, Rhodesian authorities and high-ranking Selous Scouts denied exposing their enemies to biological weapons. But the allegation that Rhodesia had been the first country to use bioweapons in war in modern history persisted. There was no proof—either that a deliberate policy had been adopted by the intelligence or military or that the Selous Scouts, or any other party, had deliberately infected the cows of Zimbabwe and thousands of people who ate them. Yet Jim Parker says he heard details about deliberate anthrax deployment from a now deceased Rhodesian Army medical officer, Sandy Kirk, now deceased but stationed at the time at a remote outpost in western Zimbabwe. He quoted Kirk in his book and confirmed the information with two sources who served with the Selous Scouts.

"It was given to the cattle through veterinary staff," Parker told Coen. "The main idea was that all the cattle would get anthrax and, as a matter of fact, if you eat that beef, you will then get anthrax and succumb to it." Parker said he was amazed to find, years later, the extent to which the operation was a success. "It was the whole country, the whole country. Went through the lot." By the end of 1979, one third of Tribal Trust Lands was infected with anthrax, according to Nass' study—this included close to 20 percent of the country where no cases of bovine anthrax had ever been reported—to total over 10,000 cases in two years, spiking from an average of about thirteen human cases annually.

Heightening the morbidity of the pervasive anthrax infections was the isolation of its victims. Rhodesia during the bush war was a patchwork of boundaries and no-go areas, crippled by curfews, military bivouacs, terrorist hunting grounds and government cantonments. "Everything was laagered into its own little parochial area," explained Parker. "If you were thirty or forty kilometers away and you needed medical attention, you couldn't get there because there were curfews, and the army would shoot you if you moved at night, and the terrorists would abduct you if you moved through the day. So these people were stuck there, again, right in the middle of it all. A lot of them just couldn't get treatment." Officially, 182 people died of untreated gastrointestinal anthrax contracted from poisoned meat. Many observers assume that double that many died in agonizing isolation, during or after the brutal last years of the war, their fates undocumented.

With the numbers of victims uncertain (and in all likelihood growing as Zimbabwe's buried anthrax regenerates and its national health system degenerates), the most certain legacy of Rhodesia's biological battles in the bush can be found not in its rural areas, but in the court records of South Africa's Truth and Reconciliation Commission established fifteen years later. Because, though the operatives tasked with disbursing anthrax among the Rhodesian guerillas were urged, as a former SAS guy told Parker, to "be very careful not to go too far, we don't want it ending up in Kruger National Park." In fact, that is where the dirty tricks game reconvened . . . in the hands of the apartheid regime's final champions.

A man-made Rhodesian anthrax outbreak remains a contentious affair all these years later.

Consider the case of a doctoral student at George Mason University whose dissertation thesis centered on the alleged Rhodesian use of biological agents. For months before Coen went to South Africa, the student had pressed the reporter to divulge his information including sources and methods, if possible. The fellow—wired into US law enforcement—had numerous contacts among Selous Scout veterans and had even arranged for some of them to give a series of private talks at hotels near Washington, DC, during which they denied that the Scouts had used anthrax during the war. When the journalists met with him at an outdoor café in Virginia in spring 2007, they asked for a copy of his dissertation. He demurred, explaining that it was locked in a safe and "embargoed for twenty-five years," the result of classified US material within. "That must be a helluva dissertation," Nadler cracked. "You bet," the graduate student answered without cracking a smile.

PROJECT COAST

Most countries developing biological weapons in the late-twentieth century did so behind an (often bogus) pretense of self-defense. South Africa did so as well; and though the program it operated from 1981 until the end of the apartheid era in 1993 was clearly offensive in nature, South Africa had perhaps the most legitimate claim to defensive necessity of any nation using the pretext. After all, by 1970 it was surrounded on all sides by hostile parties supported in some measure by the Soviet Union, which was known to have one of the most advanced caches of biological weapons on the planet. South Africa had signed onto the Geneva Convention only in 1963, and cleaved tightly to the protocol's proviso allowing for retaliatory use of unconventional weapons in the face of chemical attack. That presumed threat, though never definitively confirmed, was enough to warrant an inconsistent and spotty application of chemical agents by all parties involved in regional conflicts. While toxins were almost certainly present across many guerilla theaters of southern Africa, it was impossible to verify who was responsible for releasing them. Thus, no South African Defence Force (SADF) counterinsurgent would think to drink from an Angolan well, assuming that it was poisoned either by one of several rebel groups or by his own comrades-in-arms before him.

The fact that Africa is saddled with numerous endemic blood-borne diseases and infectious illnesses spread by substandard sanitation, like cholera and gastroenteritis, helped popularize the notion that communist foes were releasing biological agents against South Africa and its proxies. The South African army sought to make use of the incertitude—troops employed chemical deception, firing clouds of smoke skyward in the hopes that the enemy would scramble to don gas masks and protective suits and slow their advance. But Pretoria and its white rulers had little capability to wage a sophisticated germ war until the SADF tapped an obscure Army cardiologist named Wouter Basson to go on a global fact-finding tour of the unknown frontiers of biological weaponry.

South Africa had once contributed to and benefited from the biological arms programs of its post-World War II Western allies, but by the 1970s the racial policies of apartheid had officially strained diplomatic relations. South African military/intelligence ties with both the US and UK went dark just as reports of chemical weapons surfaced on the battlefields of the Angolan civil conflict, a Cold War proxy battle next door. The bloody fight pitted Cuban and Soviet troops against US and South African-supported forces. South African Defence Minister P.W. Botha announced a military response of "Total Onslaught" against the foes on all its borders. South Africa faced a Red enemy at large, and a Black enemy at home. It was in this siege mentality in 1981 that Project Coast was initiated by the defense force. The concept—to bolster counterinsurgency capabilities with unconventional weapons—owed a great deal to the "dirty games" techniques of the Selous Scouts and the clever poisons of Symington's lab.

Wouter Basson was President P.W. Botha's thirty-year-old private physician when he was tapped to perfect a "blueprint" for South Africa's chemical and biological weapons program. Prior to his appointment at the helm of Project Coast, Basson was a medical officer with the Seventh Medical Battalion, which frequently accompanied SADF counterinsurgency troops into

Angola. Basson, who held a master's degree in medical virology, and with only six years military service under his belt, was given *carte blanche* in his efforts to fill South Africa's biological armory. His SADF superiors encouraged him to troll the international arms bazaar with an unlimited budget and a mandate to come home with more information than he shared abroad.

Exactly what Basson and his team of biospies bought, borrowed and stole on behalf of their country has proved exceedingly difficult to ascertain. The operation was first publicly revealed in testimony gathered by the investigators of South Africa's unique Truth and Reconciliation Commission (TRC).

The commission, convened in 1995 by the new National Unity Government to offer amnesty to former officials of the apartheid regime willing to describe their roles in human rights abuses committed over thirty years, had heard only the broad outlines of the secret program: Dr. Daan Goosen, a veterinarian who headed the Roodeplaat Research Lab (RRL) where Project Coast's biological work was centered, described a network of front companies that, in contrast to military facilities, could attract top scientists with generous salaries and gain access to the international scientific community; Jan Lourens, a mechanical engineer who ran a Project Coast front company called Protechnik, elaborated on an assassin's factory turning out poison-tipped umbrellas and spring-loaded screwdrivers armed with toxic polycarbonate balls undetectable to a coroner; Dr. Schalk van Rensburg acknowledged that he was ordered to develop a vaccine to prevent fertility to be employed in "population control" of the country's rebellious black townships.

In 1999, one year after the TRC rested, Wouter Basson was indicted on sixty-seven criminal charges, including drug trafficking, fraud and the murder of 229 individuals. Where the TRC was limited in its scope to address only cases of human rights abuses by Project Coast scientists, the criminal case drew from three separate investigations dating back to the 1990s. It presented a history of subversive activities ranging from seditious attempts to undercut a negotiated post-apartheid political settlement to drug-trafficking, and from conspiracy to murder to the embezzlement of funds meant for protective suits for SADF troops. While the evidence was abundant, it was also confusing. Moreover, having been generated by Basson himself, much of the documentation was in the end no more reliable than the defendant's own testimony.

The same scientists who testified at the Truth and Reconciliation Commission took the stand at Basson's trial to confirm that Project Coast had developed the use of deadly pathogens and experimented with illegal drugs like methaqualone, MDMA and LSD to create new kinds of "incapacitants" and crowd control substances. Other witnesses had been operatives on the receiving end of Project Coast's supply lines. Assassins from the Civil Cooperation Bureau—some of whom were former Selous Scouts—described "elimination" operations for which Pacific Coast supplied anthrax-laced cigarettes, vials of cholera and botulism. Some victims, they said, were drugged and then pushed out of a plane into the sea. Also at the trial, testimony emerged about a man-made cholera epidemic. International drug runners testified for the prosecution that Basson had choreographed elaborate deals to secure quaaludes and a chemical hallucinogen called BZ in exchange for Croatian warbonds, and had landed in a Swiss jail for a few days in the process. Other dealers suggested that Basson was selling popular street drugs to make money at the expense of suffering townships.

Finally, there were the charges of fraud to contend with. The state called on witnesses to address a list of alleged illegal financial transactions that was several hundred pages long. These witnesses conveyed various manners in which government funds were rerouted into commercial entities owned by Basson and his cronies. A forensic auditor, Hennie Bruwer, testified that Project Coast's laboratory for chemical agents, Delta G Scientific, alone had cost the government 100 million rand from its establishment to its sale five years later. Yet the company apparently had produced only CR tear gas and a supply of methaqualone. At one point, Judge Willie Hartzenberg took the extraordinary step of moving the trial from Pretoria all the way to Jacksonville, Florida for three days to hear the testimony of an American associate of Basson's. Attorney David Webster testified that just one of Basson's businesses, WPW Group, owned assets including a $3.2 million Jetstar airplane, and multi-million properties including a Pretoria mansion called Merton House, Fairclough Cottage in Warfield, England, a few apartments in Brussels, and an Orlando, Florida condominium. For weeks, Judge Hartzenberg was regaled with details of offshore accounts, cooked books, complex bank transfers and the minutiae of stock allocations during the privitization of Project Coast's four main divisions in 1995.

Having early on dismissed fifteen of the sixty-seven charges against Basson, including all of the alleged murders that took place outside of South Africa, Judge Hartzenberg proved himself a clear holdover from the *ancien régime*. He professed to be "bored to death by all of this." And he limited some of the state's evidence with such arrogance that lead prosecutor Alan Ackerman asked that he recuse himself on the grounds of bias. The judge refused.

Basson was the only witness for the defense. His voice soft and his demeanor gentle, he assured the judge that Project Coast's science was valid and its accounting unblemished. He dismissed the testimony of 153 witnesses with a combination of withering scorn, haughty arrogance and a technique that, while unorthodox for a defendant, apparently worked exceedingly well on Judge Hartzenberg—the boldfaced doctrine of implausible denial. Basson insisted that he knew nothing about Civil Cooperation Bureau hit men who were known to have used the very lethal substances that Project Coast was stockpiling. Prosecuting attorney Tori Pretorius then asked him on cross-examination where the CCB would have acquired such toxins if not from Project Coast. "Either," Basson answered calmly, "they never used such poisons or there was another source."

For fifty-six days in the witness box, Basson maintained that everything that the judge had been told in regard to his activities was either false or information taken out of context. With a brazenness that might be called cheeky if it weren't so sinister, Basson declared the 20 million rand spent on the trial a travesty of misused funds that could have been better spent on drugs for the millions of HIV-infected South Africans. It was an additional waste of time, he declared, of the 150 witnesses who perjured themselves in court.

In the end, Judge Hartzenberg—between yawns—clearly relished Basson's stories of how he had gained entry to closed countries by marrying multiple wives; how he had acquired information from the Library of Congress in the US under the guise of a draft dodger; and how Project Coast hardware was smuggled into the country from England by a little old lady who packed it in consumer electronics packaging. Ultimately, the judge sided with the defense, essentially declaring each of the remaining charges mere "conjecture." The bulk of the testimony, he asserted, was fatally compromised. Project Coast staffers and Civil Cooperation Bureau assassins had an obvious self-interest in condemning Basson for crimes that they were implicated in. Without definitive evidence linking Basson to the bodies tossed into the sea, or proving that drugs he acquired were for anything other than research, Hartzenberg surmised, "the prosecution decided in advance what the truth was." The offshore accounts and businesses, he concluded, were for legitimate Project Coast affairs, and the fraud charges "totally unreasonable." As for the drug trafficking, Hartzenberg believed Basson's story that he was in fact trying to return the 1,000 caplets of MDMA that he was busted with in Pretoria's Magnolia Dell gardens to their real owner, who had unintentionally delivered them to Basson in a case of wine.

"We kind of expected that it wouldn't go our way," recalled attorney Tori Pretorious when Coen had tracked him down on his third day in-country. "But being found not guilty on all the charges was a shock. Getting all the operatives to come and give evidence, to spill the beans and put this all on the table and them not being believed . . ." Pretorius sighed and shrugged his shoulders.

In effect, Hartzenberg's report declared Project Coast—an entity that had grown under Basson into an operation with 200 scientists working for a smorgasbord of front companies, a private jet, multiple safe houses throughout Europe and an annual budget of about $10 million with virtually no oversight or mandate—a great success, and Basson . . . a top-notch secret agent.

Basson's smoke and mirror skills were quite effective. During his Project Coast years, Basson and a team of biospies knocked on doors from Pyongyang to Baghdad, from Tehran to Taipei. He apparently managed to overcome ideological considerations with cold cash. He was able to secure technological data from the Kremlin's biolabs and boasted that he had convinced actors throughout the NATO bloc to ignore its own embargo to help Project Coast. He traveled constantly, all while holding absolute control over his home operation for which he alone was responsible for creating cover stories and disinformation. Wouter Basson was a major operator.

But how much of a real threat was Project Coast?

This was the question that Coen put to Chandré Gould. From 1996 to 1999 she was an investigator with the Truth and Reconciliation Commission. Throughout the Basson trial she was responsible for compiling weekly reports on the proceedings as part of the Centre for Conflict Resolution's chemical and biological warfare research project.

"Globally speaking it was a very small program, rather bizarre, somewhat flaky if you like, in terms of what it was looking at," she said. "Their offensive work was not on a large scale—[not] weapons of mass destruction, but far more focused on individual assassination weapons . . . you know, classic spy stuff."

Indeed, the highlights of the trial for most reporters had been the 007-style toys: the poisoned screwdrivers and sugared salmonella, the cyanide chocolates and thallium beer cans. During Basson's trial, Andre Immelman, a former research director at Roodeplaat Research Lab, testified that the facility held "cases and cases" of pathogens and that he was told by Basson to keep the now-infamous "Verkope" sales list of poisons available for purchase from RRL. There were diabolical stories of clothing smeared with toxic gunk and of captives administered lethal injections. But for every admission of murder or mayhem, there was another story of a botched hit. There was the Reverend Frank Chikane, a leading anti-apartheid figure, whose suitcases were given a good dose of the nerve agent organophosphate just before his 1989 visit to America. After three trips to the emergency room in as many days, the good reverend was finally given a new wardrobe by US Health Secretary Donna Shalala and made a full recovery. There was testimony by one witness of a "disposal flight" gone awry because they forgot the drugs and had to bludgeon the detainees to death instead. Another attempt to put cholera in the water supply of a Namibian refugee camp came to nothing because the supply was too chlorinated. Perhaps the most brazen of all concerned the plot to poison the imprisoned Nelson Mandela with thallium—not necessarily to kill him, clarified Dr. Schalk van Rensburg, one of the RRL scientists involved in the scheme, but to render him a completely useless leader once he was released.

Bob asked Chandré Gould about anthrax. "They had a pretty good collection," she said. "All of which had been collected in the Kruger National Park."

Coen had to smile. He was thinking of the Selous Scouts, and Jim Parker telling of some forgotten major's concern that human error might add to the abundance of natural anthrax found in South Africa's biggest wildlife reserve. But he was also thinking that Chandré Gould, like many experts on Project Coast, knew perhaps more than she was willing to tell. In dismissing Project Coast as junk science and focusing on Basson's alleged penchant for money-laundering and drug-trafficking, spinners in Mandela's government diverted attention from more sensitive concerns—that there was evidence that showed a connection between Project Coast and Western governments. The US and UK wanted all Project Coast stocks and records destroyed. Instead, when the new government discovered that Basson had saved Project Coast documents and stashed them in steamer trunks, the authorities classified them on national security grounds and placed them in a secure strong box. That's where they remain to this day. In 1996, the Mandela government told TRC commissioners in 1996 that revelations therein, especially those detailing secret meetings between American and British diplomats and Project Coast scientists, could jeopardize the nation's international relations.

CHAPTER EIGHT

The Ghost of Larry Ford

THE MAD HATTER

When observers look over the range of Project Coast activities with an eye to which of its shady purposes might have been of value to other regimes, it is hard to ignore the operation's diabolical flirtation with a "black bomb."

Both the Truth and Reconciliation Commission and the criminal trials had heard testimony that Basson ordered research into ethnically targeted bioagents that would work only on black people. To date, there is no evidence that such a viable weapon was actually designed. But Coen and Nadler saw nothing assuring in the intensity of the effort.

"Project Coast was the godchild, if not in fact the brainchild, of white supremacists," Nadler insisted to Coen. "Intention is half the journey to success."

They also realized that the working knowledge of anyone involved in such a task would surely have been of great interest not only to the apartheid government, but also to any other state challenged with a restive ethnic minority. *How many interested parties were there outside of Pretoria?* Nadler and Coen wondered. Some nations—Israel, China—came to mind. But for a variety of reasons, they decided to focus on a Mormon doctor with a bizarre double-life: His name was Larry Ford, and he was as an alarming a case as you could ever hope to find.

Larry Ford was an American gynecologist interested in HIV, STDs and all things South African. He was still a postdoc in his twenties when a colleague named Jerry Nilsson—a big-mouthed Californian and fellow surgeon who claimed long-standing ties with the Rhodesian Special Forces and was a fan of the racist government next door—invited him to South Africa, sparking a lifelong interest in the biological potentials of the bush. Ford and Nilsson traveled frequently to South Africa in the 1980s. Soon the young doctor was hanging the heads of buffalos from the veldt in his half-million dollar home in Irvine just south of Los Angeles. In time, Ford embarked on a more esoteric quarry in South Africa and in the United States: He was hunting amniotic fluid for use in devising a "wonder drug."

To most of the world outside Pretoria, Larry Ford was a brilliant scientist, a Mormon of good standing and a celebrity gynecologist who treated Margaux Hemingway and Bianca Jagger. It was only after he killed himself in March 2000 with one of the dozens of rifles he kept close at hand, that Dr. Ford's inner Mr. Hyde took center stage.

Larry Ford's suicide on March 2, 2000, had a backstory made for Hollywood, a week's worth of tabloid headlines and more than one segment of *Inside Edition*. It came days after a botched murder attempt on James Riley, his business partner, which had turned the respected doctor into a wanted man overnight. The police had pulled in a friend of Ford's who had driven the getaway car for the hit man, and they had questioned Ford's assistant, who was his mistress for eighteen years. The note Ford wrote before putting a twelve-gauge shotgun in his mouth read, "I was set up by evil."

The subsequent investigation gained manpower with a tip from an FBI informant that any search of Ford's house include the ground beneath the swimming pool. That's where police discovered a cache of military-grade weapons and explosives. In his refrigerator they found baby food jars full of deadly germs.

The informant was a former theater actor turned Paramount Studios security guard named Peter Fitzpatrick. "He was mutating germs," Fitzpatrick told Coen and Nadler as he drove them years later through the well-groomed community that had been evacuated for four days when officials discovered Ford's deadly trove. "He had perfected these germs and mutated them to the point that they had absolutely no known antidote. No. Known. Antidote." The germs, Fitzpatrick explained, had been secreted away in a slapdash fashion, next to exposed electrical wires and volatile substances like aged ether. "If there had been an explosion in the house, and the house had been levelled, all of these germs would be blowing all over beautiful southern California. It would have been a catastrophe of biblical proportions, believe me!" he exclaimed as they circled the manicured cul-de-sacs and well-watered lawns of the dead doctor's affluent neighborhood.

For reasons known only to him, Fitzpatrick decided to infiltrate Larry Ford's inner circle in the 1980s via Gideon Bouwer, the LA-based highflying, big-talking South African trade attaché, who befriended the ex-actor in a bar one night and regaled him with tales of international hijinks and derring-do. Fitzpatrick, a transplant from Brooklyn, insinuated himself into Bouwer's opulent Beverly Hills lifestyle and into a position that was one part business and two parts schmooze. He walked the attaché's dog and ordered the liquor for Bouwer's perpetual parties . . . and then he told the FBI about the sanctions-busting schemes hatched in the hot tub.

"It was nonstop partying. I mean we had some really good times despite all of the dark stuff that was going on," he said of the time he spent squiring Bouwer's out-of-town guests, exchanging gossip and hanging out with "the South African girls, [who] are among the most beautiful on the planet."

As Fitzpatrick passed on information about Bouwer's associates to the FBI, he assumed that the agency would eventually act—particularly when it came to Larry Ford, a frequent guest of Bouwer who had boasted of parachuting behind enemy lines to take blood samples from dead rebels and of "wiping out" entire Angolan villages in 1986. That same year Fitzpatrick told his handlers that Gideon Bouwer had set up a meeting between Ford and the then-Surgeon General of South Africa's Army, Niel Knobel. The meeting, Fitzpatrick warned them, would include a handover by the American of some extremely deadly gifts.

"I was waiting for a SWAT team to show up, an FBI SWAT team," he recalled. "I waited until two o'clock in the morning. No SWAT team showed up. And Dr. Knobel left with the germs. What happened with those germs in South Africa? They were killing people."

Bouwer had told Fitzpatrick that in addition to unrecognizable strains of plague and cholera, the satchel handed over to Knobel that night included a new breed of germs engineered to target specific DNA—"Kaffir killers," "Kaffir" being the N-word of choice for South African racists. So when the FBI let Knobel return to Africa with his suitcase full of genocide, Fitzpatrick was baffled. Though inured to the extremism of South Africa's most dyed-in-the-wool racists, he reassured himself that the bulk of what Bouwer had asserted could only be fiction.

"This is where it goes beyond crazy," said Fitzpatrick to Nadler and Coen as they toured the hills where Bouwer's opulent former home still stands. "[Bouwer] told me that God's plan was that they were going to release these germs . . . from the Sahel region on down, there were going to be these overlapping circles of contamination which were going to so overwhelm all of the health facilities in these nations, that people were going to be dying off by the tens of millions. The population of the continent of Africa essentially would cease to be, especially the black population. God's plan, according to him, was to reduce the population of the earth from its six billion down to a few hundred million, which would be much more manageable."

During his South African trip, one of the first things Coen had noticed when he entered the study of Knobel in Pretoria was a photograph on the wall of Larry Ford and a thick binder labelled "Larry" resting on the bookshelf. The retired general was unequivocal about his relationship with the dead doctor.

"Bob, I must be really honest with you," said Knobel with a look of profound sadness. And then he described a friendship, "a relationship almost like a father to son. It was personal."

Binding the friendship was a common cause, said Knobel, a belief that the world could be cured of HIV/AIDS and that Africa was the most promising arena in which to engineer its fall.

"At the time, there were lots of publications worldwide, which speculated about where this virus had originated and whether it was in fact a virus that originated naturally or whether it was a man-made virus, within the test tubes," Knobel recalled. Larry Ford, he said, was extremely knowledgeable about HIV's epidemiology and could speak at length about the many scenarios by which the virus originated and spread from primates to humans. It was during these discussions, said Knobel, that Ford suggested that he had substantial expertise in the fields of biological and chemical weapons as well as sexually transmitted disease and fertility, and he hinted that he had gained the expertise with the CIA's assistance.

But Knobel would not pass judgment on Ford's covert activities. Nor would he accept that the doctor was an attempted murderer or a suicide or a white supremacist. He was far too smart, he said, and even spiritual. "Larry was emotional. He share[d] the vision of getting a solution for Africa's problem of HIV. Now that doesn't sound to me like a person who's a radical or a racist." Then the general deviated a bit to praise the Mormon Tabernacle Choir, which he and his wife had so enjoyed on their trip to Brigham Young University organized by Larry, and to show Coen a few of the fawning notes the gynecologist had sent, including one that read, "To Niel, the General that embodies the best of the genius of General MacArthur, the guts of General Patton, the compassion and concern of General Bradley with, most importantly, the love of God . . . country and family."

Knobel clearly liked Dr. Ford, and was impressed with his "inside knowledge" of chemical and biological warfare matters, which he surmised may have been gained at top-level US government facilities. "I am still uncertain about whether he was part of the CIA," he said, eyebrow arched before adding the coup de grâce. "And I am still not certain that he committed suicide."

Coen and Nadler weighed the various accounts: Larry Ford's interactions with Project Coast had either been an instance of sophisticated germ weaponeers humoring a loose cannon in their midst as he lectured them on ways to coat girlie magazines with lethal germs (as other Project Coast veterans told TRC researcher Chandré Gould); or they constituted a promising scientific and entrepreneurial endeavor, implying that it was Ford who suffered fools gladly in order to achieve his own vision of a medical breakthrough.

"Of course there's a third, simpler answer," posited Nadler. "Ford was a sketchy doctor, a worse spy and a really bad guy."

Ford's diabolical research in South Africa centered on amniotic fluid, which he believed could be harvested to create a "wonder drug." Ford, said his confidante Niel Knobel, was unable to collect enough of the stuff in the US to continue his research. South Africa, and its friendly senior medical official, opened the door for Ford to collect unlimited quantities of what he called "UAFs," or unidentified amniotic fluids. According to Helen Purkitt, an instructor at the US Naval Academy who, with Stephen Burgess, wrote a book titled *South Africa's Weapons of Mass Destruction*, Ford was in fact able to collect "huge amounts" of UAFs with the cooperation of the South African Medical Service, which was headed by none other than Wouter Basson.

Ford was free to move forward boldly with this edgy research given that South Africa's regulation procedure for new drugs was "a lot shorter and a lot quicker," in Knobel's words. Even the Reagan-era FDA process impeded Larry Ford in his quest to get another invention to market. This was his patented "Inner Confidence," a female suppository that combined spermicide and microbicide to offer contraception, STD prevention and protection from HIV. It was a product that Ford assumed would be of great interest to the apartheid regime; and as Coen would soon ascertain, he wasn't entirely wrong. What is less clear is why.

"To this day, I don't think we know exactly what was the purpose of that [amniotic fluid] project, I mean, if there was a dark side to that project," US Naval Academy's Professor Purkitt told Coen and Nadler. "But it was very controversial. After the transition, the new South African surgeon general was very suspicious about all this work. By then, the AIDS epidemic was full-blown, and there was always a suspicion that perhaps Project Coast was the cause of HIV/AIDS."

In the end, it was Dr. Ford's domestic endeavors that got him in real trouble.

In addition to his gynecological practice, Ford ran a company called BioFem. His partner in the venture was a man named James Riley. By 2000, Ford and Riley were on the cusp of achieving a longtime dream, having just secured millions of dollars in funding for their breakthrough contraceptive/microbicide, "Inner Confidence." Riley believed it would be his golden goose; Ford had delusions of a Nobel Prize for his invention.

Instead, Riley was shot in the face as he walked across BioFem's parking lot by an assailant quickly linked to his own business partner. The car that picked the gunman up at the scene was tracked to Dino D'Saachs, a close friend and associate of Larry Ford. Ford, when quizzed by police, could not come up with a plausible reason for D'Saachs' car on the scene, nor could he explain why D'Saachs had called him from his cell phone minutes before the hit. It looked bad for the gynecologist, and a few days later a shot from his home rang out signaling his death. Another apparent suicide on the long list of biologists and their mysterious deaths.

A two-month-long investigation into the attack on Riley ended in the conclusion, sealed in court papers, that Ford had "masterminded the assassination of the victim for financial gains related to the business activities of BioFem." Riley's assailant has never been identified. Dino D'Saachs, now serving twenty-six to life, is still not talking. Riley has grown a mustache to hide the bullet scar and professes to be "traumatized" by the betrayal of his partner. But there are other Ford victims—such as the women who claim to be the unwitting guinea pigs in Ford's quest to perfect "Inner Confidence." Their stories came, quite literally, out of the woodwork following Ford's death, when detectives uncovered the files of eighty-three patients under a false floorboard in the doctor's pretty house.

Since the Ford story has become public, eight former patients have come forward to divulge information about their treatment. Six of them complained of illnesses ranging from abdominal infections to cancer. One woman claimed to have been poisoned in 1987 by Ford after she spurned his attentions. She said he had called it an "alpha-bug" and that she has suffered from debilitating vertigo ever since. The medical connections are unproven and perhaps untenable—epidemiologists who interviewed the patients concluded there was no pattern to suggest deliberate infection and no risks of a public health epidemic.

But the case of Tami Tippit was enough to get Stephen Dresch on board. He stayed there, searching for proof, urging more digging into the secrets of BioFem's dark genius.

"There was a whole series of front companies and a very sleazy group of people all clearly pumping money into Ford," he told Coen during a long debriefing in 2006.

Dresch had worked closely with Vic Ray, the Irvine police force's lead detective on the Ford case, who had called the story he uncovered "the most bizarre friggin' thing" he had ever investigated. It was Ray who first gathered some hard data that Ford had a CIA connection—getting confirmation of the relationship from a FBI officer who liaisoned with Langley. But after months of muscular gumshoeing, the detective was abruptly bumped from the case. "Iced-out," suggested Dresch, to prevent the public disclosure of Ford's US and South African bioweapons activities. With Detective Ray off the case, the FBI seized and the gonvernment sealed Ford's papers. But Dresch fought to open the records with the help of a Washington law firm. It was, he argued, a matter of life and death. It was another uphill struggle; Dresch's health was worsening, and so was Tami Tippit's. Tami Tippit had been an attractive blonde model hired and romanced by Ford under the pretext of pushing his line of face creams. By the time Dresch reached her late in 2006, she was a living corpse, poisoned, she claimed, by the insane gynecologist whose advances she spurned.

Nadler and Coen kept intermittent tabs on Tippit, and Dresch kept up a steady drumbeat of pressure on the Feds to release Ford's file, which he argued could contain some indication of an antidote for Tippit's ailments. One morning, he called the journalists with the news that one of Tami's doctors, an expert on biotoxins and neurological ailments, had had an . . . incident. He had been rushed to a hospital in LA after he spontaneously started bleeding from numerous orifices. It appeared that his car's door handle had been dusted with some sort of toxin.

Over the course of the next two years, Tippit drifted further from reach in a morphine slumber. She was eventually moved into a seedy nursing home, where Dresch occasionally visited. She died in 2006. Two years later, Coen and Nadler were finally able to get hold of the FBI file on Larry Ford. It was almost entirely redacted, but the news that memos on Dr. Ford were prepared for Attorney General Richard Thornburgh and Hugh Price, the associate deputy director for counter-intelligence at the CIA, was clear. Diligent censors may have erased the traces of Larry Ford's work on a race weapon and a relationship with the CIA, but there remained evidence that he had had very real interactions with the South Africans involved in Project Coast—including the man who ran it.

ANTHRAX . . . NOT JUST FOR APARTHEID

Getting Wouter Basson to sit down for an interview on camera was not an easy proposition, and even if he agreed to sit down, Coen and Nadler expected a difficult session.

"How do you interview a man who once advised soldiers who had been captured for interrogation to, quote, 'spin him any story that you like . . . talk as much rubbish as you can within the first 24 hours so that your comrades have enough time to get away,'" Nadler asked Coen on the Skype hook-up from Brooklyn. "He's a smooth operator."

"His nickname is 'Dr. Death' and he's free to walk the streets today," answered Coen in Pretoria. "That, in itself, is quite remarkable."

Five years after his acquittal, Basson was again practicing medicine in the army hospital where he had begun his career. He had taken up the cloak of respectability, having been reinstated as cardiologist at the Groote Schuur Hospital in Cape Town—the same hospital, Nadler had pointed out, where Dr. Christiaan Barnard had pioneered the human heart transplant in 1967.

At first blush, it seemed that Basson, when asked to talk about the role of Project Coast in forging a new biological arms race, would have nothing to gain from reminding the world of his decidedly checkered past. But Coen had bet, rightly, that there was unfinished business in Basson's debriefing. He might take justifiable pride in having upheld his own innocence, but Dr. Death wouldn't be fully exonerated, mused Coen, until he had the chance to prove that neither self-interest, conviction in apartheid or even love of country alone explained his actions entirely. In essence, Coen had snagged an interview with Basson by offering him the chance to lay part of the blame for Project Coast's excesses at the doorsteps of other states which remained in the shadows.

Basson had agreed to meet Coen in Cape Town on a Saturday night in May 2008 after he was done lecturing students at the University of Cape Town Medical School. He instructed the journalist to find a suitable place to conduct the interview. Coen rented a conference room in a hotel not far from the university and set up the lights with apprehension. Would he show up or would he change his mind? At the appointed time, Coen waited on a couch near the hotel entrance, looking up nervously every time someone walked in with the cold wind in tow. Finally, there was Basson, meticulously dressed in an expensive suit seeming a bit apprehensive yet soon enough quite game. The two men shook hands and Coen ushered him down the corridor to a conference room with two chairs set up bathed in film lights. As microphones were secured to jacket lapels, Coen began making the usual small talk of Africa, the weather, the landscape and headlines. "I hear the crime rate has gone through the roof," Coen said, and Basson tested his voice levels and began:

"In actual fact, there can be no opinion of what was done in Project Coast, because of the vast amount of work that was done, only a small percentage has been made known," Basson told Coen when the lights were adjusted and the camera rolling. "I don't know if anybody in the world, at this stage, except myself and maybe five or six colleagues, can in any way express an opinion on what was done in Project Coast, because they don't know it.

"If you're running a research team, it's not in your interest or in their interest to have the full picture, so each member of the research team had a certain part of the picture. And what happened in the court cases was that . . . when those members were pushed, they came up with the facts that they knew as well as the interpretation. So each of them made their own interpretation as to what was done," Basson paused, as if to let the full misguidedness of the courts sink in. "The state took the information and ran with it because they believed these people—not realizing that this was pure conjecture."

Coen took this in and wondered how best to respond to the assertion that there was no truth in pieces of truth. "So you deny the assassination team?" he asked.

"I don't have to deny it. The court said it didn't exist. I don't have to say a word about that; you can go and read the judgment," replied Basson.

Finally, Coen gave Basson his target by asking: Was South Africa isolated at the time it started to build Project Coast and if so, how did he get the project up and running so quickly?

The answer, as Coen had suspected, came from the West.

"What we basically did is we did a decent threat analysis, and after having done the decent threat analysis, we decided to find those organizations in the world that could help us with technology, and, of course, they were mostly in the UK, in America, odd few stations in Europe," said Basson. "And we then visited these places, explained to them what was our problem was, and then, of course, we told them what the information was that we needed, and we then eventually got some of the information from them. The rest we bought, borrowed and stole. Strangely enough in America and in the UK, the help that came from there was ideological."

Throughout most of Project Coast's existence, the CIA and MI6 kept files on Wouter Basson, and the Western intelligence agencies had a pretty fair idea of his activities. South Africa may have been entered into the list of violators of the weapons ban, but both the US and the UK governments essentially turned a blind eye to this breach. The *noblesse oblige* was in accordance with the policies of President Ronald Reagan, who authorized "constructive engagement" with the apartheid government, a euphemism for financial support to allow the South African government to continue its opposition to majority rule.

Surgeon General Niel Knobel had earlier confirmed to Coen that the lack of censure went beyond disinterest: "Whenever I visited any of those countries and had the opportunity of meeting some of my colleagues within the military medical services, at some or other point, somebody would say, 'By the way, we know what you're doing, and we're giving you all the support we have until it's going to be become known internationally, but don't quit.'"

In fact, many experts believe that Project Coast may have acted as a convenient outsourcing actor for institutes like Porton Down and Fort Detrick, which were constrained in their research ambitions as signatories to the 1979 Biological Weapons Convention. Project Coast's interest in designing undetectable stealth assassination tools would have been of interest to any intelligence agency, regardless of their avowed compliance to certain treaty standards. Why not let South Africa do the "dirty work," which, after all, could always be disavowed by Western governments.

The notion that the West helped stoke the fires of biological battles in Africa's wars of independence has gained currency over the years. Some sources suggest that the United States and Britain were aiding the biowar as early as "Operation Winter," the covert transfer of Rhodesian assets into South Africa, on the eve of Zimbabwean independence through the use of American transport planes and the advice of British government ministers. Later, Project Coast scientists confirmed that Roodeplaat Research Lab head Schalk van Rensburg had gone so far as to hire consultants from Porton Down to help build the lab's first Biosafety Level 4 facility, a decision that apparently caused the consternation of colleagues concerned that van Rensburg would "blow RRL's cover." But no matter how persistent and damning the conjectural evidence, the tracks of American and British influence on Basson's operation are not readily visible. Solid, corporeal evidence was something all sides worked hard to avoid.

Coen asked Basson straight up if he knew David Kelly. The South African acknowledged having met the Englishman on "three or four occasions," but remained evasive on whether the meetings had occurred at Porton Down.

"Did you visit Fort Detrick?"

"Yes, I did."

At a request for details, Dr. Death became testy: "I mean, you know, the next question that I get asked is, who, who arranged it, and why, and what, and where, and then, you know, I already have hassles with the UK and American governments, I don't need any more, thank you, it's enough for me. But, suffice it to say, we went there, with no objective of ever doing any damage to either the UK or the USA, our sole objective was to make sure, or to determine what they could do to help us, and how we could enhance our own program based on their knowledge."

And with that, the good doctor refused to give any more details about foreign entanglements. But he did offer a few nuggets about the enigmatic Dr. Larry Ford, whom he called a "mad hatter."

And while Army Surgeon General Niel Knobel had nothing but fondness for his young friend, describing him "eccentric to the extreme," Wouter Basson was reserved with his praise. In answer to Coen's question about Ford, Dr. Death began with the blank-faced sarcasm that Coen was beginning to recognize as an attempt to stall. "Larry was a wonderful fellow," he said flatly. "He would rock up in South Africa, having flown in on intercontinental flights with a trousers pocket full of goodies. Concealed vials that he claimed were new and wonderful organisms and could do the most wonderful things on Earth." As far as Basson was concerned, or as far as he was willing to tell Coen, Larry Ford's pockets were ultimately full of "junk." He called him a "rogue" planted by the CIA to nose into Project Coast. It was Basson's job, he said, to control Ford's scientific activities while in South Africa, to serve him a few helpings of disinformation and send him back home. Nothing more.

Coen next assaulted Dr. Death with questions about the "black bomb." Although he began by jokingly call it "the most fun I've ever had in my life," Basson said that talk of such a thing in the popular press was misconstrued. That, in fact, the only research specifically directed at his nation's black population was an infertility project—which in itself was always planned as voluntary and which, incidentally, was performed at the behest of another, unnamed, country with a "population explosion."

This answer raised alarming questions in Coen's head. What country could possibly have been challenged with a population explosion? Basson refused to answer. Coen believed there were several candidates, but none that, as of this writing, could be confirmed. And if Basson's scientists were close to a breakthrough on a vaccine intended to limit black women's fertility, what did that say of other ethnically targeted medical interventions they might have? What did it say of the elephant in South Africa's living room? What did it say of African AIDS?

If the United States and the UK had kept a low profile in setting up, contributing and perhaps benefiting from Project Coast, they were less coy about making their influence known in shutting the operation down. It happened in the early 1990s, when Wouter Basson began taking all-too-frequent trips to Libya.

Western intelligence officers interpreted this new relationship with Gaddafi as an indication that Basson was seeing the decommissioning handwriting on the wall. All-white rule was drawing to a close, and as the de Klerk government negotiated with the African National Congress for a role in the Mandela government, it was clear that Project Coast was in its sunset years. The fear was that Wouter Basson, in need of new employment, was going rogue. And that spooked the thus-far complacent signatories to the biological weapons ban who leaned hard on the apartheid regime, and later on Mandela's government, to reign in its Project Coast scientists. Around the time that the US and the UK sent demarches to the new government in South Africa that it destroy Project Coast stocks and weapons, they also insisted that the loose cannon Basson be rehired as a South African National Defence Force doctor after his dismissal from Project Coast.

It was an understandable concern, noted state Prosecutor Tori Pretorius. Pretorious mused on the fate of Project Coast science falling into the hands of "criminal gangs and terrorists." Coen thought to himself that Basson and his crew qualified as both. "So it's important to look after the scientists that were involved," continued Pretorius. "It's important to look after the human beings that were involved."

THE SHY FISH GREEN CARD CAPER

In 1993 Project Coast was officially disbanded. President F.W. de Klerk ordered that all original documents be destroyed, along with the weapons stockpiles in Project Coast labs. He put Dr. Wouter Basson in charge of the electronic archiving of the documents. It was a bit like putting the fox in charge of the henhouse. Basson declined to shred the program's paper trail, instead stashing key documents in two large steamer trunks found after he was caught trying to sell drugs in the Magnolia Dell gardens in Pretoria. Still, he continues to assert that he fulfilled the final orders pertaining to the biological material. No one, he told Coen, would ever be able to recreate Project Coast's illicit inventory, which had been deep-sixed into oblivion somewhere off the coast of South Africa.

"I have no idea where it happened. I was sitting in the back of the airplane. The pilot should know where he went—I don't know. And at a specific time he opened the doors and we dumped the stuff out and then we went back home." Basson sniffed lightly and settled back into his chair with his arms folded across his chest. He had tossed his life's work into the ocean and was quite ready for the next question.

Basson claimed that the legacy stocks of Project Coast's twelve-year dalliance with death had been dumped at sea . . . every last sample. But this appeared to be an example of Basson's proclivity to "spin any story," for in the summer of 2002, with the FBI hot on the trail of the anthrax letter killer in the United States, former Project Coast scientist Daan Goosen offered to sell Washington the very same germs that had been reportedly destroyed in the South Atlantic. He thought the Pentagon might be particularly interested in the seventy-some strains of anthrax and an anthrax anti-serum developed in Roodeplaat Research Labs.

Goosen, the former head of RRL, was a witness for the state in Basson's trial. He had testified that Surgeon General Niel Knobel had considered the proposed infertility agent "the most important project in the country" and that Dr. Death had abused his authority. The microbiologist had fared poorly in the post-Project Coast years. Bumped from the operation after he suffered a "nervous breakdown," Goosen was reduced, in Dresch's words, to "artificially inseminating cows." But he apparently had an ace up his sleeve—one that the United States might want in the new hand dealt in the bio-paranoid post-9/11 games.

For three years beginning in 2001, Dresch had been gathering details on the real fate of the Project Coast legacy stocks. At the center of it all was a man who said he represented Dr. Goosen in high-level negotiations with the US to purchase South African germs and viruses on the black market. He was Donald Mayes, an arms dealer with CIA connections. It had taken months of courting, but Dresch's perseverance paid off when he found himself in May 2004 on Mayes' doorstep in Vera Cruz, Mexico and was invited in for a chat.

A few days later Dresch returned to New York and plunked down at Coen and Nadler's office a piece of paper stamped "Top Secret"—a letter ostensibly from Niel Knobel to Nelson Mandela confirming that the army's bioweapon legacy stocks had been dumped at sea, just as Basson had said.

"Voila," Dresch announced to the journalists. "And now let me tell you why that document is a lie," whereupon Dresch launched into what he called "The Shy Fish Green Card Caper."

Dresch laid out what he had learned: While attending a

conference in Washington, DC, during the 2001 anthrax attacks, Daan Goosen approached the Pentagon officials and offered to supply the US government with anthrax countermeasures developed by Project Coast. He was told to tell his story to the experts working on the anthrax vaccine in Lansing, Michigan, at BioPort, the company with the contract for the US anthrax vaccine. He claimed that he did just that during a trip to Lansing, but later told associates that he essentially got a quick brush-off there and returned to South Africa a bit depressed.

Back home, he turned to Tai Minaar, a major general in the South African Defence Force, and a hands-on intelligence expert said to be close to a Civil Cooperation Bureau assassination team suspected in the murder of Swedish Prime Minister Olaf Palme in 1986. Minaar had a resume listing years as an undercover agent in Europe, Cuba, South America and the US. The general promised to be of service to Goosen.

In November 2001, Minaar approached an American contact, Donald Mayes, a fellow useful to the CIA in high-tech arms deals, and a man whose quest for obscurity earned him a nickname from Dresch: "Shy Fish." Dresch traveled down to Veracruz, Mexico, debriefed Mayes and reported to Coen and Nadler:

"Minaar told Mayes there were some Project Coast veterans who wanted $5 million and seventeen green cards in exchange for a valuable collection of germs and viruses, including anti-anthrax potions." Minaar described the cache as so extensive that he himself didn't know what they contained. But it was intimated that the goods could change the balance of a biowar. Mayes informed the CIA and the CIA, because of the anthrax attacks, hands him over to the FBI—in particular to Barbara Martinez, deputy director of the National Domestic Preparedness Office.

"Mayes arranges to bring samples in for Martinez's inspection, and his associate Bob Zlockie heads off to South Africa where Goosen prepares some samples. Zlockie empties out a tube of toothpaste, pumps some cooling gel into it and shoves capsules of genetically modified E. coli spliced with *Clostridium perfringens* in as well.

"Zlockie closes the tube of toothpaste up, throws it in his shaving kit or whatever, climbs on a plane and flies home to Florida. Gets home to Islamorada, an hour or so south of Miami, and calls the FBI and says 'all right I've got the stuff.' A young lady FBI agent came out and picked it up from him.

"So then the FBI lab has to analyze the stuff. When they confirm what it is, the negotiations begin in earnest. The biggest issue is how to get the stocks of the stuff (and the people) out of the country discreetly."

At the sit-down at FBI headquarters in May 2002, Mayes and Zlockie worked out logistics with Agent Martinez. Joby Warrick and John Mintz of the *Washington Post* later reported the arrangements:

> A private aircraft would land at a remote airfield 600 miles from coastal city of Durban. From a waiting camper-trailer on the runway, the bacteria in two cryogenic canisters would be loaded onto the plane along with two of the South African scientists. The canisters were to be labeled "oxygen" to avoid suspicion. One of the canisters was to contain more than 20 liters of antiserum and other antidotes, documents show. The other would contain 200 glass vials of biological material described as "extremely harmful to people and the environment." An inventory later provided to the FBI listed the contents of those vials as more than 150 strains of bacteria, including six that were marked as genetically modified.

Dresch continued the saga: "Martinez then asked for a list of names of the South African scientists who wanted green cards, according to Mayes' version of events. Zlockie obliged, and Martinez excused herself to work out some kinks with the plan. 'We'll be in touch,' she says. So, Mayes and Zlockie wait into the evening at their hotel for the FBI call. "Instead," Dresch continued, "in comes a call comes in from General Minaar in South Africa: 'What the fuck happened?' he screams, 'Shit is going down here! Goosen's been raided by National Security. What have you guys done?'"

The FBI had ratted out Goosen to the South African authorities. Agent Martinez never called.

But even after the DC sting, Goosen kept peddling his germ wares on the street with Tai Minaar as his mediator. Soon they had buyers on the line—including a Nazi treasure hunter with "mining operations" in Czechoslovakia and an Arab sheik.

And then things got really dodgy. On September 9, 2002, General Minaar had a beer with his girlfriend, took ill and died. Postmortem, the medical examiner was stunned to see Minaar's corpse swollen to more than double its normal size. The cause of death was recorded as heart attack; the girlfriend went into hiding.

For his part, Goosen insisted all along that he was looking for responsible buyers who might want to stem the proliferation of germ weapons as well as legitimate job opportunities for him and his colleagues. He had hoped that the Centers for Disease Control in Atlanta might fund the furthering of groundbreaking germ research begun in South Africa. He professed to be surprised by the sudden US no-go. And he later told the South African press that had no comment on General Minaar's demise.

Dresch was willing to consider Goosen's explanation. And he was just as willing to turn it on its head: "Of course the other interpretation, the other more sinister possibility is that the 2001 anthrax letter attacks were designed only to produce an American market for the anti-toxins. Recall that the origin of the anthrax letters has never been determined. It's certainly not inconceivable that whoever controlled the anti-toxin with or without Goosen's knowledge, was responsible for the anthrax letters. And that the anthrax letters as their only or primary purpose was the creation of a market for the anti-toxin."

Dresch had been sharing his sources and leads with one of South Africa's leading investigative reporters, and in January 2003, Sam Sole of the *Mail & Guardian* broke the story of the Shy Fish Caper.

Coen had all this in his mind when he met with Sam Sole just before he left Cape Town in the spring of 2008. "The reason why the Americans backtracked on the whole operation has never been satisfactorily explained," said Sole. "When we wrote the story we contacted the FBI. We phoned the CIA and tried to get some kind of comment and of course got nothing, but it was an amusing experience. So, yes, there's still a lot of loose ends . . . in this story."

Coen asked Sole about Goosen's character.

"I would say that he's a credible person," responded Sole after a moment's thought. "I wouldn't say that I always believed that his motivations were, you know, 100 percent above board. He wouldn't have got involved in this program, I think, if he'd had, you know, an impeachable ethical principle, because I think from the start, it was a program with huge ethical problems. But, that said, I haven't come across things that he said to me, where I have found that he's been lying to me or he's wrong."

Sole passed on messages to Goosen that Coen wanted to film him. Finally, Goosen phoned back. "Why are you doing this?" he asked. Coen said truth was important in these murky waters. “Send me a list of questions,” Goosen requested. Coen did so, and a meeting was arranged for the next day in the “public place” Goosen desired—a coffee shop in a Pretoria strip mall. Goosen arrived with a man he identified as another Project Coast veteran. He insisted that they sit inside, and not at Coen’s outdoor table. Despite an hour of repeated entreaties, Goosen refused to give Coen new details of the fate of the Project Coast legacy stocks: “I can’t get into this now. It’s just too damn dangerous, and I’ve been burned before. Maybe one day I’ll tell the true story. Not now.”

CHAPTER NINE

The Ghost of Sunshine

THE WILD WEST

Coen jetted back to the States with photocopies of Project Coast documents in hand, and his head filled with questions about apartheid, "Kaffir-killing" germs, David Kelly and the CIA. He was now deep inside Stephen Dresch's rabbit hole, where there were few straight lines, but where the real-life promises he made of an exciting "spiral" path, stretching exponentially over geography and time, were actually being fulfilled.

Back at the office, Coen unpacked his film gear, secured the shoot's digital data and placed some African souvenirs in the setting sunlight across his desk. He BlackBerried a meeting with Nadler for the next morning and laid his hands upon his laptop. He sat for a moment watching the East River tugboats gliding outside the window, savoring this American Moment.

Coen and Nadler had picked up evidence that the CIA and British intelligence may have used South Africa as an offshore testing ground for their own germ war interests. At the very least, it was clear that, officially, the West had turned a blind eye towards South Africa's Dr. Death and his potions.

They had also learned of the Western response to Soviet bio-duplicity.

The chessboard was active: Dresch had uncovered that the US, trying to take advantage of the nano-moments of post-Soviet transparency, had asked the Russians to supply samples of the antibiotic resistant anthrax they had developed—perhaps Biopreparat's Anthrax 836.

Several ranking Russians at first agreed to a handover of deadly potions, but ultimately Moscow refused to give them a thing. As a result, the US, using CIA subcontractor Battelle, of Ohio, began to design its own super-anthrax—so as to develop a vaccine that would kill it. This according to a *New York Times* scoop implying that the US was back in the germ war game in a big way, that the international treaty banning biological weapons was in tatters and that we may be living in the midst of a secret germ-war arms race. The front-page article by William Broad, Stephen Engleberg and Judith Miller, published in early September 2001, reported that the Pentagon was working on the creation of a genetically engineered anthrax strain—one analogous to the one the Soviets had developed—and was also researching germ bomb delivery systems.

The *Times* piece also revealed that the Pentagon's Defense Threat Reduction Agency was at work in the Nevada desert putting together a prototype of what a crude "terrorist germ lab" might look like. And while the *Times* sources insisted that the material used in the lab was benign, its location—the very same testing grounds that had hosted more than 800 nuclear test blasts during the Cold War—raised plenty of eyebrows.

Elisa Harris, President Clinton's germ war specialist on the National Security Council at the time, was forced to admit to the *Times* that she had "no idea" that the covert directorates were up to such mischief. A huge admission, but revealing of the contempt that the covert world had for political bureaucrats, especially in a Democrat's administration.

Alas, the *New York Times* story published on September 4, 2001, was too-soon forgotten in the wake of other more terrible news on September 11.

But still Coen thought it was important to look deeper into the corporate–government nexus of US biodefense. For on the day before he left South Africa, he had taken the time to examine the 1980s travel records of the Project Coast scientists, boxed in a basement storeroom maintained by the South Africa History Archive. He found itineraries of trips all across America. One particular mission caught his eye. A senior scientist had gone to San Antonio, Texas, home of the world's largest primate testing complex—a sprawling campus that housed the Southwest Research Institute (SRI). His appointment was with a man named Dr. G.T. Moore, a member of an SRI scientific team under contract to the US Army Medical Research Institute of Chemical Defense doing research on the effects of deadly nerve gasses on baboons. In a peer-reviewed article, Moore and his colleagues reported that they administered very toxic soman and sarin agents to the captive primates; they notated the rapid onset of "apnea and cardiac arrhythmias," as well as the signs of "impaired hemodynamics [blood flow] and persistent lung injury." Unsaid was the fact that baboons were the test animals most resembling humans.

"I remember that visit quite well," Dr. Moore told Nadler years later. "I met at SRI with a fine fellow named Dr. Daan Goosen, and in fact, I later took up his invitation and lectured about my work in a South African tour Goosen arranged . . . Our wives hit it off."

This Texas outfit was most interesting. Coen and Nadler had actually decided to go there some months earlier, when they heard that SRI's sister location was these days home to the world's only privately held Biosafety Level 4 laboratory, where the most dangerous germs and viruses—always fatal, no antidote, no cure—are handled. "What the hell is going on in that Texas wilderness surrounded by US military bases?" Nadler wondered, staring at the Google Earth map of San Antonio on his laptop. "Who are these guys?" And so, in the early winter days of 2007, the pair took off for San Antonio, known in the Lone Star State as "Military City."

The Southwest Foundation for Biomedical Research (SFBR) is spread over 400 acres of suburban Texas—a vast scientific compound not too far from the state's Sea World park and Lackland Air Force Base. Established in the years after World War II, when San Antonio was a far cry from a metropolis, the research campus represented, according to the company's promotional literature, the ambition of its founder to "dare to imagine a city of science in South Texas."

Thomas B. Slick, said visionary and founder, was the prep-schooled Ivy-educated son of an oil magnate—a well-heeled dynastic hopeful who palled around with Howard Hughes and had an uncommon sense of adventure. He was esteemed by his fans as an entrepreneurial catalyst, a philanthropist, and even a peacemaker, but it was Slick's escapades as a cryptozoologist that particularly endeared the man to his biographer Loren Coleman, known himself as the world's leading researcher of undiscovered animals. "A handsome, lean, prematurely white-haired man, soft-spoken, with a slight Southern drawl," proclaimed Nadler, reading from one of Coleman's works about Slick, marvelously titled *Tom Slick and the Search for the Yeti.*

Yes—in addition to medical research, petrodollars and the perfect wife, Slick spent his colorful life in pursuit of the Abominable Snowman, the Loch Ness Monster and Bigfoot.

Slick was killed in 1962 in a Buddy Holly-style airplane tragedy—an accident that Coleman asserts could have been caused by a bomb on the small aircraft planted by rival researchers upset with Slick's increasing interest and expenditure on Sasquatch tracking. Just forty-six when he died, this "son of a wild-catter" had found time in his truncated life to expand his research empire until it encompassed five separate foundations and to crisscross the world in search of the unknown. "A life legends are made of," pronounced Nadler, still reading aloud.

In another book, *Tom Slick: True Life Encounters in Cryptozoology*, Coleman fashions a muscular footnoted argument that Slick was also an old school spy, recruited by the World War II spy shop the OSS, headed by Colonel "Wild Bill" Donovan, whose services were called upon time and again by intelligence associates during the Cold War.

Coleman uncovered evidence that Slick's fleet of cargo planes—Slick Airways—worked in concert with the CIA's proprietary Air America fleet in Asia and Latin America as things got hot.Most intriguingly, he links Tom Slick's search for the Yeti with a CIA effort to smuggle the Dalai Lama out of China in the late 1950s. Coleman's book has been optioned for the screen by actor Nicholas Cage.

Slick's vision endured into the twenty-first century, and today SFBR is one of the largest biotech research centers in the world. Since the anthrax attacks in 2001, the foundation's scientists have received funding from federal agencies to study exotic pathogens like Marburg virus and Lassa fever. To do so, the foundation established its Biosafety Level 4 lab, which provides maximum containment conditions for working with deadly pathogens. It is the only BSL-4 lab in private hands in the world. And while this fact hasn't received much public attention, SFBR officials are quite proud of their achievement.

"The BSL-4 lab is the first to be operated outside of the two federal labs, and again is just an example of the ability of an independent non-profit organization like this to make a strategic commitment in the area of research that was sort of ahead of its time," crowed SFBR President John Kerr, when the journalists met him in his office.

When first approached, Kerr and his staff had treated the filmmakers with the wariness that most facilities engaged in large-scale animal testing reserve for investigative journalists. The primate compound was a bull's eye on the front gate of SFBR, which had learned to treat such outside interest as a Trojan Horse sent from PETA. But when Nadler and Coen assured the PR department that they were more concerned with terrorists than monkeys, and more interested in lab capability than the conditions in the baboon cages, the response was cordial. Coen described their work-in-progress about the international response to bioterrorism. "We understand that you are doing cutting-edge research at your facilities," he explained. The doors were opened.

John Kerr, according to a profile published in a 2007 *San Antonio Business Journal* article, is "a man who lives and breathes biomedical progress on many levels." One of those levels, perhaps the entry-level, was his marriage to Tom Slick's niece. On a less local but equally influential level is the friendship he maintains with his neighbor from childhood—George W. Bush. (The one-time White House dog-in-chief—Millie—was named for Kerr's mom, he confirmed.) The photographs lining the walls of his office attest to the importance of both these connections. Coen asked him about the foundation's ties to the government and Kerr answered readily. He asserted that the foundation is a "charitable scientific research institute," funded primarily by the

National Institutes of Health. But the asset of having a BSL-4 lab, he continued, meant that "in addition . . . we have a number of other federal research contracts with a number of federal agencies, including research that's being done to understand and develop ways of dealing with these select agents like anthrax that have been weaponized and could be used in bioterrorism."

The readiness of SFBR's top-level lab allowed the facility to have a major role in the Amerithrax forensic work, Coen and Nadler learned from Kerr. When the mail scare subsided, Tom Slick's foundation was in a position to handle a fresh wave of biodefense research generated by the Pentagon and Homeland Security. Because after 9/11, "there was a lot more money being given," Jean Patterson, head of SFBR's Department of Virology and Immunology, said in an interview with Coen and Nadler. "So we expanded our program into the hemorrhagic fevers like Ebola, Marburg. And SARS erupted and we were able to work on that right away because we had all the facility. And we also worked with plague and tularemia and other select agents, those things the governments have predetermined to be potential biological weapons."

Coen wanted to know exactly "how researchers derived antivirals from potential biological weapons material." Nadler wanted to know just "how dangerous this whole process was." For a few moments, Patterson talked about the intricacies of "aerosolization and recombinant DNA" and then became disarmingly frank: "Well, it's like cooking basically. You throw things in and mess with it." This was not reassuring.

The anthrax attacks, and SFBR staffers' ability to "mess" with the stuff in their moonlab suits, put Tom Slick's dreams in a new light. The "city of science" Slick had imagined as a "tool . . . by which we can improve the physical side of our lives" was giving up ever increasing space to the deadly machinery of biowar. Where once his scientists developed solutions primarily to known health problems—safe contraceptives and a cure for cancer—today they were also contemplating Armageddon: weaponized Marburg, late stage antibiotic-resistant anthrax toxins, Ebola. Coen and Nadler left SFBR thinking that the fate of Moore's primates, the South African's toxic gas interest, the need for a BSL-4 lab, and the bid to acquire more funding from agencies playing with virulent fire, put the SFBR campus on a map with decidedly dark spots. What was the real mission of this decidedly spooky place? Nadler and Coen eventually asked for details in a follow-up email: Was SFBR conducting classified research for the government in its BSL-4 lab? If so, did any of it involve anthrax?

"We are prohibited from answering these questions due to regulatory/security restrictions imposed by the federal government," responded SFBR's newly hired press consultants.

The journalists had their answer, and it gave them a chill.

The Southwest Foundation for Biomedical Research was 1,100 miles down the road from the next key anthrax hot spot on the team's itinerary, Utah's Dugway Proving Ground, where the US government conducts its most secret weapons testing.

In the wake of the anthrax letters, the *Baltimore Sun* reported US Army scientists in Utah had been making weapons-grade anthrax and shipping it to Fort Detrick. The anthrax spores were virtually identical to those mailed to Congress.

Coen, Nadler and cameraman Verrechia made the drive from Texas to Utah on Interstates 10 and 40. The highway snaked through some desert, then beautiful lunar-like landscapes and the breathtaking Wasatch Mountain Range, which reminded Coen of portions of South Africa. Passing through the valleys that were important portals during the movement west of the Mormons 100 or so years earlier, Coen considered a possible reason for the affinity between Mormon Larry Ford and his pals among the Afrikaaners, who also claimed an arduous historical trek as a proud part of their legacy.

En route, the team took a few detours that touched on their bioterrorism investigations. First, to Henderson, Nevada to look for the abandoned silver mine where Larry Ford had supposedly stashed some of his anthrax-making equipment. They never found it, though the local gunsmith they met outside town remembered lots of police and media activity at the time. They also went in search of the gold mine being worked by the Searchlight Mineral Corporation, the last corporate manifestation of Vladimir Pasechnik's phage-for-profit operation. This one they found just outside Searchlight, the three-stoplight hometown of US Senate Majority Leader Sen. Henry Reid. The mine was behind a barbed wire fence. The access road gate was padlocked and No Trespassing signs were clearly posted.

Perhaps the strangest thing they experienced on their own trek west was the song on the radio that looped repeatedly through the better part of the forty-hour drive through the desolation—a blues spiritual about Moses. The station broadcasting the song never identified itself, as FCC regulations require; there was no announcer or commercial interruptions, just that damn song over and over again, beamed out with a signal that never seemed to waver. Tuning to the station hundreds of miles later, the song was still on; three days later they were able to pick up the signal and the song was still playing. It would haunt the three men to the present day.

"If we get to Dugway, and they are playing that song on the elevator, I'm gonna lose it," Nadler warned.

Though it spans an area the size of Rhode Island, Dugway Proving Ground is easily overlooked as it hides in plain site in the vast Utah wilderness. It was chosen as an ideal testing site because it encompasses a vast area called the Great Basin where all rivers and waterways flow to its center. In other words, nothing can leak out. Nadler and Coen stood on the side of the road and gazed through binoculars at a single corner of what their guide, an environmental activist named Steve Erickson, called a "national sacrifice for military projects."

"This part of the country has been subjected to a lot of abuses and a lot of sacrifices on behalf of the rest of the nation," said Erickson. "All of this airspace is controlled by the military. We have not just the chemical and biological testing here at Dugway, but one mountain range further to the west and north of here is both a toxic waste incinerator and a radioactive waste landfill. You've got . . . a bombing range as well to the north. And then when we go back to the east, over this mountain range, there's the chemical weapons stockpile and incinerator. So we've got a potpourri of nasties out here. And there's a lot of space to keep a secret."

Dugway has been the military's testing site for more than a half century. Its biological lab is listed on the National Historic Register for its role in testing germ agents. In fact Frank Olson visited regularly—his son remembered how his father told him about the big sky and rugged wilderness. More than 1,000 open-air chemical weapons tests were performed at Dugway in the decades since its opening in 1942, including one in 1968 that killed about six thousand sheep. A former head of Fort Detrick's USAMRIID has claimed that anthrax was weaponized there by the pound. Erickson's group, the Citizens Education Project, claims responsibility for torpedoing a plan to build a Biosafety Level 4 lab at Dugway, but has come up against silence in trying to ascertain specifics regarding current expansion plans. As ground zero for Cold War weapons testing, Dugway has a classified pedigree. Much of what goes on there, even today, is unknown.

"They have on the site samples of a variety of different biological agents that could be used as pathogens," said Erickson. "They store them in an icebox. We call it Pandora's Icebox. But they've never told us the contents of Pandora's Icebox, so we really don't know what their stockpile consists of."

But Erickson believes that biological weapons testing at Dugway has doubled since 9/11, under the auspices of a new counter-terrorism directive. And he believes that directly or indirectly, Dugway Proving Ground is responsible for spawning the new emphasis on counter-terrorism: He believes the anthrax in the letters to Daschle and Leahy was in fact milled at Dugway.

As the visitors stood on a bluff overlooking the base, a pair of F-16 jets screamed across the sky, scattering the herd of pronghorn antelope on the plains below.

The process of gaining access to Dugway for filming had gone unexpectedly smoothly. All the Army wanted in return was the chance to review the transcript for accuracy and national security's sake. At the gates, they were met by the director of public relations for Dugway, a cheerful and helpful woman named Paula Nicholson, who noted that Dugway's isolation amid vast tracts of restricted air and land space "makes customers very happy if they want privacy for testing conditions." Coen raised his eyebrows at the flack as she merrily continued, "We have customers from all over the Department of Defense because we test for joint services—Army, Air Force, Navy, Marines and Coast Guard." Nicholson pointed out the barracks, commissaries and the post office. She noted that Dugway had a bowling alley and a strip mall. She said the wild deer and the antelope lived peaceably alongside the biowarriors in training. "They seem to sense they're safe in this area," she said happily.

En route to the "Life Science Test Facility," the journalists were shown the 11,000-foot-long airplane runway, the ridge of mountains that serve remarkably well for proxy Afghan terrain and the remnants of the models of German and Japanese villages built for war gaming with Standard Oil money during World War II. Further along there were "igloos" where chemical gasses are stored and a working wind tunnel for testing military instruments in adverse conditions. "Every piece of equipment that goes to war should have been tested at Dugway Proving Ground," said Nicholson.

At the Life Science Test Facility named after the late Dr. Lothar Salomon ("a very distinguished Jewish man" with decades of Dugway service, Nicholson cheerily offered), Coen and Nadler were introduced to Dr. Alan Jeff Mohr, an affable tour guide who proved as cheerful and ready to please as the public affairs staff. He happily accommodated the cameras by directing via microphone, several scientists working behind the small glass windows of the sealed lab doors. On command, the space-suited researchers extracted receptacles from liquid nitrogen. Small red signs on the doors of the different labs identified the toxic agents being worked with inside—including "*Bacillus anthracis*—Ames." The notorious Ames strain of the attack letters.

"You can't film that," warned Nicholson.

"Yes, for security reasons we can't allow you to show the agents we're working on," agreed Mohr. And then he named them—one by one as the cameras rolled, with sound on.

Coen was surprised at the frankness of the answer he received after he asked Dr. Mohr about the anthrax letters. "A bunch of us worked with the FBI on Amerithrax. So we know all the ins and outs and we have to be careful about that because we signed statements saying that we wouldn't talk about exactly what that anthrax looked like."

But then he told Coen and Nadler something about what it looked like and gave specifics: "It was milled down to one micron single spores, yes it was," he said, and he beckoned them over to a monitor showing, in high definition, what a one-micron single spore looks like, when magnified. "Alrighty then," he said clapping his hands and continuing on to the next room.

Mohr confirmed to the journalists that his lab was indeed weaponizing anthrax. "It's probably the only laboratory in the country that does and the reason we make it is because we test detectors." He walked them past a lab where he said Ames anthrax, Venezuelan Equine Encephalomyelitis virus and Botoxin were aerosolized. "This morning, the system under test broke, or at this moment right now we'd be aerosolizing anthrax," he noted. "So, we're air washing that chamber right now, and then we're going to go in there later on today and fix that detector so that we can go back again and resume testing tomorrow."

Mohr had been at Dugway for twenty-eight years, heading up the biological division for many of them. He was nearing a move over to the "private sector," he said, and it was clear to Coen and Nadler that he sensed a golden age approaching. Dugway's Life Science Facility had helped to revive bioweapons research in the post-9/11 era. Mohr's division had grown into a major operation.

"There's been a significant amount of money invested both in facilities and in the expertise of the scientists who work there. We have some beautiful laboratories in the chemical lab, beautiful laboratories here at life sciences," concluded Mohr proudly. "Great people, good facilities, so we can provide the soldiers with the bottom line, be able to tell them if the equipment that has been developed is worthy of being used out in the field."

At the end of their tour, Coen and Nadler conferred outside the gates with citizen activist Erickson, who laughed ruefully at the gung-ho reception the journalists had received. In his newsletter, Erickson had written of Dugway's expansion, which "will include 25 new BSL-2 and BSL-3 labs and two 1,500 litre fermenters—that's sixty times the size of what they have now." And as he stood with Coen and Nadler in the desert, he added:

"If the US were ever to embark on an offensive program, this is where it would begin."

The facilities that John Kerr at Southwest Foundation for Biomedical Research and Jeff Mohr at Dugway Proving Ground so confidently displayed for Coen and Nadler were the physical manifestations of the new biodefense boom spawned by 9/11 and the anthrax attacks. In the years since 9/11, the US government has elevated the research of biological weaponry to an unprecedented priority level. It began almost immediately, with President Bush ushering in Operation Bioshield with a $5.6 billion-dollar check in November 2001—the height of anthrax-attack hysteria. But that allocation was just the tip of the iceberg. Total spending by government agencies through 2008 on germ warfare programs topped $50 billion dollars. That's twice as much money as was spent, in relative terms, on the Manhattan Project to develop the nuclear bomb in the 1940s.

The beneficiaries of this spending spree are myriad: federal facilities like Fort Detrick's USAMRIID and Dugway Proving Ground; state universities with high-level bioresearch operations like the University of Texas and the University of Wisconsin; leading Big Pharma firms like Pfizer and Squibb; private enterprises Battelle and Southwest Foundation for Biomedical Research. The list of agencies and corporations grows daily—players in what is arguably the planet's most dangerous new business behemoth, the United States Bio-Military Industrial Complex.

Project Sunshine

In October 2007, a community organizer named Edward Hammond was called upon to testify at a congressional hearing investigating the rapid proliferation of biological laboratories. Hammond, of the Sunshine Project, testified before the House Committee on Energy and Commerce that laboratory buildings totaled about four million square feet, or ninety acres. That's the equivalent of thirty-six Wal-Marts, he offered as analogy for those who liked visuals. He detailed for lawmakers an exhaustive but still incomplete inventory of the number of high-containment labs in the United States, their capacities, and their cost. His list included more than a half-dozen future BSL-4 sites under construction or proposal, including several slated for Fort Detrick under the $1.2 billion plan for the National Interagency Biodefense Campus. He said that the media and public regularly asked him where the government published this data.

"It doesn't," was his alarming, but correct, response.

At the time of his testimony, Hammond, then of Texas, headed the Sunshine Project, the country's only independent watchdog of biological weaponry research. In his thirty-minute prepared remarks, he condoned the Pentagon's aim to maintain a defensive program, particularly following the revelations about Soviet capabilities and in the wake of the 2001 events. But the rate of lab expansion under the Bush administration, he said, "has gone far beyond what is prudent and necessary. And without a regulatory framework."

What Hammond told lawmakers that day was startling: More than 100 university, government, hospital and corporate labs were engaged in potential germ war research but were refusing to disclose details of their operations publicly. Moreover, the National Institutes of Health, the ostensible regulator of such labs, was encouraging the lack of transparency. Adding to the breakdown in regulation, said Hammond, was the fact that funding for the research came from a range of agencies across the federal government without a comprehensive oversight law.

Hammond offered case after case of private labs operating without a mandated Institutional Biosafety Committee (IBC). Others that had convened such a committee had never held a meeting. Some that had held IBC meetings had either failed to record or refused to provide minutes of the meetings. Since 2003, he said, the Sunshine Project had launched 150 written complaints to the NIH about facilities refusing to disclose their internal committee documents. The Southwest Foundation for Biomedical Research near his home base in Texas, for example, had offered up more than four years worth of correspondence with NIH that totaled just two sentences, and IBC minutes that fit on a single sheet of paper. (In an e-mail to the authors an SFBR spokesman pointed out "the operational protocols employed by SFBR staff serve as a national model. Furthermore SFBR is in compliance with all regulatory requirements.")

But the worst offenders, according to Hammond, were to be found in the most prestigious private academic institutes and among the nation's leading biotech giants. Just 18 percent of workers in the top twenty biotech firms were working at an NIH-compliant company, said Hammond, and with an estimated 15,000 people working in 400 facilities, biological weapon research was clearly an industry in need of effective oversight. Instead, there was little, if any at all.

Hammond then itemized numerous accidents of varying severity that had taken place in public labs in the past year. It was a particularly egregious incident at Texas A&M in which the university failed to report lab workers' exposure to Q fever and *Brucella* that sparked congressional interest.

A cranky Republican on the oversight subcommittee of the House Energy and Commerce Committee, a former obstetrician from North Texas named Michael Burgess took all this in, and then delivered a single question—Was it true that Hammond's Sunshine organization received funding from George Soros, the billionaire liberal? Karl Rove would have been proud. Hammond sighed and advised Rep. Burgess to check out all the donors to his one-man operation on his website.

Nadler and Coen were impressed by Hammond's testimony, which they watched live from their office. He argued for transparency and disclosure, arguing that "Americans have a right to know what research is occurring in their midst and if labs are being operated safely and legally." Like security work by contract guards in Iraq and elsewhere that the US relied upon to cloud the chain of responsibility for possible war crimes and excessive force in its War on Terror, private biowarfare labs had become a masked and hidden network—one that was beyond the Freedom of Information Act and far less answerable to the public. "We are talking about Bio-Blackwaters, no?" asked Nadler, and Hammond agreed. The name that Ed Hammond had chosen for his agency, "The Sunshine Project," was a very loud echo of Stephen Dresch's own mantra: Only sunlight killed germs, and only truth could disinfect the dirty business that had gone on for too long. So a few months later, Nadler and Coen went to visit Hammond, re-located to Berkeley, to follow up with some questions of their own. Nadler asked him why he was alone out there—why there weren't more Sunshine Projects, more public outrage, more private citizens taking up the cause.

"A lot of people are scared by this. Talking about some of the horrible things that can be done with biological weapons has scared people so much that they are willing to accept a biodefense program in the United States that poses more of a threat to its own citizens than we would have if our investment was far, far less in biodefense," Hammond answered. "We are creating a large constituency of people whose future self-interest—keeping their labs up and running—depends upon our being scared of biological weapons. Once this culture of fear gets too entrenched, it's going to be very, very, very difficult to reduce US work on biological weapons agents to a reasonable level. We simply don't need three or four hundred labs in the United States handling biological weapons agents . . . too often those threats are exaggerated."

What is not exaggerated, added Hammond, is the risk of accidents that lab proliferation poses. The brick and mortar buildup, he noted, meant increased hiring—the new labs must be staffed. Much of the manpower would come from novice researchers—young graduates who lack in experience what they hoped to make up for in expertise. During his tenure, Project Sunshine had uncovered more than a dozen accidents involving pathological agents in BSL-3 labs. There were the unauthorized handlers of *Brucella* at Texas A&M; improperly handled Ebola at Tulane University and the University of Wisconsin; accidental self-infection at the University of New Mexico and at the Medical University of Ohio. None of the accidents was reported, though the conditions of their funding called for such documentation. The federal government was not adequately aware of the substandard conditions in some of these labs, particularly the newer ones, said Hammond. "In fact, the Government Accountability Office recently determined that the government doesn't even know where all the labs are."

In September 2008, the GAO released an assessment of the security conditions at the nation's BSL-4 labs, prompted in part by Ed Hammond's testimony a year earlier. There were, by then, five of them. The report concluded that things could be much improved and urged that the Centers for Disease Control, which regulates the highest-level security labs, "take action to implement specific perimeter controls." Though none of the labs was named, the press decoded the report and noted that "Laboratory E," which was found to be in compliance with just four of the fifteen key perimeter controls set out by the CDC, was none other than San Antonio's Southwest Foundation for Biomedical Research.

Nadler laughed when he read the report, remembering his experience with SFBR's perimeter. The two filmmakers had been given permission to film the exterior, and as they did so they were struck by the compound's laid-back boundary security. Whereas government institutions like Porton Down and Fort Detrick had impressed them with their solidity—impermeable check stations, miles of barbed wire and high fences, a driving corridor that snaked back and forth to slow down suicide bombers—the perimeters of San Antonio's prize research facility were downright disquieting. The chain-link fence sagged, the surveillance cameras were few and far between, and an unarmed rent-a-cop sat sleepy-eyed in a lone guardhouse at the front entrance.

"What's with the Mickey Mouse security?" Coen, who had been spooked at Sverdlovsk's Compound 19, wondered aloud. As if in response, Nadler had begun chatting up the security guard, an affable sort listening to the radio in his guard box.

"Yeah, there have been some strange things," the guard agreed. "I've seen a baboon get out of here. They've had to shoot down with long range tranquilizer rifles from a helicopter." (Indeed, the escape was confirmed by a July 2006 news story in the *San Antonio Express-News*).

"The stuff in there," the guard continued, motioning to the area where the primates used for research are kept, "it leaks into the groundwater. My mother works across the street in that La Quinta hotel," he said. "And she says you don't ever want to drink the water. She tells that to the guests."

In a letter to Nadler, an SFBR spokesman noted that it is evaluating the GAO's recommendations and that "upgrades" are included in the budget for fiscal year 2009. And, for the record, other than the anecdotal testimony of its security guard, there is no proof that there is any groundwater leakage from SFBR. Still Nadler and Coen refused iced drinks until they were way clear of San Antonio.

Two months after his testimony on Capitol Hill—an impassioned plea that might have been a turning point after seven years of against-all-odds advocacy—Ed Hammond closed down Project Sunshine and moved to Colombia, the native land of his wife. He told Coen and Nadler over the phone that the organization had run out of money.

"I wish George Soros or someone like him *was* enthusiastic about this issue. But they say you can win on only a few things—like nukes—and that in germ research, there's just too many folks out there with vested interests—powerful corporations with deep pockets. They tell me it's a good fight, but a losing one." He said he was tired, defeated and convinced that "you only live your life once." Coen expressed his condolences and then hung up the receiver. "The news is bad," he said. "Sunshine is dead."

THE DEATH OF THE BIOLOGICAL WEAPONS CONVENTION

If Ed Hammond had hopes that research institutes like the Southwest Foundation for Biomedical Research and their confederates around the nation would one day take responsibility for their activities, Francis Boyle wants even more accountability. He wants to see the officials of the Dugway Proving Ground and their brethren indicted for criminal offenses. He has written a law to enable such measures.

The 1989 Bioweapons Anti-Terrorism Act was enacted as a measure to implement the existing 1972 Biological Weapons Convention and to make its content applicable to private citizens as well as nation states. It is now a criminal act to violate the Convention—an innovative and supposedly strong deterrent.

Boyle, a constitutional law professor at the University of Illinois and an outspoken opponent of biowarfare research and development, drafted the bill, which was passed unanimously by both houses of Congress in 1990, and signed into law by the first President Bush.

Boyle still refers to the forty-first commander-in-chief as the only one in memory who has behaved "responsibly" on biowarfare issues. He blames Reagan-era neoconservatives and defense hawks in the Clinton administration for planting the seeds of the current biowar research boom. One of the main culprits in his view is former Secretary of the Navy Richard Danzig. Danzig left government service during the George W. Bush years and joined several corporate boards, including the Maryland-based Human Genome Sciences Corp., which recently received a $1.8 billion contract from the US Department of Health and Human Services to help the government stockpile anti-anthrax antibodies. During the latest presidential maneuvering, he was one of the top foreign policy advisers to Barack Obama. He is said to be in line to succeed Robert Gates as Secretary of Defense.

In drafting the law, Boyle was particularly intent on providing a maximum punishment for violating the BWC—life imprisonment. By equating offensive bioresearch with terrorism, Boyle wanted to send a message to the men and women in the lab coats and protective suits: They could not defer to "orders," but would be held morally and legally accountable for contributing to the death sciences. Boyle, an intense academic with a fat FBI file cataloguing an active history on the left side of public debate, worries that the profligacy of biowar spending threatens the security of the nation more seriously than any potential germ weapon.

"There's too much money at stake here for anyone to say no," he told Coen and Nadler, who were visiting in his office in Champaign. Indeed, this was hard to argue with. Where the NIH allocated 5 percent of its budget to studying infectious diseases when George W. Bush came to office, today it dedicates nearly one third of its resources. Within that arena, another priority is made clear: In 2006, for example, the NIH got $120 million to combat influenza, still one of the biggest killers stalking the planet today. In comparison, it received $1.76 billion to work on biodefense. Several universities and private labs have been known to open new or expand existing biolabs purely "on spec," in hopes of winning lucrative government contracts. The country's leading biologists, not to mention the newest generation of researchers making career choices, have a very clear picture of where the money is, says Boyle.

"It's like the Wild West out there. This massive proliferation of Biosafety 3 and 4 labs all over the country, unregulated research development testing. You've had releases of biological agents [in] several places and eventually . . . this is a catastrophe waiting to happen." Boyle has heightened his call for all biowar research to be considered illegal—arguing that there is no longer a line between "defensive" and "offensive" research.

"The problem is all this technology . . . can be put simultaneously to both offensive and defensive uses and indeed, that is the nature of a biological weapon. You have to be able to launch an attack but at the same time you have to be able to defend your own troops. And so it's necessarily offensive and defensive at the same time. Otherwise you do not have an effective weapon," he told the journalists on a cold day in November 2007. "So what we've seen since September 11 confirms that that capability has now been taken care of and biological and chemical weapons are fully integrated throughout the entire US military establishment today."

The Pentagon, Boyle stated bluntly, is ready to wage anthrax war. It has asserted as much in its own public document unearthed by the indefatigable professor who pulled the papers out for the interview.

"Look at the Department of Defense's Chemical and Biological Defense Program Report to Congress, April 2007, page 22, Table 2-5. Information Systems Modernization Strategy, Mid FY09-13," he said, warming to the minutia of his subject. "Here you find a study to estimate human effects from a 5,000 weapon worldwide strike; to predict fatalities and incapacitation, both initial and delayed and to accommodate population moves including area evacuations or sheltering in place. Now how does that strike you?

"There are only two states in the entire world that by then could have the capabilities to launch an offensive first strike with 5,000 biological weapons on a worldwide basis: the United States and Russia." Boyle emphasizes, "We are not dealing here with some terrorist group or some Third World country. Clearly, the United States is today planning to be able to do this. They are developing a computer model to do it. And they are developing the capabilities to do this. The Russians can read this as well as I can."

As far as Boyle is concerned, the US government has already violated the Biological Weapons Convention with its program at Dugway Proving Ground; and therefore Dugway's researchers, under the language of the 1989 Bioweapons Anti-Terrorism Act, have committed crimes punishable by law. "A whole lotta people should be indicted, convicted and sentenced to prison, I kid you not," he said firmly. "But don't hold your breath."

It was also becoming clear that the Kremlin was taking a grave view of the proliferating US program. In his formal outgoing address to the State Council as Russian president in 2008, Vladimir Putin declared, "It's now obvious that a fresh round of a new arms race is starting..." Russia, he warned, may be forced to respond to the West's new breakthroughs in "bio, nano and information technologies." Amazingly, Putin's comments were ignored by the mainstream media in the US. "No surprise at all," said Boyle. "No surprise."

Since there are no scientific safeguards on the outcome of the work being done in ever-increasing and highly-opaque laboratories across the globe, and since only a leap of faith can establish ethical parameters, it seems that proliferation concerns can only be dealt with by the international treaty system. But there too, Boyle told Nadler and Coen, the future looks unpromising.

The Biological Weapons Convention of 1972 remains the only world agreement on germ war research and development. The BWC treaty—outlawing programs of an offensive nature but allowing plenty of room for defensive testing, a problematic distinction to be sure—has been signed by 162 nations, but it lacks the verification and inspections measures to make it an enforceable treaty. The absence of such conditions is attributable solely to the United States and Russia—the two nations with the greatest capability to violate the treaty. The United States has argued that international inspections would endanger the intellectual property secreted in corporate labs. Russia doesn't have an official excuse, officially calling for mutually verifiable transparent programs, secure in the knowledge that the US—at least before Obama—wouldn't hear of it.

And so the BWC is, for all intents and purposes, a paper tiger. But still, the UN meets every two years to try and work things out. At Boyle's suggestion, Coen, Nadler and Verrechia flew to Geneva to watch the proceedings—a bizarre charade given what they knew was happening in laboratories worldwide. The delegates from the US, Russia and South Africa courteously ducked interviews, but the journalists were able to snag a chat with Ronald Noble, the very smooth-talking executive director of Interpol, the international law enforcement agency famed more as the foil of SPECTRE and SMERSH in film and novel lore than for anything it actually does in real life. Noble, a mid-forties African American, assured them for thirty minutes that he was working tirelessly to smoke out any bioterrorists who may be praying in London mosques or Afghan caves. But he did admit he found the new threat worrisome.

"I don't sleep at night," he said bluntly. "I don't sleep at night well at all."

Among the NGO delegates gathered in Geneva in 2007 was Professor Malcolm Dando of the University of Bradford in the UK, who was even more worried than the Interpol chief. "We are in the middle of a really major scientific and technological revolution in life sciences. What confronts us is the possibility that this major revolution will be used both for hostile as well as for benign purposes. The question we have to ask is: Can we stop that from happening? The answer is, We don't know."

After two days of mind-numbing speeches, long lunches and meaningless resolutions voted upon in the UN Hall, Nadler and Coen took a train to Zurich where their brains came alive once again during an interview with Philipp Sarasin, professor of modern history at the university there and the author of *Anthrax: Bioterror as Fact and Fantasy*. Sarasin sees our modern fear of germ war reflected in older scenarios:

> Since at least the nineteenth century, people have the impression that microbes are dangerous things coming from the East or from the Arabs. Even in the Middle Ages people said "the Jews have poisoned our water supply and it was the Sultan of Baghdad who instructed the Jews to do this." So this is a really old narrative—that the Arabs, the Jews, people in the East, are trying to kill us, to attack us, poison our bodies. And I think the language of bacteriology in the late-nineteenth century also reveals that these fears invaded the scientific texts of the time. Because they also say 'out there, out of our bodies, are invisible enemies and we have to defend ourselves against this invasion of something we cannot see.' These are old fears that resurface in our culture, in our unconscious, these fears are present.

Sarasin believes that a popular culture awash in films like *Outbreak* and *Twelve Monkeys* and in television programs like 24, bioterrorism becomes a "self-fulfilling prophecy." Sarasin argues that it was *The Hot Zone*, Richard Preston's 1994 novel on an outbreak of the Ebola virus, that was vital in getting then-President Bill Clinton to increase biodefense funding and authorize biowar games like the 1999 New York City bio-attack scenario Operation Dark Winter.

"One interesting thing about Richard Preston is that he says in the book that he has some information from intelligence people, from the Pentagon . . . And then he writes this novel," said Sarasin. "The novel gets famous and then surprise, surprise, Richard Preston became an expert. He was even invited to the Senate committees to testify about the danger of biological warfare. And I think from this very moment—1998—American politics gets sort of really fascinated by this danger."

Coen and Nadler began to bring up some of the unanswered questions in their investigation but Sarasin waved them off. "I try not to know too much about it," he insisted. "I don't want to be hysteric about this. But I think bioterrorism is only one small part of this concern. What are they actually doing in the labs? That's the question."

The journalists thanked Professor Sarasin and then packed up their gear for the final leg of their journey—to talk to the man who might be able to answer the professor's final question. They were headed for Kiev.

"I JUST HOPE WE ARE NOT SO CRAZY"

Ken Alibek had been knee-deep in germ war during his stint in the West and had kept himself quite busy providing fodder to the biohawks in the late '90s with his debriefing and his sensational tell-all memoir *Biohazard*. He had stoked the fires of Iraq with his certainty that Saddam Hussein had a most dangerous bioweapons program courtesy of former Biopreparat scientists. Fifteen years after his defection, Alibek knew that he had spent half of his career thinking about germ war more from Washington's perspective than from Moscow's. But in 2007, he kind of defected from America too, and from the germ war business. Or so it seemed. Alibek, the world-renowned bioweaponeer, was finally going to honor his first calling—that of a physician. He was all about building a new pharmaceutical empire devoted to good health and a long life.

In the Ukraine.

Trailed by bodyguards.

Landing in Kiev with Verrechia, the first thing Coen and Nadler laid eyes upon in the arrivals lounge was their old guide, K, who gave them each bear hugs and suggested vodka and dumplings soon after they cleared customs. Outside the airport, they vanned down the highway and K quickly pointed out the skeleton construction sight of Alibek's new company called Max-Well, for Maximum Wellness. In the half a football field-sized warehouse-to-be, lit in the darkness by a few strings of bare bulbs, Alibek was promising to produce, stockpile and distribute enough vitamins, enzymes and supplements at generic prices to hopefully cure some cancers.

It was a long way from biological weapons. At least on paper.

The question loomed. What had made Alibek turn his back on a lucrative career as consultant to the biowarriors/defenders in Virginia and head back east—well within the reach of the authoritarian regime he had betrayed years earlier?

"Maybe he just saw the writing on the wall," said Coen. A long investigative piece by the *Los Angeles Times'* David Willman published on July 1, 2007 certainly didn't help. The article, headlined "Fear Inc.: Selling the Threat of Bioterrorism," questioned Alibek's research methods, "conflicts of interest," veracity, paid endorsements of dubious medical products and his cozy relationships with right-wing figures on the Hill who tossed a lot of biodefense research money his way—$28 million to him or companies he worked for. "His most sensational research findings, with US colleagues, have not withstood peer review by scientific specialists. His promotion of nonprescription pills—sold in his name over the Internet and claiming to bolster the immune system—was ridiculed by some scientists. He resigned as executive director of a Virginia University's biodefense center 10 months ago while facing internal strife over his stewardship," Willman wrote. "And, as Alibek raised fear of bioterrorism in the United States, he also has sought to profit from that fear."

At the time of his Ukranian venture, Alibek's American star was clearly on the wane. And still, Coen and Nadler thought he must have some set of balls or Grade-A protection from deep inside of somewhere to journey this close toward home. Alibek readily agreed to meet the team in his stylish new offices in downtown Kiev. Tea and coffee were repeatedly offered by young women who really knocked the team out with their micro-minis, elaborate cosmetics and broken English questions about New York and the intricacies of filmmaking. Alibek was a media pro who had worked the best journalists for years. He chewed a dried apricot, sipped his tea and exhaled as the interview began.

"Believe me, I was not happy when it happened," Alibek said of the US anthrax attacks. He told Coen and Nadler that yes he had been polygraphed, yes he had consulted with the FBI; sure, he had examined the spores, no, he didn't think the stuff was particularly sophisticated, and yes, a lone gunman with the right expertise and equipment could have done the job. The attack powder reminded him of some long-ago Fort Detrick stocks. This was not a case, he had decided, of Biopreparat's crown jewels falling into malevolent hands. It wasn't Iraq or Al Qaeda or Russia. "It was not even the United States," he told them in his broken but intelligible English. "Let me put it this way. It was a case when some crazy . . . scientist who want to—to become, let me say famous. It sounds like, let me say, the case of a firefighter who is saving, let me say, the family but before he can—he is setting fire. In my opinion this is the case . . . somebody wanted to become famous by defense expertise or . . . wanted to show how biological weapons would be dangerous."

It was the character sketch favored by the FBI and it fit both Hatfill and Ivins. But, noted Coen and Nadler, it sounded like Alibek, too.

Coen pressed him. Why had he suddenly left the States? Why was he sitting in an empty three corner-windowed office in the capital of the nation most defiant towards the Kremlin these days, and yet located just a short flight from Moscow? Why was the renowned bioweapon expert now engaged in making generic vitamins? And if that was really his primary occupation these days, why did a bodyguard tail his every move?

Alibek averred that he could not go into details about his sudden departure. But he did offer this: "I haven't done anything bad to any country. I was drawn to the United States; my own intention was to reduce the threat of biological weapons, to reduce the threat of biological warfare, to reduce the threat of biological terrorism."

The scientist leaned back and reflected in his thick accent and deadpan expression, "I am not young any longer. I have got maybe ten or fifteen years active life," he said. "That's why I decided to establish a pharmaceutical company and do something, let me say specifically, prolonging human life." Among other positive global impacts, Alibek hoped Max-Well might also offer some psychological therapy for its CEO and president.

"You cannot have bad dreams every single night," he said quietly. "You cannot . . . think about this stuff every single day."

The wind whipped against the glass and the bodyguard shifted his weight. Nadler took the moment to mention David Kelly and Vladimir Pasechnik—two other microbiologists and anthrax experts with whom Alibek shared a unique vocation and who had died in suspicious circumstances after the October 2001 anthrax attacks. They were two men who may well have had very bad dreams on their last night alive. Alibek's broad brow was smooth, his hands still as he replied, "If for these activities somebody could be killed, it doesn't matter where you are. In Ukraine, in United States, Great Britain, Saudi Arabia or some place else, if some body wants to kill you there is no problem for this people. I mean they are professionals, to take care of it, right? In this Ukraine, Moscow, Almaty, Washington, DC—in this case it doesn't matter. If they want to kill, they would have."

Alibek said that he was less worried of his being eliminated than he was of a bigger threat. He said that he worried that the massive spending by the US, and the new world's unchecked parameters of experimentation, were provoking risky programs in other countries. "I just hope that we are not so crazy to start creating something which could wipe out the entire mankind."

Coen noted that "we" in the quote.

It was late afternoon when Nadler and Coen exited Ken Alibek's Max-Well office complex. The scientist, an armed bodyguard leading the way, escorted them to the street where the crowd surged home from work, and he agreed to stroll around the block with Coen for a filmed "walk and talk." Nadler noticed that K, whom they had insisted remain in the van during the interview, was now busily snapping photographs of Alibek on the march, presumably a figure still of interest to Russian intelligence. When Nadler got back to the van, K wanted to know the square footage of the office. "Can you draw me a floor plan?" he asked Nadler, who declined. He hadn't brought a tape measure, he said, and the only thing he really noticed were the pretty Ukrainian girls serving tea.

K said he knew a good place to eat and soon the team was in a restaurant adorned with several huge black and white photos of Charlie Chaplin, Marilyn Monroe and the Russian Three Stooges'—Trus, Balbes and Byvaly. The food was served as the last rays of the setting sun shined in.

Coen, Nadler, Verrechia and K sat around the table, digesting their dinner and trying to make sense of what they had learned on their journey into the dark world of anthrax. A secret game with an ever-mounting toll of dead players does not yield its secrets easily, but the filmmakers knew they had penetrated a bit of what Dresch liked to call the "international bioweapons mafia." First off, was it a mafia, after all? Was that a fair characterization? Nadler and Coen thought it was. And not just thanks to the corpses and the maimed bodies of the victims of human experimentation. No matter how patriotic the original motives, "germ war" involved wet work. And then there was the bottom line—the enormous profits behind the product. This gang—just a handful of characters when you got right down to it, but whose numbers were growing daily—was peddling the latest wares in the WMD line—"antidotes" for terrorist scourges. These were big-ticket items. Indeed, the defense establishments of too many countries seemed already addicted to the "vaccines." Multinational pharmaceutical companies were bagging big contracts, the business was going legit, and claiming all the political cover that money can buy. And what about the market? The pool of "users" was growing—first the military would need these "vaccines," then first responders, the mailmen and eventually the general population. Today, the US and the UK, tomorrow—the Middle East, China, the world. The need for this new and profitable "biodefense" bulwark against terrorism is reinforced incessantly by both the news media and popular culture. Nadler and Coen predicted to K and Verrechia that a bio-attack would take place whenever the industry needed a shot in the arm.

And who the heck knew what they were doing behind closed doors in China, Israel, France? What secrets had been hijacked and bootlegged across the globe?

Yes, it *was* a mafia, the table concluded, one that operated in the shadows behind classified walls and trade secrets, largely unregulated with little effective oversight. Who indeed really knew what was going on in the labs? More than 10,000 researchers in the US alone are cleared to work with dangerous pathogens and toxins, so the "family" is growing. In the name of fighting terror, a new and terrible arms race is upon us.

"And who the hell murdered David Kelly?" Nadler said a bit too loudly as he slammed his fist down on the table. A few diners glanced up. Coen smiled and poured the last legs of a bottle of vodka into his compatriots' glasses. The men ordered dessert and finished eating in silence.

CHAPTER TEN

The Ghost of Stephen Dresch

Throughout his collaboration with Coen and Nadler, Stephen Dresch had contributed, in addition to his invaluable sources and deep file cabinets, a mild but enduring sense of paranoia.

He had raised the ire of the FBI, the suspicions of globally connected bio-businessmen, the concerns of mobsters and the blood pressure of more than one more than one high-ranking military brass. He had drawn many a morbid family tree on which the grainy photographs of a dozen dead men were taped to the limb out on which they had "gone too far." He had always been philosophical about the notion that his own picture might join them. In the end though, it was neither Big Brother nor Big Pharma nor the Big Shy Fish that got him. It was his three-pack-a-day habit.

In the spring of 2006, Dresch delivered the news to Nadler and Coen that he had terminal lung cancer and would not likely be around another year. He sounded resigned, unmotivated and very sick. Nadler was disappointed. Coen was devastated. Dresch had become more than just a source for him; he had become a friend.

Coen said he would go to Michigan immediately. Nadler agreed and strongly suggested that Coen bring his camera.

The Kauth House in Hancock, Michigan was an imposing structure—part Gothic manor, part Plantation House. It was quiet on the street outside, but Coen could hear strains of classical music coming from the house. Dresch's wife Linda greeted Coen at the door. She looked much younger than her sixty-five years. She was holding a large pair of scissors. "I was just doing a little grooming," she said.

Linda led Coen out to the deck on the back side of the house. Dresch sat with a towel around his shoulders, halfway through a haircut. His beard, like his hair, had grown long and unkempt. He looked like a haggard holy man. "This is my first day outdoors since March," he told Coen.

But Coen was soon reassured. After the haircut, the three of them had a steak dinner and Dresch drank a glass of wine with his cigarettes. Then he went upstairs to change. He was the guest speaker at an assembly of local Republicans that night at their annual Lincoln Day dinner—a showing he gilded with his own morbid wit as an "anticipatory obituary." The dinner would be attended by many of his friends, all of whom knew that Dresch's speech would be barbed. "Gotta stick it to the fat cats," he said as he rose from the table with Linda's help.

And stick it to them he did. In comments that he entitled "The Principles of a True Republicanism versus the Politics of Expediency of a Self-Serving and Self-Perpetuating Political Governing Class," the libertarian relived his battles, large and small, against corruption and his short-lived adventure in politics: "The political class could not understand my refusal to make the usual vacuous promises. . . . I will bring you full employment, I will lower your auto-insurance rates, I will guarantee a chicken in every pot," he said to laughter.

But his serious message to the Republicans that night, most of whom Dresch had already determined had been co-opted to varying degrees by the "Politics of Expediency" was this: Don't perpetuate the problem. Don't cultivate corruption. His real message was to the absent, maverick, "doomed candidate of principle, flying below the radar," far from the black-tied dinner guests. His message was "beware when the political/governing class suddenly decides to adopt you. Either you are being offered up as a sacrificial lamb, or the decision has been made that you must (and can) be corrupted into membership in that dominant class." Coen, unlike most of the audience, heard in the address a clarion call not merely about looming financial crimes or Senate-seat selling scandals. He heard a plea that the responsible men and women of Dresch's hometown and homeland put a stop to the snowballing greed, fear and cooptation that was allowing a homegrown arsenal of catastrophic proportions to flourish in America.

Coen kept a copy of the speech Dresch gave that night, parts of which stayed indelibly in his brain for years afterwards.

Three months later, Linda called to say Dresch was deteriorating rapidly. It was time for him to have his last word on the subject of the menace of biological weapons and their merchants of death. Nadler urged Coen to take his camera on the next trip to Michigan. It would be a key but, for Coen, agonizing interview.

On the drive to Michigan, Coen recalled the work they had done together—countless hours speaking by phone, trading information and mulling connections. He remembered how many times he had lain awake at night, worried by a prolonged silence from Dresch during one of his marathon interstate journeys in search of shady sources and hair-trigger witnesses. In the back of his mind, Coen had always thought that it would be an endangered malefactor who would spell the end for Dresch. That he would be bumped off in the night—meet a mysterious accident on one of the endless highways along which he left littered cigarette butts and correct conclusions. Not cancer.

When he arrived, Dresch was in bed in his attic room, listening to Mahler. Linda went up first to tell her wasted husband that Coen had arrived. The response was unexpected and audible down three flights of stairs. Expletives and coughs punctuated the dying man's express wish that Bob "go the fuck away" because he didn't want to see him.

Linda suggested they let Dresch rest. Coen agreed and lay low for a few hours. At Linda's urging, he ventured up to the attic in the early evening. He was shocked to see his friend's state. The pain was visible. Dresch was more rational but still far from docile.

"I don't know that this is a very interesting conclusion for your film," noted Dresch. "But dying last words are always sexy. So set up the lights and hand me my smokes."

The prospect of one last chance to malign the forces of indifference, negligence and collusion in the US government had clearly animated Dresch, who instantly began trashing the FBI.

By the time the fourth tape had run out, Coen was ready for a directive. Coen waited, zoomed the camera in for an extreme close-up of Dresch in a moment of jaded disillusionment. "I don't know, Bob. You're not gonna bring down a corrupt establishment, but it's always better to make it uncomfortable whenever you can. Whittle away at its security, make it nervous. But don't make it so nervous that it decides it has to rub you out."

This was the Dresch Coen knew, and he turned his camera off and slumbered on a cot next to Dresch that Linda had provided. He said he would not film the final moments, and he didn't.

One week later there was a memorial service for Stephen Dresch attended by his family and about twenty friends and associates. In the back of the chapel Linda had set up a TV. She played the video that Coen had shot two years earlier of Dresch driving his Black Maria cruiser and striding up Harrowdown Hill, full of vigor.

Coen gave a short tribute. He spoke of the courage that allowed Dresch to treat deeply dangerous subjects as the mundane manifestations of a banal evil. He spoke of Dresch's idiosyncratic refusal to take things too seriously, even his safety, as he fired off damning evidence on faxes bearing his phone numbers and addresses. He was a man, Coen told the audience at the funeral home, who was unafraid to delve where others feared to tread—a man who boldly stepped into the dark places we know are out there, but are too afraid to confront ourselves.

After the service Coen called Nadler who offered a final salute.

"'Citizen Dresch' should be the name of our film." Coen considered this as he walked along the shores of Lake Superior where the citizen's ashes had been scattered.

And for a moment, just a moment, Bob Coen felt a hint of sunshine.

Epilogue

It is an odd time on the planet.

Green seems mainstream; corporations say they love the earth; and politicians promise that they are all over inconvenient truths. Except when it comes to germ war and biodefense.

To say the power structure is tone deaf on this matter does not do justice to this moral felony. On this vital, vital issue, our culture is brain dead, toe-tagged and body-bagged. This bio-boom does not make us safer, and proliferation issues should be of great concern. Deadly germs are indeed coming to a neighborhood near you, but it's the government and not terrorists who are responsible. Consider:

- Where once there were only a handful of labs handling anthrax, today 390 labs are certified to work with microbes or toxins that might be used for bioterrorism, and 15,300 people have security clearances to work with these "select agents," a Congressional Research Service analysis reported in March 2009.

- Fort Detrick is undergoing the largest expansion in its history. The recently opened National Biodefense Analysis and Countermeasures Center at the facility contains heavily guarded and hermetically sealed chambers in which scientists will simulate terrorist attacks and use lethal germs and toxins. This, remember, is the facility that officialdom claims was the source of the only significant germ war attack on US soil. Battelle has the $250 million contract to manage the operation.
- In February 2008, the government announced it was suspending work with lethal agents at Fort Detrick to take an inventory, giving rise to legitimate questions over stock security. It is hard to argue with Francis Boyle that all this "is a catastrophe waiting to happen."

There is something profoundly ignorant and unhealthy about a political system in which the powers that be continue to declare that we are living in an extraordinary "Anthrax Emergency" and only a few lone citizens ask the first thing about it: On October 1, 2008, the Department of Health and Human Services Secretary declared that anthrax still presents "a material threat against the United States population, sufficient to affect national security" and extended total liability protection for another seven years to the government and manufacturers of the anthrax vaccine. This "emergency" is a boon to the only company distributing the vaccine today in the US—Dresch's béte noir BioPort, now called Emergent BioSolutions (EBS).

The outfit had worked hard for its government favors. From 2004 through June of 2007, it hired fifty-two lobbyists for a cool $5.3 million to work the Hill and the White House, including former aides to Vice President Dick Cheney and top GOP congressional leaders, according to David Willman of the *Los Angeles Times*. From its modest beginnings in Michigan, the company had landed almost a billion dollars in US government contracts. And despite lawsuits claiming the vaccine made some soldiers sick, the emergency status allows the government to start stockpiling it for first responders. (Full disclosure note: Emergent BioSolutions spokeswoman Tracey Schmitt, who took a few months off near the end of 2008 to work as Sarah Palin's press secretary, was cordial enough when we first asked to use an EBS corporate video in our film, but told us later it was a no-go from upstairs. No hard feelings.)

As the market tanked last fall, EBS became the hottest stock on the Street. Investors bet heavily on a vaccine useful in the next bio attack to secure their cash in an offering that was up 400 percent for the year. Jim Cramer on CNBC led a posse of analysts screaming "I LIKE!" As 2009 dawned, the company secured the rights to provide anthrax vaccine to India. For Emergent BioSolutions, the future looks bright indeed.

For guys like us who like to follow the money, this says it all.

Meanwhile, families of US servicemen came forward in 2009 to claim their loved ones were subjected to the horrors of Cold War human experimentation at US Military's Edgewood Arsenal in Maryland decades ago, and were filing suit for redress, much like the Porton Down vets a few years earlier. The horrors involving human guinea pigs was a story that wasn't going away.

And finally, regarding the anthrax attacks which began this story: Rep. Rush Holt, who represents the New Jersey district where the killer letters were mailed, has introduced a bill, H.R. 1248—"The Anthrax Attacks Investigation Act of 2009"—calling for the establishment of a national commission to study this mysterious matter further. Though Congress was preoccupied with the financial crisis when we put this book to bed, we were told the bill was still alive . . . barely. So, it's important for citizens to call their congressional representatives and demand action if they want to open this important Pandora's box. This is not a Democratic issue. This is not a Republican issue. It is not even an American issue. It is a global issue.

Acknowledgments

This book is a collaboration. First off, we thank Elizabeth Kiem, a talented writer and thinker who quickly absorbed five years' worth of material and helped us present it on a demanding schedule. Without her, this book would not exist.

To the professionals at Counterpoint, we have enjoyed our dealings with Charlie Winton, Richard Nash, Trish Hoard, Laura Mazer, Abbye Simkowitz and Jeff Miller.

On the film side, we thank our colleagues in the trenches, Dylan Verrechia, K, Natalia Viana, Kantarama Gahigiri, Isabelle Lemonnier, Natalie Dubois, Rosella Tursi, Tichafa Tongogara and Harold Crooks. We salute Christine LeGoff, Yves Jeanneau and Arnie Gelbart for all their support.

On the home front, we give big shout-outs to those who had to live too long with too many tales of anthrax, long trips, late nights and occasional paranoia. They know who they are.

And finally, we tip our hats to Stephen Dresch in the Big Black Mariah in the sky. It's been an interesting ride.

Bob Coen
Eric Nadler

Notes

Chapter One: The Ghost of Bruce Ivins

A Perfect Fall Guy

"Scientist's Suicide is Linked to Anthrax Inquiry," *New York Times*, August 2, 2008.
"Anthrax Case Renews Questions On Bioterror Effort and Safety," *New York Times*, August 3, 2008.
"Pressure is Growing for FBI to Show Evidence on Anthrax Scientist," *New York Times*, August 5, 2008.
"Justice Dept. Set to Share Details in Anthrax Case" *New York Times*, August 6, 2008.
"New Details Show Anthrax Suspect Away on Key Day," *Washington Post*, August 2008.
"From Offering Help in the Anthrax Investigation to Being Named the Suspect," *New York Times*, August 8, 2008.
"For Suspects, Anthrax Case Had Big Costs," *New York Times*, August 10, 2008.

"The Anthrax Case From Spores To A Suspect," *Science NOW Daily News*, August 12, 2008.

Transcript, FBI Briefing, August 18, 2008.

"Scientists Elaborate on the Case Against Bruce Ivins," *Los Angeles Times*, August 19, 2008.

"FBI Elaborates On Anthrax Case," *Washington Post*, August 19, 2008.

"FBI Reveals More Details of Anthrax Investigation," *Science News*, August 19, 2008.

"A Trained Eye Finally Solved Puzzle Through 'Morphing' Samples," *New York Times*, August 21, 2008.

"Seeking Details, Lawmakers Cite Anthrax Doubts," *New York Times*, September 7, 2008.

"Demand for Cipro May Be a Break for Bayer, and A Headache," *New York Times*, October 18, 2001.

Amerithrax

FBI website: www.fbi.gov/anthrax/amerithraxlinks.htm.

"Comparative Genome Sequencing for Discovery of Novel Polymorphisms in Bacillus anthracis," Paul Keim et al., *Science*, June 14, 2002.

Armed Forces Institute of Pathology newsletter, October 31, 2002.

"Anthrax Powder—State of the Art" by Gary Matsumoto, *Science*, November 28, 2003.

"Forensic Application of Microbiological Culture Analysis to Identify Mail Intentionally Contaminated with Bacillus Anthracis Spores" by Douglas J. Beecher, *Applied and Environmental Biology*, August 2006.

"Technical Intelligence in Retrospect: The 2001 Anthrax Letters Powder" by Danny Shoham and Stuart Jacobsen, Journal of Intelligence and Counter-Intelligence, March 7, 2007.

Vaccine A: The Covert Government Experiment That's Killing Our Soldiers by Gary Matsumoto, Basic Books, New York, 2004.

Richard Spertzel. Interview with authors, Jefferson, Md., August 8, 2008.

Stuart Jacobsen. Interview with authors, Prisco, Texas, November 10, 2007.

Professor Mathew Meselson. Interview with authors, Cambridge,

Mass., November 6, 2007.
Professor Jonathan King, MIT, Cambridge, Mass., November 6, 2007.
Gary Matsumoto. Interview with authors, Brooklyn, New York, October, 2007.

A Person of Interest

"The Lesson of Steven Hatfill," *SEED Magazine*, October 2, 2006.
James Watt. Phone interview from Calgary, Canada, with Coen, March 2, 2009.

Chapter Two: Enter Stephen Dresch

The Scourge of Bioport

"FBI Overlooks Foreign Sources of Anthrax" by Edward Jay Epstein, *Wall Street Journal*, December 24, 2001.
Memorandum on sale of Michigan Biologic Products Institute, prepared by Michigan House of Representatives Majority Counsel David Opplinger, September 24, 1998.
Transcript of Fuad El-Hibri's testimony before US House of Representatives Committee on Government Reform, June 30, 1999.
Stephen Dresch letter to Henry Hyde, December 10, 2001. For this and all Dresch matters, see his still-active website, www.Forensic-Intelligence.org.
Ed Epstein. Interview with authors, New York, October 26, 2007.

Chapter Three: The Ghost of David Kelly

The Dodgy Dossier

The Strange Death of David Kelly by Norman Baker, Methuen Publishing Ltd., London, 2007.
Secret War: One Hundred Years of British Intelligence Inside MI5 and MI6 by Gordon Thomas, St. Martin's Press, New York, 2009.
Gideon's Spies by Gordon Thomas, St. Martins Press, New York, 2007.
"The David Kelly Affair" by John Cassidy, *New Yorker*, December 8,

2003.

This website contains a complete version of Lord Hutton's Report investigating the circumstances surrounding the death of Dr. David Kelly: www.the-hutton-inquiry.org.uk/content/report.

Investigations

"Our Doubts About Dr. Kelly's Suicide," letter published in *The Guardian* (UK), January 24, 2004, by six medical specialists.

John Scurr. Interview with Coen, London, England, March 17, 2004.

Louise Holmes. Interview with Coen, Oxfordshire, England, August 3, 2004.

Norman Baker. Interview with authors, Lewes, England, November 5, 2006.

Interview with Coen, London, Westminster, England, April 30, 2008.

Gordon Thomas. Interview with Coen, Bath, England, October 10, 2008.

Marilyn Von Berg. Interview with authors, Monterey, Calif., March 19, 2008.

Lee Steinmetz. Interview with authors, Monterey, Calif., March 19, 2008.

Chapter Four: The Ghost of Frank Olson

Operation Antler

Wiltshire Constabulary official website: www.wiltshire.police.uk/antler/default.asp.

"Poisoned by Their Own People," *London Independent*, October 3, 2000.

"Women Used in Porton Down Chemical Tests," *Sunday Telegraph*, October 8, 2000.

"Ex-Ministers Face Police Inquiry On Porton Down Tests," *London Telegraph*, October 29, 2000.

"Porton Down Scientists Could Be Charged," BBC News, July 9, 2001.

"No Porton Down Charges," BBC News, July 8, 2003.

"No Prosecution For Scientists," *This is Wiltshire* (Wiltshire.co.uk), July 10, 2003.

"Disbelief As Prosecutions Are Ruled Out," *This is Wiltshire* (Wiltshire.co.uk), July 17, 2003.
Alan Care. Interview with Coen, Tumbridge Wells, Kent, England, July 31, 2006.
Mike Kenner, citizen activist monitoring Porton Down. Interview with Coen, Weymouth, England, May 1, 2008.

Off The Reservation

Chemical and Biological Warfare: America's Hidden Arsenal by Seymour Hersh, Doubleday, New York, 1969.
Human Smoke by Nicholson Baker, Simon and Schuster, 2008.
"The Cold War and Beyond: Covert and Deceptive American Medical Experimentation" by Susan E. Lederer, PhD., Military Medical Ethics, Vol. 2, 2003.
Julian Perry Robinson, University of Sussex. Interview with Coen, April 19, 2008.
Frank Olson Legacy Project. This site examines the death of biochemist Frank Olson in 1953: www.frankolsonproject.org.
"The Olson File: A Secret That Could Destroy the CIA" by Kevin Dowling and Phillip Knightley, *Night and Day*, supplement to *London Daily Mail*, Aug. 28, 1998.
"What Did the C.I.A. Do to Eric Olson's Father?" by Michael Ignatieff, *New York Times Magazine*, April 1, 2001.
A Voice For The Dead by James E. Starr, G.P. Putnam, New York, 2005.
Eric Olson. Interview with authors, Frederick, Md., August 8, 2008.

Chapter Five: The Ghosts of Sverdlovsk

Siberian Ulcer

"Death In the Wind" by Jim Kelly, University of Texas Medical Branch Newsletter, Galveston, Summer 2002.
"The Sverdlovsk Anthrax Outbreak of 1979" by Mathew Messelson, Jeanne Gillemin, et al., *Science*, November 18, 1994.
Biological Espionage: Special Operations of the Soviet and Russian Foreign Intelligence Services in The West by Alexander Kouzminov, Greenhill Books, London, 2005.
Mathew Meselson. Interview with authors, Cambridge, Mass.,

November 6, 2007.
Tatiana Mikailovna. Interview with authors, Yekatrinburg, Russia, December 21, 2007.
Lev Grinberg. Interview with authors, Yekatrinberg, Russia, December 22, 2007.
Raymond Zelinskas. Interview with authors, Monterey, Calif., March 19, 2008
Yuri Remnev, Russian biodefense expert. Interview with authors, Moscow, Russia, December 18, 2007.

Chapter 6: The Ghost of Vladimir Pasechnik

Biopreparat

Plague Wars by Tom Mangold and Jeff Goldberg, St. Martins Griffin, New York, 1999.
Pasechnik obituary, *London Telegraph*, November 29, 2001.
Casey Harlington. Interview with Coen, London, May 1, 2008.
Raymond Zelinskas. Interview with authors, Monterey, Calif., March 19, 2008.
Bateriorphage-Mediated Lysis Anthrax Bacteria," inventors Vladimir Pasechnik/David West/ Juan Pablo Bifani. Publication Date February 6, 2003. International filing date July 24, 2002. Co-applicant Phage Genomics, PO Box 27740, Las Vegas, Nevada.
"The Odds of That" by Lisa Belkin, *New York Times Magazine*, August 11, 2002.

Alibek

BioHazard by Ken Alibek with Stephen Handelman, Random House, New York, 1999.
Malcolm Dando. Interview with authors, Geneva, Switzerland, December 12, 2007.
Andrew McKinley. Interview with authors, London, England, November 5, 2006.
Interview with Coen, Warfield, England, May 3, 2008.

Chapter Seven: The Ghosts of Africa

The Poison Fields

Apartheid's Friends: The Rise and Fall of South Africa's Secret Service by James Sanders, John Murray Publishers, London, 2006.

Assignment Selous Scouts: Inside Story of a Rhodesian Special Branch Officer by Jim Parker. Galago Books, South Africa, April 2006.

"Anthrax Epizootic in Zimbabwe, 1978-1980: Due to Deliberate Spread?" by Meryl Nass, MD, Physicians For Social Responsibility, 1992.

Project Coast

"The Rollback of South Africa's Biological Warfare Program" by Stephen Burgess and Helen Purkitt, Institute for National Security Studies, Occasional Paper 37. US Air Force Academy, February 2001.

South Africa's Weapons of Mass Destruction by Helen E. Purkitt and Stephen F. Burgess. Indiana University Press, 2005.

Elimination Theory: The Secret Covert Networks of Project Coast by T.J. Byron, PublishAmerica, Baltimore, Md., 2004.

Secrets and Lies: Wouter Basson and South Africa's Chemical and Biological Warfare Programme by Marlene Burger and Chandre Gould, Zebra Press, South Africa, 2002.

Truth and Reconciliation Commission Summaries, Wouter Basson trial: http://ccrweb.ccr.uctc.za/archive/cbw/cbw_index.html.

Nuclear Threat Initiative South African Biological Program Profile: www.nti.org/e_research/profiles/safrica/index.html.

"The Poison Keeper" by William Finnegan, *New Yorker*, January 15, 2001.

"South Africa's Project Coast: 'Death Squads,' Covert State-Sponsored Poisonings, and the Dangers of CBW Proliferation" by Jeffrey Bale, *Democracy and Security* 2:27-59, 2006.

Helen Purkitt. Interview with authors, Annapolis, Md., March 4, 2008.

Jim Parker. Interview with Coen, Germiston, South Africa, May 7, 2008.

Meryl Nass. Interview with Coen, Brooklyn, New York, May 2002, Ft. Drum, New York, 2004, Washington, DC, September 2008.

Pat Clawson, Hatfill spokesman. Phone interview with Coen, February 2009.

James Watt. Phone interview with Coen several times, May 2002–February 2009.

Chandre Gould. Interview with Coen, Pretoria, South Africa, May 8, 2008.

Tori Pretorious. Interview with Coen, Pretoria, South Africa May 6, 2008.

Wouter Basson. Interview with Coen, Cape Town, South Africa, May 9, 2008.

Jean-Phillippe Ceppi, Swiss investigative reporter. Interview with authors, Geneva, Switzerland, December 17, 2007.

Vasily Solodovnikov, former southern Africa KGB chief and member Russian Academy of Sciences. Interview with authors, Moscow, Russia, December 20, 2007.

Chapter Eight: The Ghost of Larry Ford

The Mad Hatter

Peter Fitzpatrick. Interview with authors, Culver City, Calif., March 14, 2008.

Vic Ray. Phone interview with Coen, August 2008.

"The Medicine Man" by Edward Humes, *Los Angeles Magazine*, July 2001.

Larry Ford's redacted FBI files.

Transcript, "Dr. Death and his Accomplice," CBS "60 Minutes," November 7, 2002.

Peter Klein, CBS Producer. Phone interview with authors, September 2008.

"Calif. Doctor's Suicide Leaves Many Troubling Mysteries Unsolved" by Jo Thomas, *New York Times*, November 3, 2002.

Niel Knobel. Interview with Coen, Pretoria, South Africa May 11, 2008.

Wouter Basson. Interview with Coen, Pretoria, South Africa. May 9, 2008.

The Shy Fish Green Card Caper.

Don Mayes. Phone interview from Vera Cruz, Mexico with Coen,

August 2008.
Dan Goosen. Interview with Coen, Pretoria, South Africa, May 12, 2008.
Niel Knobel. Interview with Coen, Pretoria, South Africa, May 11, 2008.
Joby Warrick. Interview with authors, Washington, DC, April, 2008.
Sam Sole. Interview with Coen, Johannesberg, South Africa, May 12, 2008.
Helen Purkitt. Interview with authors, Annapolis, Md., March 4, 2008.
"SA General Touted Anthrax Abroad" by Sam Sole, *Guardian and Mail*, South Africa, January 24, 2003.
"South Africa's Surrender Was Only Half the Battle" by Robert Block, *Wall Street Journal*, January 31, 2003.
"Lethal Legacy: Bioweapons for Sale" by Joby Warrick and John Mintz, *Washington Post*, April 20, 2003.
"Biotoxins Fall Into Private Hands: global Risk Seen in S. African Poisons" by Joby Warrick, *Washington Post*, April 21, 2003.
Briefing to President Mandela on the Defensive Chemical and biological Warfare Programme of the SADF and the RSA's Position WRT The CVC and BWC. From Surgeon General Knobel, August 1994.

Chapter Nine: The Ghost of Sunshine

The Wild West

"US Germ Warfare Research Pushes Treaty Limits" by Judith Miller, Stephen Engelberg and William J. Broad, *New York Times*, September 4, 2001.
Germs by Judith Miller, Stephen Engelberg and William Broad, Simon and Schuster, New York, 2001.
Judith Miller. Interview with Coen, New York, November 10, 2008.
"Acute Inhalation Toxicity of Soman and Sarin in Baboons" by G. Moore et al., Fundamental and Applied Toxicology #14, 1990.
G.T. Moore. Phone interview with Nadler, March 3, 2009.
Tom Slick and the Search for the Yeti by Loren Coleman, Faber and Faber, Boston and London, 1989.
Tom Slick: True Life Encounters in Cryptozooology by Loren Coleman,

Linden Publishing Company, Fresno, Calif., 2002.

Tom Slick Mystery Hunter by Catherine Nixon Cooke, Paraview Inc., Bracey, Virginia, 2005.

John Kerr. Interview with authors, San Antonio, Texas, November 16, 2007.

Jean Patterson. Interview with authors, San Antonio, Texas, November 16, 2007.

US Government Accountability Office Report: "BioSafety Laboratories Perimeter Security Assessment of the Nation's Five BSL-4 Laboratories," September 2008.

Joel Williams, Dublin & Associates on behalf of SFBR. E-mail communication to Nadler, November 21, 2008.

Dugway Proving Ground: http://en.wikipedia.org/wiki/Dugway_Proving_Ground.

Steve Erickson. Interview with authors, Toole, Utah, March 17, 2008.

Jeff Alan Moore. Interview with authors, Dugway Proving Ground, Utah, March 18, 2008.

Project Sunshine

Written Testimony by Edward Hammond Submitted to the Subcommittee of the House Committee on Energy and Commerce for the Hearing, "Germs Viruses and Secrets: The Silent proliferation of laboratories in the United States, October 4, 2007.

Edward Hammond. Interview with authors, Berkeley, Calif., March 20, 2008.

The Death of the Biological Weapons Convention

Biowarfare and Terrorism by Francis A. Boyle, Clarity Press Inc., Atlanta, Georgia, 2005.

Bioterror and Biowarfare by Malcolm Dando, Oneworld Publications, Oxford, England, 2006.

Anthrax: Bioterror as Fact and Fantasy by Phillip Sarasin, Harvard University Press., Cambridge, Mass., 2006.

Francis Boyle. Interview with authors, Champaign, Ill., November 14, 2007.

Ronald Noble. Interview with authors, Geneva, Switzerland, December 11, 2007.

Philipp Sarasin. Interview with authors, Zurich, Switzerland, December 14, 2007.

Malcolm Dando. Interview with authors, Geneva, Switzerland, December 12, 2007.

"I Just Hope We Are Not So Crazy"

"Fear Inc.—Selling The Threat of Bioterrorism: An ex-Soviet scientist raised fears, helped shape US policy and sought to profit" by David Willman, *Los Angeles Times*, July 1, 2008.

Ken Alibek. Interview with authors, Kiev, Ukraine, December 16, 2007.

Photo Credits

Anthrax—CDC/Janice Haney Carr
Bioport vaccine—CBS
Bruce Ivins—Frederick NewsPost
Mueller—Transformer Films
Hatfill—Transformer Films
Dresch driving—Transformer Films
Dresch office—Linda Dresch
Dresch letter—Forensic Intelligence International LLC
Anthrax vacine—Associated Press
BSL 3 Lab—Transformer Films
David Kelly—Reuters

Antler Notice—UK Ministry of Defence
Frank Olson—Eric Olson
Olson passport—Eric Olson
Olson family—Eric Olson
Crew in Yekaterinburg—Bob Coen
Lev Grinberg—Transformer Films
Tatiana Mikhailovna—Transformer Films
Vladimir Pasechnik—Raymond Zilinskas
Pasechnik phage patent—UK Intellectual Property Office
Alibek—Transformer Films
Zimbabwe Anthrax child—James Watt
Jim Parker—Transformer Films
Basson—Transformer Films
Project Coast poisons—South Africa History Archives
Larry Ford—Associated Press
Niel Knobel—Transformer Films
Mandela document—Stephen Dresch
Control room—Transformer Films
Dugway—Eric Nadler
Dugway Sign—Transformer Films
CRP—US Department of Defense
Francis Boyle—Transformer Films

Index

N

Printed in the United States
by Baker & Taylor Publisher Services